PERSONAL IMPRESSIONS

Isaiah Berlin was born in Riga, capital of Latvia, in 1909. When he was six, his family moved to Russia: there in 1917, in Petrograd, he witnessed both the Social Democratic and the Bolshevik Revolution.

In 1921 his family came to England, and he was educated at St Paul's School and Corpus Christi College, Oxford. At Oxford he was a Fellow of All Souls, a Fellow of New College, Professor of Social and Political Theory and founding President of Wolfson College. He also held the Presidency of the British Academy. His published work includes *Karl Marx*, *Four Essays on Liberty*, *Russian Thinkers*, *Concepts and Categories*, *Against the Current*, *The Crooked Timber of Humanity*, *The Sense of Reality*, *The Proper Study of Mankind*, *The Roots of Romanticism*, *The Power of Ideas* and *Three Critics of the Enlightenment*. As an exponent of the history of ideas he was awarded the Erasmus, Lippincott and Agnelli Prizes; he also received the Jerusalem Prize for his lifelong defence of civil liberties. He died in 1997.

Dr Henry Hardy, a Fellow of Wolfson College, Oxford, is one of Isaiah Berlin's Literary Trustees. He has edited several other books by Berlin, and is currently preparing his letters and his remaining unpublished writings for publication.

The career of Lord Annan (1916–2000) reflects a lifelong dedication to education and the arts. He was Provost of King's College, Cambridge, Provost of University College London and Vice-Chancellor of the University of London. He was also Chairman of the Trustees of the National Gallery, a Trustee of the British Museum, and a Director of the Royal Opera House, Covent Garden. His books include *Leslie Stephen*, *Our Age* and *The Dons*.

For further information about Isaiah Berlin visit
www.wolfson.ox.ac/berlin/vl/

Also by Isaiah Berlin

✻

KARL MARX
THE AGE OF ENLIGHTENMENT
FOUR ESSAYS ON LIBERTY

Edited by Henry Hardy and Aileen Kelly

RUSSIAN THINKERS

Edited by Henry Hardy

CONCEPTS AND CATEGORIES
AGAINST THE CURRENT
THE CROOKED TIMBER OF HUMANITY
THE SENSE OF REALITY
THE ROOTS OF ROMANTICISM
THE POWER OF IDEAS
THREE CRITICS OF THE ENLIGHTENMENT

Edited by Henry Hardy and Roger Hausheer

THE PROPER STUDY OF MANKIND

PERSONAL IMPRESSIONS

ISAIAH BERLIN

Edited by Henry Hardy
With an introduction by Noel Annan

Second Edition
Including five additional essays

PRINCETON UNIVERSITY PRESS
PRINCETON, NEW JERSEY

Published in North America by Princeton University Press,
41 William Street, Princeton, New Jersey 08540

First edition first published by The Hogarth Press in 1980
Second edition first published by Pimlico in 1998

First Princeton edition, 2001

Library of Congress Cataloging-in-Publication Data

Berlin, Isaiah, Sir.
Personal impressions / Isaiah Berlin ; edited by Henry Hardy ;
with an introduction by Noel Annan.— Second ed. ;
including five additional essays.
p. cm.
Includes bibliographical references and index.
ISBN 0-691-08858-6 (pbk. : alk. paper)
1. Biography—20th century. I. Hardy, Henry. II. Title.

CT120 .B37 2001
920'.009'04—dc21 00-066863

For further information about Isaiah Berlin visit
www.wolfson.ox.ac.uk/berlin/vl/

Printed on acid-free paper. ∞

www.pup.princeton.edu

Printed in the United States of America

1 3 5 7 9 10 8 6 4 2

To the memory of
Geoffrey Wilkinson
1921–1996

CONTENTS

ILLUSTRATIONS

between pages 96 and 97

Photo credits: 1, 2, 4, 6, 10, 12, The Hulton Getty Collection; 3, Bernard Hoffmann/*Life* © Time Inc. 1945 (print supplied by the Weizmann Archives); 5, Yoram Sadeh; 7, *New York Times*; 8, 9, The Warden and Fellows of All Souls College, Oxford; 11, The Warden and Fellows of Nuffield College, Oxford; 13, 18, author's collection; 14, Ian Parsons; 15, Sylvia Salmi (print supplied by Farrar, Straus and Giroux); 16, Mrs E. Grant; 17, Chatto and Windus

AUTHOR'S PREFACE
TO THE FIRST EDITION

THIS VOLUME consists of writings that resemble what in the eighteenth century were called *éloges* – addresses commemorating the illustrious dead. All but two of these were composed in response to specific requests: the exceptions, those on Franklin Roosevelt and Lewis Namier, as well as 'Meetings with Russian Writers', were not commissioned, and were written because I believed that I had something to say which had not, so far as I knew, been said elsewhere.

The form, and to some extent the content, of these tributes was largely determined by the purposes for which they were intended. Thus the memoirs of Maurice Bowra and John Plamenatz were obituary addresses read at memorial services in Oxford; the article on Chaim Weizmann was delivered as a public lecture in London on a somewhat similar occasion; those on Richard Pares, Hubert Henderson, J. L. Austin, Aldous Huxley, Felix Frankfurter and Auberon Herbert were requested by editors of academic journals or commemorative volumes. The essay on Albert Einstein was the inaugural address read at a centenary symposium in his honour: my intention was to bring out his sharp awareness of social reality and of the importance of truths unwelcome to some of those who paid him homage as a saintly and withdrawn thinker who saw the world through a haze of vague-minded idealism. The essay on Churchill was originally a review of the second volume of his war memoirs; it was written at a time when he was Leader of the Opposition in the House of Commons and had begun to be widely and fiercely criticised, sometimes with good reason, on both sides of the Atlantic. I thought, and still think, that his part in 1940 in saving England (and, indeed, the vast majority of mankind) from Hitler had been insufficiently remembered and that the balance needed to be restored. So, too, in the case of President Franklin

Roosevelt, I wished to remind readers of the fact that for my generation – those who were young in the 1930s – the political skies of Europe, dominated by Hitler, Mussolini, Stalin, Franco, Salazar and various dictators in Eastern Europe and the Balkans, were very dark indeed; the policies of Chamberlain and Daladier held out no hope; for those who had not despaired of the possibility of a socially and morally tolerable world the only point of light seemed to many of us to come from President Roosevelt and the New Deal. This article, too, was written largely during the recriminations of the immediate post-war years.

The last essay is new and written for this volume. It deals with my visits to Russia in 1945 and 1956. I wanted to give an account principally of the views and personalities of two writers of genius whom I had met and come to know, which I had not found elsewhere, not even in the memoirs of Nadezhda Mandel'shtam and Lydia Chukovskaya, the most detailed and moving accounts that we have of the lives of writers and artists at a terrible time, to which my narrative (a part of which was delivered as a Bowra Lecture under the auspices of Wadham College, Oxford) can claim to be no more than a marginal supplement.

I wish to record my deep gratitude to my friend Noel Annan for writing the Introduction to this miscellany, and to tell him, and his readers, that I am only too well aware of what reserves of sensibility, conscience, time, sheer labour, capacity for resolving the conflicting claims of truth and friendship, knowledge and moral tact, such a task unavoidably draws upon; and to thank him for his great goodwill in agreeing to perform it. Finally, I should like to take this opportunity of once again acknowledging my deep and ever-growing debt to the Editor of this edition of my essays. No author could ask for a better, more disinterested, scrupulous or energetic editor; and I should like to offer Dr Henry Hardy my thanks for exhuming, and putting together, this collection, composed over a long period, against what must, at times, have seemed not inconsiderable odds – some of them due to the idiosyncrasies of the author.

ISAIAH BERLIN

June 1980

EDITOR'S PREFACE

THIS is the second edition of one of five volumes in which I have brought together, and prepared for reissue, most of the published essays by Isaiah Berlin which had not hitherto been made available in a collected form.[1] His many writings were previously scattered, often in obscure places; most were out of print; and only half a dozen essays had been collected and reissued.[2] These five volumes, together with the complete list of his publications which one of them (*Against the Current*) contains,[3] and subsequent volumes in which I have published much of his previously unpublished work,[4] have made much more of his *oeuvre* readily accessible than before.

The essays in the present volume are tributes to or memoirs of twentieth-century figures whom, with the exception of Roosevelt

[1] The first edition of this volume was originally published in London in 1980, and in New York in 1981; it was the last of four volumes published, in the first instance, under the collective title *Selected Writings*, which explains the author's reference on page x to 'this edition of my essays'. The other three volumes were *Russian Thinkers* (London and New York, 1978), co-edited with Aileen Kelly; *Concepts and Categories: Philosophical Essays* (London, 1978; New York, 1979); and *Against the Current: Essays in the History of Ideas* (London, 1979; New York, 1980). The fifth volume followed a decade later: *The Crooked Timber of Humanity: Chapters in the History of Ideas* (London, 1990; New York, 1991). There is also a selection of essays drawn from these volumes and their predecessors: *The Proper Study of Mankind: An Anthology of Essays*, ed. Henry Hardy and Roger Hausheer (London, 1997; New York, 1998).

[2] *Four Essays on Liberty* (Oxford, 1969; New York, 1970) and *Vico and Herder: Two Studies in the History of Ideas* (London and New York, 1976). Other collections had appeared only in translation.

[3] The currently most up-to-date version of this bibliography appears in the Pimlico paperback edition (London, 1997).

[4] *The Magus of the North: J. G. Hamann and the Origins of Modern Irrationalism* (London, 1993; New York, 1994) and *The Sense of Reality: Studies in Ideas and their History* (London, 1996; New York, 1997).

and Einstein, the author knew personally, together with a chapter on his meetings in 1945 and 1956 with Boris Pasternak, Anna Akhmatova and other Russian writers in Moscow, where he was working in 1945 for the British Embassy, and in Leningrad. Original publication details of the pieces included in the first edition are as follows. 'Winston Churchill in 1940' (with 'Felix Frankfurter at Oxford', one of only two pieces published in the lifetimes of their subjects) first appeared in 1949 in *Atlantic Monthly* 184 No 3 (as 'Mr Churchill') and *Cornhill Magazine* 981 (as 'Mr Churchill and F.D.R.'), and was reissued in book form as *Mr Churchill in 1940* by John Murray of London in 1964. 'President Franklin Delano Roosevelt' appeared in 1955 in *Political Quarterly* 26 and, as 'Roosevelt Through European Eyes', in *Atlantic Monthly* 196 No 1. 'Chaim Weizmann', the second Herbert Samuel Lecture, was published by Weidenfeld and Nicolson of London in 1958. 'Einstein and Israel', which appeared in the *New York Review of Books*, 8 November 1979, is the major part of an address given on 14 March 1979 at the opening of a symposium held to mark the centenary of Einstein's birth – the full address appeared in Gerald Holton and Yehuda Elkana (eds), *Albert Einstein: Historical and Cultural Perspectives*, the Centennial Symposium in Jerusalem (Princeton, 1982: Princeton University Press). 'L. B. Namier' was published in 1966 in Martin Gilbert (ed.), *A Century of Conflict* (London: Hamish Hamilton), and in *Encounter* 17 No 5 (November 1966). 'Felix Frankfurter at Oxford' was a contribution to Wallace Mendelson (ed.), *Felix Frankfurter: A Tribute* (New York, 1964: Reynal). 'Richard Pares' appeared in the 1958 *Balliol College Record*. 'Hubert Henderson at All Souls' was part of a supplement, devoted to Henderson, to *Oxford Economic Papers* 5 (1953). 'J. L. Austin and the Early Beginnings of Oxford Philosophy' was a contribution to Sir Isaiah Berlin and others, *Essays on J. L. Austin* (Oxford, 1973: Clarendon Press). 'John Petrov Plamenatz' was the address at Plamenatz's memorial service in the University Church of St Mary the Virgin, Oxford, in 1975, and was published privately in that year by All Souls College. 'Maurice Bowra' was the address at Bowra's memorial service, also in St Mary's, in 1971, and was published privately in that year by Wadham College. 'Auberon Herbert' was a contribution to John Jolliffe (ed.), *Auberon Herbert: A Composite Portrait* (Tisbury, 1976: Compton Russell), 'Aldous Huxley' to Julian Huxley (ed.), *Aldous Huxley* (London, 1965: Chatto and

Windus). 'Meetings with Russian Writers in 1945 and 1956', an abbreviated version of which was given as a Bowra Lecture on 13 May 1980, was first published in this volume, for which, as the author says, it was specially written.

Four essays published since 1980 have been added in this second edition. 'Yitzhak Sadeh', which appeared in *Midstream* 39 No 4 (May 1993), I constructed at the author's request from two shorter pieces he had written on Sadeh, one previously unpublished, the other, 'On Yitzhak Sadeh' (a short talk broadcast on the English-language service of Israeli radio), published in Hebrew translation in *Davar*, 5 September 1986. 'Edmund Wilson at Oxford' appeared in the *Yale Review* 76 (1987). 'Memories of Virginia Woolf' was published as 'Writers Remembered: Virginia Woolf' in *The Author* 100 (1989). 'David Cecil' appeared in *Reports for 1985–86 and 1986–87; List of Fellows and Members for 1987* (London, [1987]: Royal Society of Literature).

Apart from necessary corrections and the addition of a few references, the reprinted essays appear here essentially in their original form. I have made a few further corrections and added a few further references in this new edition.

Not included here are several other pieces in the same genre, mostly shorter than or overlapping with the pieces in this volume. Their principal subjects are Chaim Weizmann, Meyer Weisgal, Michael Tippett, Randolph Churchill, Jacob Herzog, Arthur Lehning, Jacob Talmon, Teddy Kollek, Yishayahu Leibowitz, Nahum Goldmann, Martin Cooper, David Ben-Gurion, Adam von Trott, John Plamenatz, Yehudi Menuhin, Alexander and Salome Halpern, and H. L. A. Hart; full details can be found in the bibliography already mentioned.[1]

I remain grateful for all the help I received in preparing the first edition seventeen years ago. Then, as always, Isaiah Berlin patiently answered my queries and Pat Utechin, his secretary, gave indispensable aid. Virginia Llewellyn Smith assisted me with 'Meetings with Russian Writers in 1945 and 1956'. I should also like to thank Zvi Dror, Henry Near and Yoram Sadeh for help with 'Yitzhak

---

[1] See p. xi above, note 3. Of the people I have listed, Chaim Weizmann is the subject of items 49 and 84, and the others of items 91, 97, 123, 129, 140, 171a, 173a, 181a, 188a, 191, 192, 192a, 193, 203, 203a and 215 respectively.

Sadeh', and Helen McCurdy, Rowena Skelton-Wallace and Will Sulkin for help with the second edition.

HENRY HARDY

Wolfson College, Oxford
July 1997

Postscript

Isaiah Berlin died on 5 November 1997. This new edition of *Personal Impressions* had by then been passed for press, but not actually printed. No changes have been made to the body of the book, but the opportunity has been taken to add, as an epilogue, a slightly shortened version of the address Berlin gave in Jerusalem in May 1979 when he received the Jerusalem Prize for his contribution to the idea of freedom. This moving and perceptive piece – which was printed in *Jewish Quarterly* 27 Nos 2–3 (Summer/Autumn 1979) and in *Conservative Judaism* 33 No 2 (Winter 1980) – has always seemed to me, and to others whom I have consulted, to belong in the book, since it is in effect an autobiographical personal impression. I suggested to Berlin more than once that it should be reprinted in this natural context, but he always gave the characteristic reply that it seemed to him too personal, perhaps too self-regarding, to reappear in a collection in his lifetime; thereafter, however, I should do what I thought best. To my bitter regret, I am now free to add this finishing touch to the volume.

H.H.

November 1997

INTRODUCTION

Noel Annan

THE *éloge* is not much favoured as a literary form in England today: it is hauled out of the cupboard only for use at memorial services, decently to extol the dead man's virtues. The profile and the interview, the literary forms now much in use, are designed not to praise but to cut people down to size. This was the vogue which delighted Beaverbrook: he called it 'lopping off the heads of the tall poppies'. The journalist probes for the weak spot, inserts the *banderilla*, and so goads the wretched bull that he plunges to the doom of self-exposure. Professional interviewers regard this special skill with grave self-satisfaction. They are unanimous in declaring that it does the victim a positive service: he may not appear admirable but he is at least credible.

Intellectuals disparage journalists, but the course they have been following runs alongside the journalists' trail. Social scientists have depersonalised acres of human experience so that history resembles a ranch on which herds move, driven they know not why by impersonal forces, munching their way across the prairie. Critics, like crabs in a rock-pool, scuttle sideways into the recesses of post-modernism and avoid considering how people actually speak and write; or they replace the living artist by an artificial persona composed from his works. No wonder the public buys biographies. Yet how many of the two-volume lives, arid with documentation, fill the throat with dust? Those biographers who are not frightened to paint portraits in the primary colours of virtue and vice seem often to be enslaved by the principle which the harsh-tongued father of the novelist Henry Green characterised years ago as *de mortuis nil nisi bunkum*; and those who preserve certain reticences prudently let it be known that they did so to avoid damages for libel.

Isaiah Berlin ignores these current fashions. His thought, his theories, always refer to people: the very life he leads pullulates with people. His essays on those who intrigue him are studies in praise. Like the son of Shirach he wants us to praise famous men. But it is not their fame which attracts him, it is their genius. He is not ashamed to worship heroes. He has no wish to pose as God and see with equal eye a hero perish or a sparrow fall. Heroes enhance life, the world expands and becomes less menacing and more hopeful by their very existence. To know a great man is to change one's notions of what a human being can do or be. To see Shelley plain, to meet as Berlin has done men and women such as Pasternak or Stravinsky, Virginia Woolf or Picasso, Russell or Einstein, he finds exciting. But he does not consider only geniuses. Someone whose prejudices are outrageous and whose behaviour disturbs the *bien-pensants* may exhibit reckless vitality; and that challenges Berlin to find the precise words which best convey his quality and quiddity. Nor need such people be lions or stars. An obscure scholar with an unusual combination of gifts will make him feel the world well won. He likes people to show attractive qualities: austerity is praiseworthy, but so is gaiety. His austere friend John Austin found few pleasures in life equal to that of being able to praise someone unreservedly, and Berlin, no less than Keynes, who was a devastating critic of people, revels in celebrating men and women whom he admires.

But it would be an error to dismiss these studies in praise as conventional tributes. Like all his writing, they are deceptively entertaining and conceal his true originality of mind. Newspapers picture great scientists making a breakthrough which alters the course of physics or biology, or economists are praised for producing a theory which relates both logically and paradoxically all the variables within their branch of knowledge. These are the means, so it is said, by which knowledge is advanced. But Berlin does not enlarge our understanding in this way. To have done so – to have written an abstract treatise on the history of ideas, a subject which has been distorted and misunderstood precisely because it has so often been reduced to abstractions – would have been to contradict the very message he wants us to receive. He has, of course, written on theories of freedom and on historiography; but these critiques are inadequate in themselves to convey what he has added to his own interpretation of life.

That interpretation is pluralism. How the imagination droops at the mention of that dingy word! 'We live in a pluralist age' is the castrating cliché of our times. Most people when they use the term mean that society is formed of numbers of minorities who are moved each by their own interests and values. But since the interests of all these groups conflict they have to learn to tolerate each other's existence. Indeed the institution which needs to exercise the greatest tolerance is the State itself: although it has to express politically the highest common factor of agreement in society it must be especially sensitive in accommodating those whose views are opposed to the consensus. Not only the State. Every controlling body, every institution, management in its various disguises, should respond to minority feelings. But there is a difficulty in sustaining this theory in practice. When government in all its forms is weakened and drained of blood by giving transfusions to enable minorities to flourish, it becomes incapable of resisting determined and ruthless interest-groups or parties. Having benefited by the application of pluralism, they kick over the theory and elbow the government out by taking over its most important functions; they then blandly declare the interests of all other minorities to be subordinate to their own. Must not a government so hesitant about its legitimacy collapse when its power to give orders is challenged?

Isaiah Berlin's interpretation of pluralism is far more profound. He does not spend time conjecturing how far the State should or should not yield to pressure groups. What fascinates him is not the political consequences of pluralism but its justification. It needs to be justified not only against its enemies but against many of those who preen themselves on being pluralists but would be indignant if they became aware of the implications of what Berlin is saying. For those who pay lip-service to pluralism fail to understand just how disturbing he is. He believes that you cannot always pursue one good end without setting another on one side. You cannot always exercise mercy without cheating justice. Equality and freedom are both good ends but you rarely can have more of one without surrendering some part of the other. This is dispiriting for progressives who like to believe that the particular goal which at present they are pursuing is not incompatible with all the other goals which they like to think they value as much. But Berlin, disbelieving in panaceas or total solutions, is sceptical of many remedies which purport to cure social ills and to reintegrate those said to be alienated from their society. Masterful men and implacable women, planners, moving their fellow citizens about and disposing of the future of their children, determining how and where they should live in the name of efficiency or equality, justifying the brutality of their decisions by declaring how inescapable these decisions are, do not rejoice his heart. Bureaucrats who take pleasure in defining the rules and regulations which govern everyone else's jobs awaken in him the suspicion that so far from fulfilling what people want they are more interested in manipulating them. But if for him the ideals of the powerful civil servant insult too wantonly the nature of man, he does not display much enthusiasm for the political movements which grew up to oppose the gospel of efficiency. He has reservations about populism or syndicalism. He wonders how much they care for the liberty of minorities.

But these reservations give no comfort to conservatives. Unlike Michael Oakeshott, Berlin is not sceptical of reason in politics or of theories as such. He may have no views about monetarism or deficit budgeting or on other statistical or sociological analyses: but he does not regard such efforts to apply reason to politics as valueless. Such theories, the product of abstract reason and analysis, may, if put into practice, diminish the bruising and dispiriting conflicts between good ends. Life is not one long struggle against impaling oneself on the horns of a dilemma: peaceful trade-offs are possible, nor are they always agonising. Sometimes equality and liberty may be reconciled; sometimes not; but Berlin disagrees with those who deny that tangles of this sort can be combed out. Again, participatory populism is not a form of political organisation likely to make the blood surge through his veins; but if it could be shown that it led to a clear advance towards greater equality he would not reject it. Unlike even moderate conservatives he regards equality as one of the ultimate goals for men, a sacred value, obliged no doubt to yield when other sacred values would have to suffer if they were to collide with it, but to be realised so long as it cannot be shown to be doing irreparable damage. If many people are starving and can be fed if the liberty of the few is curtailed, then the few must lose their liberty. If that gives pain, well, pain must be given. All Berlin asks is that there should be no equivocation and it should be frankly admitted that liberty was curtailed – in a good cause. Nor has he sympathy with the conservative notion that all culture is founded on inequality, nor with a view dear to some intellectuals that art is the supreme value in life which must be protected and fostered at whatever cost.

If the agonising choice had to be made between the destruction of, say, Rome, glistening with the treasures of the ages, and the loss of the independence of a nation and the subjugation of its citizens to a tyranny, Berlin would throw his lot for scorched earth and resistance. Some might guess that in his sympathy for Turgenev he would follow him in loathing the right and fearing the left; and if he were faced with the alternatives which confronted Turgenev in nineteenth-century Russia the guess would be right. Berlin finds reactionary regimes odious, and terrorist revolutionaries insupportable. But within the range of Western democratic politics he follows his fancy.

To want to maximise a particular virtue is common enough: to admit that it is not always possible to do this without fatally diminishing others is not. Unfortunately people, Berlin argues, want to be assured that in fact they can always follow simultaneously all good ends. They therefore listen respectfully to political thinkers who declare that this can be done. Such sages declare that they have discovered a better kind of freedom, positive freedom, which will reconcile the desire for justice, equality, opportunity for self-fulfilment with their wish to be as free and live under as few prohibitions as possible. Positive freedom is the benign name given to the theory which maintains that not merely wise philosophers but the State, indeed governments themselves, can identify what people would *really* want were they enlightened, if they understood fully what was needed to promote a good, just and satisfying society. For if it is true that this can be identified then surely the State is justified in ignoring what ordinary people say they desire or detest. What people say is the mere rumbling of their lower self, a pathetic underdeveloped persona insufficiently aware of all the possibilities of life, often the slave of evil passions. Who in his senses would want to be a slave to the bottle? Who would not agree that art is vital to anyone who wants to lead a full life? But since all too many people are alcoholics and vast numbers of people care not at all for art, the State is compelled to enforce sobriety and propagate art so long as it is healthy and opens men's eyes to a better future.

People are often convinced by this vision of freedom because they want to believe in a common-sense view of goodness. Surely goodness must be indivisible, surely truth is beauty and beauty truth, surely the different aspects of truth and goodness can always be reconciled. But Berlin declares that sometimes they cannot.

Ideology answers the questions 'How should I behave?' and 'How should I live?' People want to believe that there is one irrefutable answer to these questions. But there is not.

There is not, because life is more than a series of solutions to problems. Berlin's pluralism has far deeper roots than politics. It is grounded in his understanding of linguistic philosophy and of history. Other philosophers grew weary of John Austin's devastating ability to dissect a proposition and expose error in their own arguments. 'You are like a greyhound', Berlin remembers Ayer saying to Austin, 'who doesn't want to run himself, and bites the other greyhounds, so that they cannot run either.' But Berlin found Austin sympathetic, not so much for the ferocity with which he argued, but because Austin, like the later Wittgenstein, rejected the doctrine that one could assemble a logically perfect language capable of reflecting the structure of reality. Unlike Ayer, who started with the verification principle and rejected an argument if it appeared to conflict with that principle, Austin believed that the only way to analyse knowledge, belief and experience was to study how people actually use words; and he rejected distinctions between empirical and logical truths – between those terms necessary to what Berlin calls 'all or nothing' philosophies.

Austin too was a theorist. He invented the theory of the illocutionary use of language (performatory, ascriptive and prescriptive expressions), and he believed in systems and in teamwork for cracking philosophical conundrums, which Berlin did not – much. But Austin did not take problems and force them into a Procrustean bed of a single all-embracing system. Whereas some logical postivists faced with a problem reformulated it in their own terms so that it ceased to be the problem it was, or else rejected it as a pseudo-problem, Austin took every problem as it came. Like Dr Johnson, Austin had a fine scorn for determinism as a doctrine which flew in the face of all experience; and this too Berlin found sympathetic. He does not see human beings as flies struggling vainly in the cobweb of historical causation, incapable of acting as free agents.

But sympathetic as Austin was to him personally and encouraging as his precept was to consider language as an act, something people do in a particular situation, Berlin's pluralism stands independent from Oxford philosophy; and it is arguable that it is never more palpable and convincing than when he writes about people. Nobody else in our time has invested ideas with such personality; no one has given them corporeal shape and breathed life into them more than Berlin; and he succeeds in doing so because ideas for him are not mere abstractions. They live – how else could they live? – in the minds of men and women, inspiring them, shaping their lives, influencing their actions and changing the course of history. But it is men and women who create these ideas and embody them. Some are scholars enclosed in their hermetic world, despising histrionics, intrigue, ambition – the game of getting on and cashing in. They recoil when confronted with brutal discourtesy, or mere counter-assertion in argument, intended to bludgeon an opponent to the ground, because they find such behaviour intensely distasteful. And yet, wholly admirable as such men are and impressive as their standard of value is, theirs is not the only way of reflecting upon life, nor are their values the one sure guide for mankind. Isaiah Berlin has compared the murmur of Bloomsbury to chamber music: and chamber music certainly resembles that exchange of views, voice answering voice, between intellectuals, like a never-ending series of telephone calls, which so delighted him as a young don in the 1930s. But this is not the only kind of existence to be regarded as admirable or profitable. Chamber music is indeed an austere and demanding musical form: neither Beethoven nor Bach wrote more profound works than the posthumous quartets or the partitas. But symphonies, great choral works and operas demanding a huge orchestra and more than half a dozen soloists also delight and astonish us, and we would think it absurd if some pedant declared that they were all vulgar or grandiose.

Why then should we not recognise that the world of affairs has its own validity and is governed by its own rules? Why should we not admit that statesmen cannot be scholars or scholars statesmen, just as long ago the Church divided mankind into the laity, the secular clergy and 'religious'? 'Life', writes Berlin, 'may be seen through many windows, none of them necessarily clear or opaque, less or more distorting than any of the others.' Bloomsbury had a right to their own scale of values: but they were in error when they assumed that all sensible and intelligent individuals should conform to it. It is all very well to believe that you have discovered the truth about ethics, history, painting and personal relations; but to declare that anyone in the vast world who does not accept these conclusions is either a fool or a knave is grotesque. Statesmen must, therefore, display very different qualities and live by ideals far removed from those of the scholars who later interpret them. Pluralism means the acceptance of a multitude of ideals appropriate in different circumstances and for men of different callings. Indeed there are different kinds of statesmen and it would be foolish to judge that one type inspired by one set of ideas is necessarily worse than another type acting under the influence of a different set of ideas. At one point, in describing Roosevelt, Berlin contrasts two types of statesmen, the first consisting of men of single principle and fanatical vision, ignoring men and events and bending them to their powerful will, the second consisting of men who possess delicate antennae which enable them to sense how events are moving and how their fellow citizens feel, to divine where the means lie for effecting what they desire; 'the distinction I am drawing', writes Berlin, 'is not a moral one, not one of value but one of type'. In each category some are noble or attractive, some dubious or deplorable. On the one hand there stand Garibaldi, Trotsky, Parnell, de Gaulle, Woodrow Wilson and Hitler; on the other Bismarck, Lincoln, Lloyd George, Masaryk, Gladstone and Roosevelt.

Immediately we begin to see that many of the moral judgements commonly made about politics are simply untrue. It is not true that good men alone bring dignity and prosperity to their people. But neither is it true, as so-called realists like to argue, that desirable ends in politics are nearly always achieved by employing undesirable means. Honourable and conscientious men have all too often failed ignominiously to govern well, while ruffians and fanatics have imposed law and order upon chaotic conditions and replaced enfeebled popular governments by vigorous despotic regimes. But it is also true that tyrants such as Hitler have died seeing the empire they created crumbling before their eyes, while indomitable leaders such as Ben-Gurion, pursuing justice and independence, lead their compatriots out of the wilderness and die lapped by the waves of their gratitude. Berlin is no Mosca or Michels, the kind of political realist who relishes telling his readers that, if the State is to defy its enemies, society to be stable and the masses happy, the ticket you buy for such a performance will cost you dear in lost liberties, the deaths of innocent creatures and the execution of opponents of the regime. Too high a price and Berlin, like Ivan Karamazov, would return his ticket.[1] He is not a party man. He joins no camp and

---

[1] Karamazov says: 'too high a price has been placed on harmony. We cannot

excludes as few visionaries as possible. Both Tolstoy and Marx he considers mistaken but far fuller of truth than of error, and worthy of the deepest respect. Belinsky, a fierce believer in one ideology after another, dedicated to propagating the truth as he saw it, intolerant of anyone whom he considered to be wilfully living a life of error, is most unlike Weizmann, the politician whom Berlin so admires; but the human race would be impoverished without men such as Belinsky. That is why he chooses the *éloge* as his paradigm. It is a way of expressing the variety of life, or reminding us how in someone who at first sight seems antipathetic or perverse good qualities abound: how the person in question lives by standards entirely appropriate to his calling. For unless society acknowledges that men both do and should live according to different ideals, the men and women within it will not be free.

Like all thinkers of importance Isaiah Berlin writes in a style which is entirely his and his alone and without which he could not express his meaning. In recent years it has become even more personal as he records what he has to say on tape and amends the transcript to produce the final draft. Such a method would be ruinous for most writers; but Berlin's mind is of such distinction that he thinks and speaks, whether in a room among friends or on the rostrum delivering a lecture, in long periods, clause upon clause, the predicate lengthening out into a profusion of participles, a manner which in the hands of other men would have become a cumbersome imitation of Cicero. He is not a Henry Moore shaping a great mass of stone which relates human beings to the elemental forces of nature. Rather he resembles a Seurat, a *pointilliste* who peppers his canvas with a fusillade of adjectives, epithets, phrases, analogies, elucidations and explanations so that at last a particular idea, a principle of action, a vision of life emerges before our eyes in all its complexity; and no sooner have we comprehended it than he begins using the same methods to create a conflicting or, it may be, a complementary vision of life, so that by contrast we may understand the first conception better. He will always use two words where one will not do. He has no fear that his reader will get lost in the labyrinth of his sentences because they have the rhythm and the spring of the spoken word. He

afford to pay so much for admission. And therefore I hasten to return my ticket of admission.' *The Brothers Karamazov*, book 5, chapter 4, trans. David Magarshack (Harmondsworth, 1958), vol. 1, p. 287.

defends what he calls Churchill's Johnsonian prose. The self-conscious revival of the style of a bygone age, such as the Gothic Revival, need not be fake; it can be genuine. And Churchill's prose is a projection of himself and his vision of history, highly coloured, vivid, big, bright, unsubtle, addressed to the world at large, not a vehicle for introspection or the private life, but suffused with deep sentiment for his own country and its place in the hierarchy of nations. Berlin's style reflects his own sense of values no less faithfully.

For, of course, he is a man with a sharp sense of right and wrong. No one should suppose that a pluralist is a relativist. He is as much entitled to his vision of life as the Catholic or the Marxist. Berlin reminds us that a vision should not be expected to be as precise as an equation.

> Nor do we complain of 'escapism' or perversion of the facts [he writes] until the categories adopted are thought to do too much violence to the 'facts'. To interpret, to relate, to classify, to symbolise are those natural and unavoidable human activities which we loosely and conveniently describe as thinking. We complain, if we do, only when the result is too widely at variance with the common outlook of our own society and age and tradition.

That is, not the conventional wisdom or even the accepted beliefs of a culture, but the very concepts and categories in which we can hardly help thinking, being who we are and when and where we exist. What, then, is Isaiah Berlin's own vision of life and what are the virtues he particularly esteems?

His heart has always been given to the life of the mind and to Oxford. Oxford has sustained him as a scholar and he has tried to repay the debt by helping to found a graduate college and assuming other duties he would not otherwise have willingly performed. He has deliberately chosen to praise men very different in temperament from himself, austere or withdrawn figures, not perhaps noted for their ebullient humour, scholars who thought a day lost if fourteen hours had not been spent in the Bodleian, college men whose minds sucked up like a sponge details in the accounts such as the singular low rate of interest earned by the reserve building fund. He practised pluralism in life: he genuinely admired those who were, like himself, indisputably intellectuals but more severe and dry. Yet even among such he cannot help making us aware that it is useless to expect them all to exhibit the same good qualities. Hubert Henderson and Richard Pares were good college men, but would it not be ludicrous to blame the shy Plamenatz for detesting committees and the noise of repartee in the common room after a feast? And would it not be equally ludicrous to condemn those who liked noise, such as Maurice Bowra, who preferred vehemence to reticence, pleasure to austerity, exuberance to melancholy, intellectual gaiety and the deflating of the establishment, the self-important and the pompous, to *pietas* and *gravitas*? High spirits are also part of what a university should prize. Professors such as Felix Frankfurter, effervescent, dispelling the prim self-consciousness that is the bane of academic communities, preferring the company of his younger colleagues to the right-thinking conventional men who consider themselves to be the arbiters of academic life – they too are essential to a great university.

Nowhere does Isaiah Berlin better reveal his commitment to Oxford and the life of the mind than in his incomparable essay on John Austin, worthy to rank with Keynes's memories of his early beliefs, in which he describes Austin pursuing truth without regard for friend or foe or for the consequences, and with a single-mindedness which Berlin found later only when he got to know Keynes's mentor G. E. Moore. There will be some who will regard his description of what was actually discussed in that seminar as final proof that British philosophy loses itself in a wilderness of pedantry. They will be wrong. Philosophers of every age, Plato's disciples, the Schoolmen, Cartesians, Hegelians, have always worked on minute points, or upon sharply defined problems such as perception and epistemology. Berlin is not complacent. Looking back, he thinks those young dons such as himself who took part in Austin's seminar were too self-centred to publish much. They were gratified enough if one of their points won acceptance from the rest of the group. But, as he says, those who have never believed that they and their colleagues were discovering for the first time new truths which would have profound consequences for their subject, 'those who have never been under the spell of this kind of illusion, even for a short while, have not known true intellectual happiness'.

Scholars are often bores – even the greatest among them. One day when Berlin was a young man a scholar called on him who was regarded by some people as a genius and by others as a champion among bores. This was Namier and, as Berlin says, 'He was, in fact, both.' Not that Berlin was bored. Not even when Namier explained to him slowly and at length, not once but several times, that he was wasting his life because Marx was someone unworthy to occupy his attention and because ideas were merely the product of men's sub-conscious drives for power, glory, wealth and pleasure, was he cast down. When Namier explained that the reason why England was a Great Power, at once humane and civilised, was precisely that the English recognised how unimportant ideas were and kept intellectuals firmly in their place, he became even more interested and over the years treasured with amusement examples of Namier's more terrifying insults. For this mounting interest there were two reasons. Unlike other scholars who when told that their subject is worthless write off their persecutor as a maniac, Berlin asked himself why it was that Namier thought as he did and what sort of a man he was. Namier seemed to him to be both the most anti-metaphysical of rationalists, at one with the analyses of Mach and Freud or later of the Vienna circle, yet at the same time a Jew and, like Disraeli, a nationalist and a romantic. What was more he was an East European Jew. What was best he was a Zionist.

From the time that he was a boy at St Paul's Isaiah Berlin has been a Zionist. This loyalty has inspired some of his finest writing. Some Zionists despise and hate Jews who assimilate successfully to the culture of the country in which they live: but not Berlin. He has no quarrel with the children or grandchildren of those whom Namier called 'trembling Israelites', men and women of Jewish descent who have long ceased to tremble, and live happily among their neighbours, accepted for what they are, who are free from envy, anxiety and apprehension and who do not observe Jewish rituals or festivals and indeed may be hostile to religion as such. He may, it is true, regard as faintly odious the contortions of those Jews who attract attention to their origins by their efforts to suppress them, who wince at hearing the name of Zion mentioned and would prefer to be strolling in the Long Room at Lord's wearing the tie of the Marylebone Cricket Club. Similarly, although he does not seek out their company, he would not decline to talk to those Foreign Office officials whose whole training has been devoted to fostering sound pro-Arab policies and distrust of Israel. He knows well that some of those whom he fascinates harbour in their secret heart mild anti-Semitic views, upper-class people who almost forget he is a Jew because, devoid of anxiety or resentment about the matter, he is as secure in his Jewishness as they are in their cocoon. Indeed he has a keen eye for those snubs, insults, pin-pricks and acts of exclusion to which even now Jews are subjected in ordinary life. Others, smooth as Jacob's hands, may make light of such things or ignore them; but for him such humiliations convince him of the necessity of the State of Israel. He did not become a Zionist because the Jews should inhabit their natural land promised them by Jehovah. He became a Zionist because he wanted there to be somewhere on earth where Jews are not always in a minority, fearful that, if they did not behave well and ape an alien culture, the Gentiles would despise them – or even murder or expel them. You feel that he speaks for himself when, writing about Weizmann, he notes how 'martyrs, failures, casualties, victims of circumstance or of their own absurdities – the stock subjects of the mocking, sceptical Jewish humour – filled him with distress and disgust'. The mordant, sophisticated jokes of central European Jews ('I have bad luck: every time I buy a dwarf it grows') – jokes full of avant-garde sophistication, cynicism, and vulgarity masking a desperate political fanaticism – are not for him. Again, when he speaks of Weizmann's love of England, the respect which as an East European Jew he had for its humane democracy, its civil liberty, legal equality, toleration, moderation, dislike of extremes and lack of cruelty, even its taste for the odd and the eccentric, Berlin is saying something about his own love for the country in which his parents settled.

For a few years during the War Berlin worked on the staff of the British Embassy in Washington, and he has measured all the imponderables, the might-have-beens, the swing of the pendulum of fate which led to the collapse of his hopes and those of Weizmann that Britain might have been the willing midwife at the birth of Israel. He never excuses his own misapprehensions but nor does he admit error when in fact despite events he was at the time right.

Some may have wondered whether he suffered from divided loyalties. Such doubts used long ago to be entertained about Catholics and there were plenty of worldly-wise establishmentarians such as Harold Nicolson who considered that it was unwise to employ Jews in the Foreign Office because they were 'not one of us' and could hardly be expected to recognise that British oil interests in Arab States were paramount. Dual allegiance can create tensions and strain loyalty; it is untrue to deny that the problem exists. But it did not exist for Berlin. He had no doubt that he was a servant in Washington of the British Government, of his own country, a country which had not conscripted him or compelled him to hold views and pursue policies deeply repugnant to him. He was under no constraint. As a civilian he was free, even in wartime, to resign. And being free he had no right to disobey or cavil. He took for granted the supremacy of total loyalty to England, which at one time had stood alone against Hitler. The clarity and purity of his moral perception relieved him of those fearful upheavals and soul-searchings which lesser men suffered over such issues as the atom bomb. Occasionally, of course, in discussing the Middle East with his colleagues in the embassy, most of whom were anti-Zionist, he found himself in disagreement and hence in some discomfort. Again, it was painful for him when some fanatical Zionists considered him tainted by his British allegiance. But discomfort or pain are different from moral contortion and strain. For had he suffered in that way then indeed the contention held by the Nicolsons of this world that no one can loyally serve two ideals would gain credence and provide tinder for xenophobia in general and anti-Semitism in particular. Nor does he stop at dual loyalties. As a pluralist he sees no contradiction in observing quadruple or quintuple loyalties.

Nevertheless it was perhaps the experiences of those years which determined him, except for a short sojourn in Moscow, never to work again for any government. Nor was he dazzled by the powerful, and if they sought him out he did not necessarily respond. After the War Beaverbrook, who had heard of Berlin's renowned weekly telegram to the Foreign Office, a commentary on the Washington political scene, summoned him and used all his repertoire of blandishments to inveigle Berlin to write for his papers. Beaverbrook was incredulous when his overtures were not immediately accepted. 'Why, Arnold Bennett wrote for me until the last breath he drew' – why should not Mr Berlin accept? There could be luxurious living which he, Beaverbrook, knew well how to arrange. There could be – and it was an offer, he declared, which was not made to many – there could be a discreet flat where Berlin could entertain – a lady; indeed ladies, if need be, could even materialise. The offer was not taken up. Shortly after, Berlin was denounced by one of Beaverbrook's minions in a leading article. Berlin enormously enjoyed the episode.

'The Jews are a peculiar and difficult people in many ways,' he has written, 'not least because their history has contradicted most of the best-known and most admired theories of historical causation.' In the history of the Jews and in the creation of the State of Israel Berlin finds his most telling argument against those who maintain that history is the study of classes and social movements, impersonal forces such as demography and climatic changes, of technological development and terms of trade. In Braudel's great work, *The Mediterranean and the Mediterranean World in the Age of Philip II*, the Spanish King makes his appearance only well on into the second volume, and for the most part, along with other princes and geniuses of that time, does not cut much of a figure. That is not how Berlin sees history. The foundation of the State of Israel was inherently improbable. That it came about was principally due, in Berlin's view, to a great statesman, Chaim Weizmann. No explanation of how it came about which eliminated Weizmann would hold water. And so little is history inevitable or determined that Weizmann's own reasonable assumptions and policies for bringing about the birth of the State were blown away by incalculable and fortuitous events.

The foundation of the State of Israel is not the only example in our times of the actions of individuals confounding determinism in history. The resistance by the British in 1940, or Hitler's invasion of Russia a year later, are as telling. If Weizmann was a great man because by his intervention in history he made the improbable happen, so were Churchill and Roosevelt. But the question immediately bursts in the sky like a shower of fireworks: how are we to regard great men? Berlin would vehemently deny that great men are beyond moral scrutiny, as Hegel declared they were. In praise of Weizmann he declares: '[He] committed none of those enormities for which men of action, and later their biographers, claim justification, on the ground of what is called *raison d'état* ... Weizmann, despite his reputation as a master of *realpolitik*, forged no telegrams, massacred no minorities, executed and incarcerated no political opponents.' Politicians should not sacrifice, even when trapped in a crisis, the accepted standards of private morality to the alleged claims of the State or some interest group. Yet at the same time, while you may, if you choose, ask questions about a great man which would be perfectly appropriate if you were considering the life of one of your friends – whether he was kind, sensitive, good company – you should recognise that these are not the most important questions. It is more appropriate to ask what this statesman achieved, what was his vision of life and how it affected his policies. Just as Matthew Arnold declared that any translation of Homer should recognise that Homer was noble and sublime and wrote in the grand manner, so Berlin suggests that Roosevelt's critics should recognise that it was due to his personality that America was regarded on his death as the natural champion of democracy and of humane social policies. It was Roosevelt who gave Americans a status both inside and outside their country which they had never had before; and in achieving this he never sacrificed any fundamental political principle to retain power nor whipped up wicked passions to crush his enemies. And similarly Churchill was recognised all over the world as the man who had saved his country and prevented Europe from falling under an evil power. Both men had, and will always have, their critics, and part of what these critics say will be true. But their criticisms pale beside the qualities, the style and the achievements which these men displayed; and they displayed them because they were animated each by a vision of life – Churchill ruling his days and controlling his passions by his sense of the past and of his place in history, Roosevelt understanding the future and shaping his policies so as to give Americans the maximum scope to deal with its problems. Devoted though he is to the virtues of the private life, Berlin has a just estimate of public virtue.

Few of us have the imagination or the integrity to see life as a whole, but you do not have to be a statesman or an artist to have a vision of life. There are people in every class in society who do so and Berlin records how in 1946, when staying at the embassy in Paris, he met such a person. This was Auberon Herbert, who having held him not in conversation but in monologue long after everyone else had retired, when Berlin was hoping for a few hours' sleep before departing at five the next morning, followed him to his bedroom and stayed talking. Berlin says he did not find this strange; he could hardly have done so, since in those days he was capable of doing exactly that himself if, as was always so, plenty was still left to say. Berlin came to realise then and in the subsequent years of friendship that Herbert did not merely hold strong, quixotic, eccentric and sometimes deplorable views, but that he lived under the spell of a code, in part that of the landed aristocracy, but made all the more piquant by a singular fastidious-ness and generosity of spirit. It was a limited vision; it was a prejudiced vision; but it was not an ignoble vision. As Berlin puts it, Herbert disliked philistines, cowards and hypocrites more than he disliked liars, barbarians or cunning adventurers. Bizarre as some of the ends were which he pursued without regard to whether the means existed to attain them, Herbert's contempt for utilitarian principles was admirable precisely because his religion checked his natural lack of moderation.

It is more difficult for an intellectual to see the point of eccentricity in another intellectual – eccentricity not in his habits but in his rational and dispassionate analysis of phenomena. That Berlin was charmed by Aldous Huxley, a man of singular sweetness of nature, humility and range of mind, is not surprising. What is unusual is the way Berlin rejects the assumption common among intellectuals that Huxley wasted his maturity investigating paranormal psychology. On the contrary: perhaps no one since Spinoza has believed as unswervingly as Huxley that knowledge liberates; and Berlin praises Huxley for extending the panorama of knowledge to include occult as well as open knowledge. He believes that Huxley had an insight into what may prove to be the field in which the greatest advances will be made in the next century: in the relation of body to mind and of myth and ritual to empirical investigation.

No one should suppose that these *éloges* emerge from a vapid disposition. Dear people exist who have never been heard to say a harsh word about anyone: for the good reason that they have taught themselves to live in a world of their own imagining where none hear, see or speak evil. Berlin is not one of them. He is not blind to human failings and is quick to spot the feet of clay of those he likes or esteems as well as of those whom he thinks of little account. As Jack Gallagher at Cambridge used to say, each of us has awful friends; and we are all somebody's awful friend. But if Isaiah Berlin cannot help regarding some awful people with sympathy and affection, even if they embarrass him, there are others who seem to him not merely awful but unattractive because they are insensitive or inhuman. He distinguishes between the awful and the bad. It is bad to be the kind of careerist who begins life as an oily opportunist only too willing to betray his friends in a crisis and ends it by gratuitously harming others in order to feed his unappeasable appetite for power and position. Others are worse than bad: downright evil or sinister or both. The sinister and evil are quite different from certain able and successful men and women whom he would rather not meet but, if he did, would make the best of it. They are different again from certain types of celebrities or snobs or complacent *bien-pensants* or proud and corrupt European aristocrats who lie on the other side of his frontier of tolerance. The sinister and evil give him the horrors and, if faced by them, he melts from the room like a displeased ghost vanishing.

Unlike some who have such a sharp eye he is not interested – none less so – in doing others down. He may be censorious but, unlike many moralists, censoriousness is not a state of mind in which he finds pleasure. In the act of observing a crook or a charlatan, a dullard or a devious fellow, he enjoys discovering redeeming features. Redemption not condemnation, merits not failings, stimulate him to write; and when he writes he chooses those he wants to praise and particularises only their good qualities. He hardly ever attributes defects: defects he generalises. For instance, if he saw fit to praise a man for the style, even the abandon, with which he dressed, he would contrast him with those who are natty or trendy – and leave his reader to guess who they were. Like Hamlet he stands amazed at what a piece of work is a man; unlike Hamlet he delights in man.

Human beings delight him because he possesses a special gift which some of those who make sapient judgements upon people singularly lack. That is an irrepressible sense of humour. Its special qualities are spontaneity, playfulness, delight in absurdity. It is not entirely English: it owes something to his Russian origins. It is like the humour which bubbles up like a spring in Dostoevsky and is at the heart of Chekhov. Not for nothing did he regard the composer, Nicolas Nabokov, whose sense of comedy was highly developed, with special affection: he loves jokes and lightheartedness even when they spring from the facetious schoolboy humour with which Churchill used to discomfit his enemies, entertain his friends and hearten his countrymen.

These tributes, then, are not sketches thrown on one side, the refuse of the artist's studio. They are as much part of Isaiah Berlin's *oeuvre* as are his essays on liberty and on the intellectuals of the Enlightenment and the nineteenth century. No one can understand ideas unless he sees them as the expression of the passions, desires, longings and frustrations of human beings; and the word 'life' itself has no meaning unless it calls to mind men and women – past, present and to come.

WINSTON CHURCHILL IN 1940

I

IN THE now remote year 1928, an eminent English poet and critic
published a book dealing with the art of writing English prose.[1]
Writing at a time of bitter disillusion with the false splendours of
the Edwardian era, and still more with the propaganda and
phrasemaking occasioned by the First World War, the critic
praised the virtues of simplicity. If simple prose was often dry and
flat, it was at least honest. If it was at times awkward, shapeless and
bleak, it did at least convey a feeling of truthfulness. Above all, it
avoided the worst of all temptations – inflation, self-dramatisation,
the construction of flimsy stucco façades, either deceptively
smooth or covered with elaborate baroque detail which concealed a
dreadful inner emptiness.

The time and mood are familiar enough: it was not long after
Lytton Strachey had set a new fashion by his method of exposing
the cant or muddleheadedness of eminent Victorians, after Bertrand Russell had unmasked the great nineteenth-century meta-
physicians as authors of a monstrous hoax played upon generations
eager to be deceived, after Keynes had successfully pilloried the
follies and vices of the Allied statesmen at Versailles. This was the
time when rhetoric and, indeed, eloquence were held up to
obloquy as camouflage for literary and moral Pecksniffs, unscrupulous charlatans who corrupted artistic taste and discredited the
cause of truth and reason, and at their worst incited to evil and led
a credulous world to disaster. It was in this literary climate that the
critic in question, with much skill and discrimination, explained
why he admired the last recorded words spoken to Judge Thayer
by the poor fish-pedlar Vanzetti[2] – moving, ungrammatical
fragments uttered by a simple man about to die – more than he did

---

[1] Herbert Read, *English Prose Style* (London, 1928).
[2] ibid., p. 165.

the rolling periods of celebrated masters of fine writing widely read by the public at that time.

He selected as an example of the latter a man who in particular was regarded as the sworn enemy of all that the author prized most highly – humility, integrity, humanity, scrupulous regard for sensibility, individual freedom, personal affection – the celebrated but distrusted paladin of imperialism and the romantic conception of life, the swashbuckling militarist, the vehement orator and journalist, the most public of public personalities in a world dedicated to the cultivation of private virtues, the Chancellor of the Exchequer of the Conservative Government then in power, Winston Churchill.

After observing that 'These three conditions are necessary to Eloquence – firstly, an adequate theme; then a sincere and impassioned mind; and lastly a power of sustainment or pertinacity', the writer drove his thesis home with a quotation from the first part of Churchill's *World Crisis*, which had appeared some four years previously, and added: 'Such eloquence is false because it is artificial . . . the images are stale, the metaphors violent. The whole passage exhales a false dramatic atmosphere . . . a volley of rhetorical imperatives.' He went on to describe Churchill's prose as being high-sounding, redundant, falsely eloquent, declamatory, derived from undue 'aggrandisation of the self' instead of 'aggrandisation of the theme'; and condemned it root and branch.[1]

This view was well received by the young men who were painfully reacting against anything which appeared to go beyond the naked skeleton of the truth, at a time when not only rhetoric but even noble eloquence seemed outrageous hypocrisy. Churchill's critic spoke, and knew that he spoke, for a post-war generation; the psychological symptoms of the vast and rapid social transformation then in progress, from which the government in power so resolutely averted its gaze, were visible to the least discerning critics of literature and the arts; the mood was dissatisfied, hostile and insecure; the sequel to so much magnificence was too bitter, and left behind it a heritage of hatred for the grand style as such. The victims and casualties of the disaster thought they had earned the right to be rid of the trappings of an age which had heartlessly betrayed them.

Nevertheless the stern critic and his audience were profoundly

[1] ibid., pp. 191–2.

mistaken. What he and they denounced as so much tinsel and hollow pasteboard was in reality solid: it was this author's natural means for the expression of his heroic, highly coloured, sometimes over-simple and even naïve, but always genuine, vision of life. The critic saw only an unconvincing, sordidly transparent pastiche, but this was an illusion. The reality was something very different: an inspired, if unconscious, attempt at a revival. It went against the stream of contemporary thought and feeling only because it was a deliberate return to a formal mode of English utterance which extends from Gibbon and Dr Johnson to Peacock and Macaulay, a composite weapon created by Churchill in order to convey his particular vision. In the bleak and deflationary 1920s it was too bright, too big, too vivid, too unstable for the sensitive and sophisticated epigoni of the age of imperialism, who, living an inner life of absorbing complexity and delicacy, became unable and certainly unwilling to admire the light of a day which had destroyed so much of what they had trusted and loved. From this the critic and his supporters recoiled; but their analysis of their reasons was not convincing.

They had, of course, a right to their own scale of values, but it was a blunder to dismiss Churchill's prose as a false front, a hollow sham. Revivals are not false as such: the Gothic Revival, for example, represented a passionate, if nostalgic, attitude towards life, and while some examples of it may appear bizarre, it sprang from a deeper sentiment and had a good deal more to say than some of the thin and 'realistic' styles which followed; the fact that the creators of the Gothic Revival found their liberation in going back into a largely imaginary past in no way discredits them or their achievement. There are those who, inhibited by the furniture of the ordinary world, come to life only when they feel themselves actors upon a stage, and, thus emancipated, speak out for the first time, and are then found to have much to say. There are those who can function freely only in uniform or armour or court dress, see only through certain kinds of spectacles, act fearlessly only in situations which in some way are formalised for them, see life as a kind of play in which they and others are assigned certain lines which they must speak. So it happens – the last war afforded plenty of instances of this – that people of a shrinking disposition perform miracles of courage when life has been dramatised for them, when they are on the battlefield; and might continue to do so if they were constantly in uniform and life were always a battlefield.

This need for a framework is not 'escapism', not artificial or abnormal or a sign of maladjustment. Often it is a vision of experience in terms of the strongest single psychological ingredient in one's nature: not infrequently in the form of a simple struggle between conflicting forces or principles, between truth and false-hood, good and evil, right and wrong, between personal integrity and various forms of temptation and corruption (as in the case of the critic in question), or between what is conceived as permanent and what is ephemeral, or between the material and the immaterial, or between the forces of life and the forces of death, or between the religion of art and its supposed enemies – politicians or priests or philistines. Life may be seen through many windows, none of them necessarily clear or opaque, less or more distorting than any of the others. And since we think largely in words, they necessarily take on the property of serving as an armour. The style of Dr Johnson, which echoes so frequently in the prose of *Their Finest Hour*, particularly when the author indulges in a solemn facetiousness, was itself in its own day a weapon offensive and defensive; it requires no deep psychological subtlety to perceive why a man so vulnerable as Johnson – who belonged mentally to the previous century – had constant need of it.

II

Churchill's dominant category, the single, central, organising principle of his moral and intellectual universe, is a historical imagination so strong, so comprehensive, as to encase the whole of the present and the whole of the future in a framework of a rich and multicoloured past. Such an approach is dominated by a desire – and a capacity – to find fixed moral and intellectual bearings, to give shape and character, colour and direction and coherence, to the stream of events.

This kind of systematic 'historicism' is, of course, not confined to men of action or political theorists: Roman Catholic thinkers see life in terms of a firm and lucid historical structure, and so, of course, do Marxists, and so did the romantic historians and philosophers from whom the Marxists are directly descended. Nor do we complain of 'escapism' or perversion of the facts until the categories adopted are thought to do too much violence to the 'facts'. To interpret, to relate, to classify, to symbolise are those natural and unavoidable human activities which we loosely and conveniently describe as thinking. We complain, if we do, only when the result is too widely at variance with the common outlook of our own society and age and tradition.

Churchill sees history – and life – as a great Renaissance pageant: when he thinks of France or Italy, Germany or the Low Countries, Russia, India, Africa, the Arab lands, he sees vivid historical images – something between Victorian illustrations in a child's book of history and the great procession painted by Benozzo Gozzoli in the Riccardi Palace. His eye is never that of the neatly classifying sociologist, the careful psychological analyst, the plodding anti-quary, the patient historical scholar. His poetry has not that anatomical vision which sees the naked bone beneath the flesh, skulls and skeletons and the omnipresence of decay and death beneath the flow of life. The units out of which his world is constructed are simpler and larger than life, the patterns vivid and repetitive like those of an epic poet, or at times like those of a dramatist who sees persons and situations as timeless symbols and embodiments of eternal, shining principles. The whole is a series of symmetrically formed and somewhat stylised compositions, either suffused with bright light or cast in darkest shadow, like a legend by Carpaccio, with scarcely any nuance, painted in primary colours, with no half-tones, nothing intangible, nothing impalp-able, nothing half spoken or hinted or whispered: the voice does not alter in pitch or timbre.

The archaisms of style to which Churchill's wartime speeches accustomed us are indispensable ingredients of the heightened tone, the formal chronicler's attire, for which the solemnity of the occasion called. Churchill is fully conscious of this: the style should adequately respond to the demands which history makes upon the actors from moment to moment. 'The ideas set forth', he wrote in 1940 about a Foreign Office draft, 'appeared to me to err in trying to be too clever, to enter into refinements of policy unsuited to the tragic simplicity and grandeur of the times and the issues at stake.'

His own narrative consciously mounts and swells until it reaches the great climax of the Battle of Britain. The texture and the tension are those of a tragic opera, where the very artificiality of the medium, both in the recitative and in the arias, serves to eliminate the irrelevant dead level of normal existence and to set off in high relief the deeds and sufferings of the principal characters. The moments of comedy in such a work must necessarily conform to the style of the whole and be parodies of it; and this is Churchill's practice. When he says that he viewed this or that 'with stern and tranquil gaze', or informs his officials that any 'chortling' by them over the failure of a chosen scheme 'will be viewed with great disfavour by me', or describes the 'celestial grins' of his collaborators over the development of a well-concealed conspiracy, he does precisely this; the mock-heroic tone – reminiscent of *Stalky & Co.* – does not break the operatic conventions. But conventions though they be, they are not donned and doffed by the author at will: by now they are his second nature, and have completely fused with the first; art and nature are no longer distinguishable. The very rigid pattern of his prose is the normal medium of his ideas not merely when he sets himself to compose, but in the life of the imagination which permeates his daily existence.

Churchill's language is a medium which he invented because he needed it. It has a bold, ponderous, fairly uniform, easily recognisable rhythm which lends itself to parody (including his own) like all strongly individual styles. A language is individual when its user is endowed with sharply marked characteristics and succeeds in creating a medium for their expression. The origins, the constituents, the classical echoes which can be found in Churchill's prose are obvious enough; the product is, however, unique. Whatever the attitude that may be taken towards it, it must be recognised as a large-scale phenomenon of our time. To ignore or deny this would be blind or frivolous or dishonest. The utterance is always, and not merely on special occasions, formal (though it alters in intensity and colour with the situation), always public, Ciceronian, addressed to the world, remote from the hesitancies and stresses of introspection and private life.

III

The quality of Churchill's volumes on the Second World War is that of his whole life. His world is built upon the primacy of public over private relationships, upon the supreme value of action, of the battle between simple good and simple evil, between life and death; but, above all, battle. He has always fought. 'Whatever you may do,' he declared to the demoralised French ministers in the bleakest hour of 1940, 'we shall fight on for ever and ever and ever', and under this sign his own whole life has been lived.

What has he fought for? The answer is a good deal clearer than in the case of other equally passionate but less consistent men of action. Churchill's principles and beliefs on fundamental issues have never faltered. He has often been accused by his critics of inconstancy, of veering and even erratic judgement, as when he changed his allegiance from the Conservative to the Liberal Party, to and fro. But with the exception of the issue of protection, when he supported the tariff as Chancellor of the Exchequer in Baldwin's cabinet in the 1920s, this charge, which at first seems so plausible, is spectacularly false. Far from changing his opinions too often, Churchill has scarcely, during a long and stormy career, altered them at all. If anyone wishes to discover his views on the large and lasting issues of our time, he need only set himself to discover what Churchill has said or written on the subject at any period of his long and exceptionally articulate public life, in particular during the years before the First World War: the number of instances in which his views have in later years undergone any appreciable degree of change will be found astonishingly small.

The apparently solid and dependable Baldwin adjusted his attitudes with wonderful dexterity as and when circumstances required it. Chamberlain, long regarded as a grim and immovable rock of Tory opinion, altered his policies – more serious than Baldwin, he pursued policies, not being content with mere attitudes – when the Party or the situation seemed to him to require it. Churchill remained inflexibly attached to first principles.

It is the strength and coherence of his central, lifelong beliefs that have provoked greater uneasiness, more disfavour and suspicion, in the central office of the Conservative Party than his vehemence or passion for power, or what was considered his wayward, unreliable brilliance. No strongly centralised political organisation feels altogether happy with individuals who combine independence, a free imagination and a formidable strength of character with stubborn faith and a single-minded, unchanging view of the public and private good. Churchill, who believes that 'ambition, not so much for vulgar ends but for fame, glints in every mind', believes in and seeks to attain – as an artist his vision – personal greatness and personal glory. As much as any king conceived by a Renaissance dramatist or by a nineteenth-century historian or moralist, he thinks it a brave thing to ride in triumph through Persepolis; he knows with an unshakeable certainty what he considers to be big, handsome, noble and worthy of pursuit by someone in high station, and what, on the contrary, he abhors as being dim, grey, thin, likely to lower or destroy the play of colour and movement in the universe. Tacking and bending and timid compromise may commend themselves to those sound men of sense whose hopes of preserving the world they defend are shot through with an often unconscious pessimism; but if the policy they pursue is likely to slow the tempo, to diminish the forces of life, to lower the 'vital and vibrant energy' which he admires, say, in Lord Beaverbrook, Churchill is ready for attack.

Churchill is one of the diminishing number of those who genuinely believe in a specific world order: the desire to give it life and strength is the most powerful single influence upon everything which he thinks and imagines, does and is. When biographers and historians come to describe and analyse his views on Europe or America, on the British Empire or Russia, on India or Palestine, or even on social or economic policy, they will find that his opinions on all these topics are set in fixed patterns, set early in life and later only reinforced. Thus he has always believed in great States and civilisations in an almost hierarchical order, and has never, for instance, hated Germany as such: Germany is a great, historically hallowed State; the Germans are a great historic race and as such occupy a proportionate amount of space in Churchill's world picture. He denounced the Prussians in the First World War and the Nazis in the Second; the Germans scarcely at all. He has always entertained a glowing vision of France and her culture, and has unalterably advocated the necessity of Anglo-French collaboration. He has always looked on the Russians as a formless, quasi-Asiatic mass beyond the walls of European civilisation. His belief in and predilection for the American democracy are the foundation of his political outlook.

His vision in foreign affairs has always been consistently romantic. The struggle of the Jews for self-determination in Palestine engaged his imagination in precisely the way in which the Italian Risorgimento captured the sympathies of his Liberal forebears. Similarly his views on social policy conform to those Liberal principles which he received at the hands of the men he most admired in the great Liberal administration of the first decade of this century – Asquith, Haldane, Grey, Morley, above all Lloyd George before 1914 – and he has seen no reason to change them, whatever the world might do; and if these views, progressive in 1910, seem less convincing today, and indeed reveal an obstinate blindness to social and economic – as opposed to political –

injustice, of which Haldane or Lloyd George can scarcely be accused, that flows from Churchill's unalterable faith in the firmly conceived scheme of human relationships which he established within himself long ago, once and for all.

IV

It is an error to regard the imagination as a mainly revolutionary force – if it destroys and alters, it also fuses hitherto isolated beliefs, insights, mental habits, into strongly unified systems. These, if they are filled with sufficient energy and force of will – and, it may be added, fantasy, which is less frightened by the facts and creates ideal models in terms of which the facts are ordered in the mind – sometimes transform the outlook of an entire people and generation.

The British statesman most richly endowed with these gifts was Disraeli, who in effect conceived that imperialist mystique, that splendid but most un-English vision which, romantic to the point of exoticism, full of metaphysical emotion, to all appearances utterly opposed to everything most soberly empirical, utilitarian, anti-systematic in the British tradition, bound its spell on the mind of England for two generations.

Churchill's political imagination has something of the same magical power to transform. It is a magic which belongs equally to demagogues and great democratic leaders: Franklin Roosevelt, who as much as any man altered his country's inner image of itself and of its character and its history, possessed it in a high degree. But the differences between him and Churchill are greater than the similarities, and to some degree epitomise the differences of continents and civilisations. The contrast is brought out vividly by the respective parts which they played in the war which drew them so closely together.

The Second World War in some ways gave birth to less novelty and genius than the First. It was, of course, a greater cataclysm, fought over a wider area, and altered the social and political contours of the world at least as radically as its predecessor, perhaps more so. But the break in continuity in 1914 was far more violent. The years before 1914 look to us now, and looked even in the 1920s, as the end of a long period of largely peaceful development, broken suddenly and catastrophically. In Europe, at least, the years before 1914 were viewed with understandable nostalgia by those who after them knew no real peace.

The period between the Wars marks a decline in the development of human culture if it is compared with that sustained and fruitful period which makes the nineteenth century seem a unique human achievement, so powerful that it persisted, even during the war which broke it, to a degree which seems astonishing to us now. The quality of literature, for example, which is surely one of the most reliable criteria of intellectual and moral vitality, was incomparably higher during the War of 1914–18 than it has been after 1939. In Western Europe alone these four years of slaughter and destruction were also years in which works of genius and talent continued to be produced by such established writers as Shaw and Wells and Kipling, Hauptmann and Gide, Chesterton and Arnold Bennett, Beerbohm and Yeats, as well as such younger writers as Proust and Joyce, Virginia Woolf and E. M. Forster, T. S. Eliot and Alexander Blok, Rilke, Stefan George and Valéry. Nor did natural science, philosophy and history cease to develop fruitfully. What has the more recent war to offer by comparison?

Yet perhaps there is one respect in which the Second World War did outshine its predecessor: the leaders of the nations involved in it were, with the significant exception of France, men of greater stature, psychologically more interesting, than their prototypes. It would hardly be disputed that Stalin is a more fascinating figure than Tsar Nicholas II; Hitler more arresting than the Kaiser; Mussolini than Victor Emmanuel; and, memorable as they were, President Wilson and Lloyd George yield in the attribute of sheer historical magnitude to Franklin Roosevelt and Winston Churchill.

History, we are told by Aristotle, is 'what Alcibiades did and suffered'.[1] This notion, despite all the efforts of the social sciences to overthrow it, remains a good deal more valid than rival hypotheses, provided that history is defined as that which historians actually do. At any rate Churchill accepts it wholeheartedly, and takes full advantage of his opportunities. And because his narrative deals largely in personalities and gives individual genius its full and sometimes more than its full due, the appearance of the great wartime protagonists in his pages gives his narrative some of the quality of an epic, whose heroes and villains acquire their stature not merely – or indeed at all – from the importance of the

---

[1] *Poetics* 1451^{b}11.

events in which they are involved, but from their own intrinsic human size upon the stage of human history; their characteristics, involved as they are in perpetual juxtaposition and occasional collision with one another, set each other off in vast relief.

Comparisons and contrasts are bound to arise in the mind of the reader which sometimes take him beyond Churchill's pages. Thus Roosevelt stands out principally by his astonishing appetite for life and by his apparently complete freedom from fear of the future; as a man who welcomed the future eagerly as such, and conveyed the feeling that whatever the times might bring, all would be grist to his mill, nothing would be too formidable or crushing to be subdued and used and moulded into the pattern of the new and unpredictable forms of life into the building of which he, Roosevelt, and his allies and devoted subordinates would throw themselves with unheard-of energy and gusto. This avid anticipation of the future, the lack of nervous fear that the wave might prove too big or violent to navigate, contrasts most sharply with the uneasy longing to insulate themselves so clear in Stalin or Chamberlain. Hitler, too, in a sense, showed no fear, but his assurance sprang from a lunatic's violent and cunning vision, which distorted the facts too easily in his favour.

So passionate a faith in the future, so untroubled a confidence in one's power to mould it, when it is allied to a capacity for realistic appraisal of its true contours, implies an exceptionally sensitive awareness, conscious or half-conscious, of the tendencies of one's milieu, of the desires, hopes, fears, loves, hatreds of the human beings who compose it, of what are impersonally described as social and individual 'trends'. Roosevelt had this sensibility developed to the point of genius. He acquired the symbolic significance which he retained throughout his presidency largely because he sensed the tendencies of his time and their projections into the future to a most uncommon degree. His sense, not only of the movement of American public opinion but of the general direction in which the larger human society of his time was moving, was what is called uncanny. The inner currents, the tremors and complicated convolutions of this movement seemed to register themselves within his nervous system with a kind of seismographical accuracy. The majority of his fellow citizens recognised this – some with enthusiasm, others with gloom or bitter indignation. Peoples far beyond the frontiers of the United States rightly looked to him as the most genuine and unswerving spokesman of democracy of his time, the most contemporary, the most outward-looking, the boldest, most imaginative, most large-spirited, free from the obsessions of an inner life, with an unparalleled capacity for creating confidence in the power of his insight, his foresight, and his capacity genuinely to identify himself with the ideals of humble people.

This feeling of being at home not merely in the present but in the future, of knowing where he was going and by what means and why, made him, until his health was finally undermined, buoyant and gay: made him delight in the company of the most varied and opposed individuals, provided that they embodied some specific aspect of the turbulent stream of life, stood actively for the forward movement in their particular world, whatever it might be. And this inner *élan* made up, and more than made up, for faults of intellect or character, which his enemies – and his victims – never ceased to point out. He seemed genuinely unaffected by their taunts: what he could not abide was, before all, passivity, stillness, melancholy, fear of life or preoccupation with eternity or death, however great the insight or delicate the sensibility by which they were accompanied.

Churchill stands at almost the opposite pole. He too does not fear the future, and no man has ever loved life more vehemently and infused so much of it into everyone and everything that he has touched. But whereas Roosevelt, like all great innovators, had a half-conscious premonitory awareness of the coming shape of society, not wholly unlike that of an artist, Churchill, for all his extrovert air, looks within, and his strongest sense is the sense of the past.

The clear, brightly coloured vision of history in terms of which he conceives both the present and the future is the inexhaustible source from which he draws the primary stuff out of which his universe is so solidly built, so richly and elaborately ornamented. So firm and so embracing an edifice could not be constructed by anyone liable to react and respond like a sensitive instrument to the perpetually changing moods and directions of other persons or institutions or peoples. And, indeed, Churchill's strength (and what is most frightening in him) lies precisely in this: that, unlike Roosevelt, he is not equipped with numberless sensitive antennae which communicate the smallest oscillations of the outer world in all its unstable variety. Unlike Roosevelt (and unlike Gladstone and Lloyd George for that matter) he does not reflect a contemporary social or moral world in an intense and concentrated fashion; rather he creates one of such power and coherence that it becomes a reality and alters the external world by being imposed upon it with irresistible force. As his history of the War shows, he has an immense capacity for absorbing facts, but they emerge transformed by the categories which he powerfully imposes on the raw material into something which he can use to build his own massive, simple, impregnably fortified inner world.

Roosevelt, as a public personality, was a spontaneous, optimistic, pleasure-loving ruler who dismayed his assistants by the gay and apparently heedless abandon with which he seemed to delight in pursuing two or more totally incompatible policies, and astonished them even more by the swiftness and ease with which he managed to throw off the cares of office during the darkest and most dangerous moments. Churchill too loves pleasure, and he too lacks neither gaiety nor a capacity for exuberant self-expression, together with the habit of blithely cutting Gordian knots in a manner which often upset his experts; but he is not a frivolous man. His nature possesses a dimension of depth – and a corresponding sense of tragic possibilities – which Roosevelt's light-hearted genius instinctively passed by.

Roosevelt played the game of politics with virtuosity, and both his successes and his failures were carried off in splendid style; his performance seemed to flow with effortless skill. Churchill is acquainted with darkness as well as light. Like all inhabitants of inner worlds, and even transient visitors to them, he gives evidence of seasons of agonised brooding and slow recovery. Roosevelt might have spoken of sweat and blood, but when Churchill offered his people tears, he spoke a word which might have been uttered by Lincoln or Mazzini or Cromwell, but not by Roosevelt, great-hearted, generous and perceptive as he was.

V

Not the herald of the bright and cloudless civilisation of the future, Churchill is preoccupied by his own vivid world, and it is doubtful how far he has ever been aware of what actually goes on in the heads and hearts of others. He does not react, he acts; he does not mirror, he affects others and alters them to his own powerful measure. Writing of Dunkirk he says:

> There is no doubt that had I at this juncture faltered at all in the leading of the nation I should have been hurled out of office. I was

sure that every Minister was ready to be killed quite soon, and have all his family and possessions destroyed, rather than give in. In this they represented the House of Commons and almost all the people. It fell to me in these coming days and months to express their sentiments on suitable occasions. This I was able to do because they were mine also. There was a white glow, overpowering, sublime, which ran through our Island from end to end.[1]

And on 28 June of that year he told Lord Lothian, then ambassador in Washington, 'Your mood should be bland and phlegmatic. No one is down-hearted here.'[2]

These splendid sentences hardly do justice to his own part in creating the feeling which he describes. For Churchill is not a sensitive lens which absorbs and concentrates and reflects and amplifies the sentiments of others; unlike the European dictators, he does not play on public opinion like an instrument. In 1940 he assumed an indomitable stoutness, an unsurrendering quality on the part of his people, and carried on. If he did not represent the quintessence and epitome of what some, at any rate, of his fellow citizens feared and hoped in their hour of danger, this was because he idealised them with such intensity that in the end they approached his ideal and began to see themselves as he saw them: 'the buoyant and imperturbable temper of Britain which I had the honour to express' – it was indeed, but he had a lion's share in creating it. So hypnotic was the force of his words, so strong his faith, that by the sheer intensity of his eloquence he bound his spell upon them until it seemed to them that he was indeed speaking what was in their hearts and minds. Doubtless it was there; but largely dormant until he had awoken it within them.

After he had spoken to them in the summer of 1940 as no one has ever before or since, they conceived a new idea of themselves which their own prowess and the admiration of the world has since established as a heroic image in the history of mankind, like Thermopylae or the defeat of the Spanish Armada. They went forward into battle transformed by his words. The spirit which they found within them he had created within himself from his inner resources, and poured it into his nation, and took their vivid reaction for an original impulse on their part, which he merely had the honour to clothe in suitable words. He created a heroic mood

[1] *Their Finest Hour* [*The Second World War*, vol. 2] (London, 1949), p. 88.
[2] ibid., p. 201.

and turned the fortunes of the Battle of Britain not by catching the mood of his surroundings (which was not indeed, at any time, one of craven panic or bewilderment or apathy, but somewhat confused; stout-hearted but unorganised) but by being stubbornly impervious to it, as he has been to so many of the passing shades and tones of which the life around him has been composed.

The peculiar quality of heroic pride and a sense of the sublimity of the occasion arises in him not, as in Roosevelt, from delight in being alive and in control at a critical moment of history, in the very change and instability of things, in the infinite possibilities of the future whose very unpredictability offers endless possibilities of spontaneous moment-to-moment improvisation and large imaginative moves in harmony with the restless spirit of the time. On the contrary, it springs from a capacity for sustained introspective brooding, great depth and constancy of feeling – in particular, feeling for and fidelity to the great tradition for which he assumes a personal responsibility, a tradition which he bears upon his shoulders and must deliver, not only sound and undamaged but strengthened and embellished, to successors worthy of accepting the sacred burden.

Bismarck once said that there was no such thing as political intuition: political genius consisted in the ability to hear the distant hoofbeat of the horse of history – and then by superhuman effort to leap and catch the horseman by the coat-tails. No man has ever listened for this fateful sound more eagerly than Winston Churchill, and in 1940 he made the heroic leap. 'It is impossible', he writes of this time, 'to quell the inward excitement which comes from a prolonged balancing of terrible things', and when the crisis finally bursts he is ready, because after a lifetime of effort he has reached his goal.

The position of the Prime Minister is unique: 'If he trips he must be sustained: if he makes mistakes they must be covered; if he sleeps he must not be wantonly disturbed; if he is no good he must be pole-axed', and this because he is at that moment the guardian of the 'life of Britain, her message and her glory'. He trusted Roosevelt utterly, 'convinced that he would give up life itself, to say nothing about office, for the cause of world freedom now in such awful peril'. His prose records the tension which rises and swells to the culminating moment, the Battle of Britain – 'a time when it was equally good to live or die'. This bright, heroic vision of the mortal danger and the will to conquer, born in the hour when defeat seemed not merely possible but probable, is the product of a burning historical imagination, feeding upon the data not of the outer but of the inner eye: the picture has a shape and simplicity which future historians will find it hard to reproduce when they seek to assess and interpret the facts soberly in the grey light of common day.

VI

The Prime Minister was able to impose his imagination and his will upon his countrymen, and enjoy a Periclean reign, precisely because he appeared to them larger and nobler than life and lifted them to an abnormal height in a moment of crisis. It was a climate in which men do not usually like – nor ought they to like – living; it demands a violent tension which, if it lasts, destroys all sense of normal perspective, overdramatises personal relationships, and falsifies normal values to an intolerable extent. But, in the event, it did turn a large number of inhabitants of the British Isles out of their normal selves and, by dramatising their lives and making them seem to themselves and to each other clad in the fabulous garments appropriate to a great historic moment, transformed cowards into brave men, and so fulfilled the purpose of shining armour.

This is the kind of means by which dictators and demagogues transform peaceful populations into marching armies; it was Churchill's unique and unforgettable achievement that he created this necessary illusion within the framework of a free system without destroying or even twisting it; that he called forth spirits which did not stay to oppress and enslave the population after the hour of need had passed; that he saved the future by interpreting the present in terms of a vision of the past which did not distort or inhibit the historical development of the British people by attempting to make them realise some impossible and unattainable splendour in the name of an imaginary tradition or of an infallible, supernatural leader. Churchill was saved from this frightening nemesis of romanticism by a sufficiency of that libertarian feeling which, if it sometimes fell short of understanding the tragic aspects of modern despotisms, remained sharply perceptive – sometimes too tolerantly, but still perceptive – of what is false, grotesque, contemptible in the great frauds upon the people practised by totalitarian regimes. Some of the sharpest and most characteristic epithets are reserved for the dictators: Hitler is 'this evil man, this monstrous abortion of hatred and defeat'. Franco is a 'narrow-minded tyrant' of 'evil qualities' holding down a 'blood-drained people'. No quarter is given to the Pétain regime, and its appeal to tradition and the eternal France is treated as a repellent travesty of national feeling. Stalin in 1940–1 is 'at once a callous, a crafty, and an ill-informed giant'.

This very genuine hostility to usurpers, which is stronger in him than even his passion for authority and order, springs from a quality which Churchill conspicuously shared with President Roosevelt – uncommon love of life, aversion for the imposition of rigid disciplines upon the teeming variety of human relations, the instinctive sense of what promotes and what retards or distorts growth and vitality. But because the life which Churchill so loves presents itself to him in a historical guise as part of the pageant of tradition, his method of constructing historical narrative, the distribution of emphasis, the assignment of relative importance to persons and events, the theory of history, the architecture of the narrative, the structure of the sentences, the words themselves, are elements in an historical revival as fresh, as original and as idiosyncratic as the neo-classicism of the Renaissance or the Regency. To complain that this omits altogether too much by assuming that the impersonal, the dull, the undramatic are neces-sarily also unimportant may well be just; but to lament that this is not contemporary, and therefore in some way less true, less responsive to modern needs, than the noncommittal, neutral glass and plastic of those objective historians who regard facts and only facts as interesting and, worse still, all facts as equally interesting – what is this but craven pedantry and blindness?

VII

The differences between the President and the Prime Minister were at least in one respect something more than the obvious differences of national character, education, and even temperament. For all his sense of history, his large, untroubled, easygoing style of life, his unshakeable feeling of personal security, his natural assumption of being at home in the great world far beyond the confines of his own country, Roosevelt was a typical child of the twentieth century and of the New World; while Churchill for all his love of the present hour, his unquenchable appetite for new knowledge, his sense of the technological possibilities of our time, and the restless roaming of his fancy in considering how they might be most imaginatively applied, despite his enthusiasm for Basic English, or the siren suit which so upset his hosts in Moscow – despite all this, Churchill remains a European of the nineteenth century.

The difference is deep, and accounts for a great deal in the incompatibility of outlook between him and the President of the United States, whom he admired so much and whose great office he held in awe. Something of the fundamental unlikeness between America and Europe, and perhaps between the twentieth century and the nineteenth, seemed to be crystallised in this remarkable interplay. It may perhaps be that the twentieth century is to the nineteenth as the nineteenth was to the eighteenth. Talleyrand once made the well-known observation that those who had not lived under the *ancien régime* did not know what true *plaisir de vivre* had been. And indeed, from our distant vantage-point, this is clear: the earnest, romantic young men of the early part of the nineteenth century seemed systematically unable to understand or to like the attitude to life of the most civilised representatives of the pre-revolutionary world, particularly in France, where the break was sharpest; the irony, the sharpness, the minute vision, the perception of and concentration upon fine differences in character, in style, the preoccupation with barely perceptible dissimilarities of hue, the extreme sensibility which makes the life of even so 'progressive' and forward-looking a man as Diderot so unbridgeably different from the larger and simpler vision of the romantics – this is something which the nineteenth century lacked the historical perspective to understand.

Suppose that Shelley had met and talked with Voltaire, what would he have felt? He would most probably have been profoundly shocked – shocked by the seemingly limited vision, the smallness of the field of awareness, the apparent triviality and finickiness, the almost spinsterish elaboration of Voltaire's malice, the preoccupation with tiny units, the subatomic texture of experience; he would have felt horror or pity before such wanton blindness to the large moral and spiritual issues of his own day – causes whose universal scope and significance painfully agitated the best and most awakened minds; he might have thought him wicked, but even more he would have thought him contemptible, too sharp, too small, too mean, grotesquely and unworthily obscene, prone to titter on the most sacred occasions, in the holiest places.

And Voltaire, in his turn, would very probably have been dreadfully bored, unable to see good cause for so much ethical eloquence; he would have looked with a cold and hostile eye on all this moral excitement: the magnificent Saint-Simonian vision of one world (which so stirred the left-wing young men half a century later), altering in shape and becoming integrated into a neatly organised man-made whole by the application of powerfully concentrated scientific, technical and spiritual resources, would to him have seemed a dreary and monotonous desert, too homogeneous, too flavourless, too unreal, apparently unconscious of those small, half-concealed but crucial distinctions and incongruities which give individuality and savour to experience, without which there could be no civilised vision, no wit, no conversation, certainly no art deriving from a refined and fastidious culture. The moral vision of the nineteenth century would have seemed to him a dull, blurred, coarse instrument unable to focus those pin-points of concentrated light, those short-lived patterns of sound and colour, whose infinite variety as they linger or flash past are comedy and tragedy – are the substance of personal relations and of worldly wisdom, of politics, of history, and of art.

The reason for this failure of communication was not a mere change in the point of view, but the kind of vision which divided the two centuries. The microscopic vision of the eighteenth century was succeeded by the macroscopic eye of the nineteenth. The latter saw much more widely, saw in universal or at least in European terms; it saw the contours of great mountain ranges where the eighteenth century discerned, however sharply and perceptively, only the veins and cracks and different shades of but a portion of the mountainside. The object of vision of the eighteenth century was smaller and its eye was closer to the object. The enormous moral issues of the nineteenth century were not within the field of its acutely discriminating gaze: that was the devastating difference which the great French Revolution had made, and it led to something not necessarily better or worse, uglier or more beautiful, profounder or more shallow, but to a situation which above all was different in kind.

Something not unlike this same chasm divides America from Europe (and the twentieth century from the nineteenth). The

American vision is larger and more generous; its thought tran-
scends, despite the parochialism of its means of expression, the
barriers of nationality and race and differences of outlook, in a big,
sweeping, single view. It notices things rather than persons, and
sees the world (those who saw it in this fashion in the nineteenth
century were considered Utopian eccentrics) in terms of rich,
infinitely mouldable raw material, waiting to be constructed and
planned in order to satisfy a world-wide human craving for
happiness or goodness or wisdom. And therefore to it the differences and conflicts which divide Europeans in so violent a fashion
must seem petty, irrational and sordid, not worthy of self-respect-
ing, morally conscious individuals and nations; ready, in fact, to be
swept away in favour of a simpler and grander view of the powers
and tasks of modern man.

To Europeans this American attitude, the large vista possible
only for those who live on mountain heights or vast and level
plains affording an unbroken view, seems curiously flat, without
subtlety or colour, at times appearing to lack the entire dimension
of depth, certainly without that immediate reaction to fine distinctions with which perhaps only those who live in valleys are
endowed, and so America, which knows so much, to them seems
to understand too little, to miss the central point. This does not, of
course, apply to every American or European – there are natural
Americans among the natives of Europe and vice versa – but it
seems to characterise the most typical representatives of these
disparate cultures.

VIII

In some respects Roosevelt half-consciously understood and did
not wholly condemn this attitude on the part of Europeans; and
even more clearly Churchill is in many respects in instinctive
sympathy with the American way of life. But by and large they do
represent different outlooks, and the very high degree to which
they were able to understand and admire each other's quality is a
tribute to the extraordinary power of imagination and delight in
the variety of life on the part of both. Each was to the other not
merely an ally, the admired leader of a great people, but a symbol
of a tradition and a civilisation; from the unity of their differences
they hoped for a regeneration of the Western world.

Roosevelt was intrigued by the Russian sphinx; Churchill

instinctively recoiled from its alien and to him unattractive attributes. Roosevelt, on the whole, thought that he could cajole Russia
and even induce her to be assimilated into the great society which
would embrace mankind; Churchill, on the whole, remained
sceptical.

Roosevelt was imaginative, optimistic, episcopalian, self-confident, cheerful, empirical, fearless, and steeped in the ideas of social
progress; he believed that with enough energy and spirit anything
could be achieved by man; he shrank as much as any English
schoolboy from probing underneath the surface, and saw vast
affinities between the peoples in the world, out of which a new,
freer and richer order could somehow be built. Churchill was
imaginative and steeped in history, more serious, more intent, more
concentrated, more preoccupied, and felt very deeply the eternal
differences which could make such a structure difficult of attain-
ment. He believed in institutions and the permanent characters of
races and classes and types of individuals. His government was
organised on clear principles; his personal private office was run in
a sharply disciplined manner. His habits, though unusual, were
regular. He believed in a natural, a social, almost a metaphysical
order – a sacred hierarchy which it was neither possible nor
desirable to upset.

Roosevelt believed in flexibility, improvisation, the fruitfulness
of using persons and resources in an infinite variety of new and
unexpected ways; his bureaucracy was somewhat chaotic, perhaps
deliberately so. His own office was not tidily organised, he
practised a highly personal form of government. He maddened the
advocates of institutional authority, but it is doubtful whether he
could have achieved his ends in any other way.

These dissimilarities of outlook went deep, but both were large
enough in scope and both were genuine visions, not narrowed and
distorted by personal idiosyncrasies and those disparities of moral
standard which so fatally divided Wilson, Lloyd George and
Clemenceau. The President and the Prime Minister often disagreed;
their ideals and their methods were widely different; in some of the
memoirs and gossip of Roosevelt's entourage much has been made
of this; but the discussion, at all times, was conducted on a level of
which both heads of government were conscious. They may have
opposed but they never wished to wound each other; they may
have issued contrary instructions but they never bickered; when
they compromised, as they so often did, they did so without a

sense of bitterness or defeat, but in response to the demands of history or one another's traditions and personality.

Each appeared to the other in a romantic light high above the battles of allies or subordinates: their meetings and correspondence were occasions to which both consciously rose; they were royal cousins and felt pride in this relationship, tempered by a sharp and sometimes amused, but never ironical, perception of the other's peculiar qualities. The relationship born during the great historical upheaval, somewhat aggrandised by its solemnity, never flagged or degenerated, but retained a combination of formal dignity and exuberant high spirits which can scarcely ever before have bound the heads of States. Each was personally fascinated not so much by the other as by the idea of the other, and infected him by his own peculiar brand of high spirits.

The relationship was made genuine by something more than even the solid community of interest or personal and official respect or admiration – namely, by the peculiar degree to which they liked each other's delight in the oddities and humours of life and their own active part in it. This was a unique personal bond, which Harry Hopkins understood and encouraged to the fullest degree. Roosevelt's sense of fun was perhaps the lighter, Churchill's a trifle grimmer. But it was something which they shared with each other and with few, if any, statesmen outside the Anglo-American orbit; their staffs sometimes ignored or misunderstood it, and it gave a most singular quality to their association.

Roosevelt's public utterances differ by a whole world from the dramatic masterpieces of Churchill, but they are not incompatible with them in spirit or in substance. Roosevelt has not left us his own account of his world as he saw it; and perhaps he lived too much from day to day to be temperamentally attracted to the performance of such a task. But both were thoroughly aware of their commanding position in the history of the modern world, and Churchill's account of his stewardship is written in full consciousness of this responsibility.

It is a great occasion, and he treats it with corresponding solemnity. Like a great actor – perhaps the last of his kind – upon the stage of history, he speaks his memorable lines with a large, unhurried and stately utterance in a blaze of light, as is appropriate to a man who knows that his work and his person will remain the object of scrutiny and judgement to many generations. His narrative is a great public performance and has the attribute of formal magnificence. The words, the splendid phrases, the sustained quality of feeling, are a unique medium which conveys his vision of himself and of his world, and will inevitably, like all that he has said and done, reinforce the famous public image, which is no longer distinguishable from the inner essence and the true nature of the author: of a man larger than life, composed of bigger and simpler elements than ordinary men, a gigantic historical figure during his own lifetime, superhumanly bold, strong and imaginative, one of the two greatest men of action his nation has produced, an orator of prodigious powers, the saviour of his country, a mythical hero who belongs to legend as much as to reality, the largest human being of our time.

PRESIDENT
FRANKLIN DELANO ROOSEVELT

I NEVER met Roosevelt, and although I spent more than three years in Washington during the War, I never even saw him. I regret this, for it seems to me that to see and, in particular, to hear the voice of someone who has occupied one's imagination for many years must modify one's impression in some profound way, and make it somehow more concrete and three-dimensional. However, I never did see him, and I heard him only over the wireless. Consequently I must try to convey my impression without the benefit of personal acquaintance, and without, I ought to add, any expert knowledge of American history or of international relations. Nor am I competent to speak of Roosevelt's domestic or foreign policies: or their larger political or economic effect. I shall try to give only a personal impression of the general impact of his personality on my generation in Europe.

When I say that some men occupy one's imagination for many years, this is literally true of Roosevelt and the young men of my own generation in England, and probably in many parts of Europe, and indeed the entire world. If one was young in the 1930s, and lived in a democracy, then, whatever one's politics, if one had human feelings at all, the faintest spark of social idealism, or any love of life whatever, one must have felt very much as young men in Continental Europe probably felt after the defeat of Napoleon during the years of the Restoration, that all was dark and quiet, a great reaction was abroad: and little stirred, and nothing resisted.

It all began with the great slump of 1931, which undermined the feeling, perhaps quite baseless, of economic security which a good many young people of the middle classes then had. There followed the iron '30s, of which the English poets of the time – Auden, Spender, Day Lewis – left a very vivid testament: the dark and leaden '30s, to which, alone of all periods, no one in Europe wishes to return, unless indeed they lament the passing of Fascism. There came Manchuria, Hitler, the Hunger Marchers, the Abyssinian War, the Peace Ballot, the Left Book Club, Malraux's political novels, even the article by Virginia Woolf in the *Daily Worker*, the Soviet trials and purges, the conversions of idealistic young liberals and radicals to Communism, or strong sympathy with it, often for no better reason than that it seemed the only force firm enough and strong enough to resist the Fascist enemy effectively; such conversions were sometimes followed by visits to Moscow or by fighting in Spain, and death on the battlefield, or else bitter and angry disillusionment with Communist practice, or some desperate and unconvinced choice between two evils of that which seemed the lesser.

The most insistent propaganda in those days declared that humanitarianism and liberalism and democratic forces were played out, and that the choice now lay between two bleak extremes, Communism and Fascism – the red or the black. To those who were not carried away by this patter the only light that was left in the darkness was the administration of Roosevelt and the New Deal in the United States. At a time of weakness and mounting despair in the democratic world Roosevelt radiated confidence and strength. He was the leader of the democratic world, and upon him alone, of all the statesmen of the '30s, no cloud rested – neither on him nor on the New Deal, which to European eyes still looks a bright chapter in the history of mankind. It is true that his great social experiment was conducted with an isolationist disregard of the outside world, but then it was psychologically intelligible that America, which had come into being in the reaction against the follies and evils of a Europe perpetually distraught by religious or national struggles, should try to seek salvation undisturbed by the currents of European life, particularly at a moment when Europe seemed about to collapse into a totalitarian nightmare. Roosevelt was therefore forgiven, by those who found the European situation tragic, for pursuing no particular foreign policy, indeed for trying to do, if not without any foreign policy at all, at any rate with a minimum of relationship with the outside world, which was indeed to some degree part of the American political tradition.

His internal policy was plainly animated by a humanitarian purpose. After the unbridled individualism of the 1920s, which had led to economic collapse and widespread misery, he was seeking to establish new rules of social justice. He was trying to do this without forcing his country into some doctrinaire strait-jacket, whether of socialism or State capitalism, or the kind of new social organisation which the Fascist regimes flaunted as the New Order. Social discontent was high in the United States, faith in business-men as saviours of society had evaporated overnight after the famous Wall Street Crash, and Roosevelt was providing a vast safety-valve for pent-up bitterness and indignation, and trying to prevent revolution and construct a regime which should provide for greater economic equality and social justice – ideals which were the best part of the tradition of American life – without altering the basis of freedom and democracy in his country. This was being done by what to unsympathetic critics seemed a haphazard collection of amateurs, college professors, journalists, personal friends, freelances of one kind or another, intellectuals, ideologists, what are nowadays called eggheads, whose very appearance and methods of conducting business or constructing policies irritated the servants of old-established government institutions in Wash-ington and tidy-minded conservatives of every type. Yet it was clear that the very amateurishness of these men, the fact that they were allowed to talk to their hearts' content, to experiment, to indulge in a vast amount of trial and error, that relations were personal and not institutional, bred its own vitality and enthusi-asm. Washington was doubtless full of quarrels, resignations, palace intrigues, perpetual warfare between individuals and groups of individuals, parties, cliques, personal supporters of this or that great captain, which must have maddened sober and responsible officials used to the slower tempo and more normal patterns of administration; as for bankers and businessmen, their feelings were past describing, but at this period they were little regarded, since they were considered to have discredited themselves too deeply, and indeed for ever.

Over this vast, seething chaos presided a handsome, charming, gay, very intelligent, very delightful, very audacious man, Franklin Delano Roosevelt. He was accused of many weaknesses. He had betrayed his class; he was ignorant, unscrupulous, irresponsible. He was ruthless in playing with the lives and careers of individuals. He was surrounded by adventurers, slick opportunists, intriguers. He made conflicting promises, cynically and brazenly, to individu-als and groups and representatives of foreign nations. He made up, with his vast and irresistible public charm, and his astonishing high spirits, for lack of other virtues considered as more important in the leader of the most powerful democracy in the world – the virtues of application, industry, responsibility. All this was said and some of it may indeed have been just. What attracted his followers were countervailing qualities of a rare and inspiring order: he was large-hearted and possessed wide political horizons, imaginative sweep, understanding of the time in which he lived and of the direction of the great new forces at work in the twentieth century – technological, racial, imperialist, anti-imperialist; he was in favour of life and movement, the promotion of the most generous possible fulfilment of the largest possible number of human wishes, and not in favour of caution and retrenchment and sitting still. Above all, he was absolutely fearless.

He was one of the few statesmen in the twentieth or any other century who seemed to have no fear at all of the future. He believed in his own strength and ability to manage, and succeed, whatever happened. He believed in the capacity and loyalty of his lieutenants, so that he looked upon the future with a calm eye, as if to say 'Let it come, whatever it may be, it will all be grist to our great mill. We shall turn it all to benefit.' It was this, perhaps, more than any other quality, which drew men of very different outlooks to him. In a despondent world which appeared divided between wicked and fatally efficient fanatics marching to destroy, and bewildered populations on the run, unenthusiastic martyrs in a cause they could not define, he believed in his own ability, so long as he was at the controls, to stem this terrible tide. He had all the character and energy and skill of the dictators, and he was on our side. He was, in his opinions and public action, every inch a democrat. All the political and personal and public criticism of him might be true; all the personal defects which his enemies and some of his friends attributed to him might be real; yet as a public figure he was unique. As the skies of Europe grew darker, in particular after war broke out, he seemed to the poor and the unhappy in Europe a kind of benevolent demigod who alone could and would save them in the end. His moral authority – the degree of confidence which he inspired outside his own country, and far more beyond America's frontiers than within them at all times – has no parallel. Perhaps President Wilson, in the early days, after the end of the First World War, when he drove triumphantly through Paris and London, may have inspired some such feeling; but it disappeared quickly and left a terrible feeling of disenchantment behind it. It was plain even to his enemies that President Roosevelt would not be broken as President Wilson was. But to his prestige and to his personality he added a degree of political skill – indeed virtuosity – which no American before him had ever possessed. His chance of realising his wishes was plainly greater; his followers would be less likely to reap bitter disappointment.

Indeed he was very different from Wilson. For they represent two contrasting types of statesman, in each of which occasionally men of compelling stature appear. The first kind of statesman is essentially a man of single principle and fanatical vision. Possessed by his own bright, coherent dream, he usually understands neither people nor events. He has no doubts or hesitations and by concentration of will-power, directness and strength he is able to ignore a great deal of what goes on outside him. This very blindness and stubborn self-absorption occasionally, in certain situations, enable him to bend events and men to his own fixed pattern. His strength lies in the fact that weak and vacillating human beings, themselves too insecure or incapable of deciding between alternatives, find relief and peace and strength in submitting to the leadership of a single leader of superhuman size, to whom all issues are clear, whose universe consists entirely of primary colours, mostly black and white, and who marches towards his goal looking neither to right nor to left, buoyed up by the violent vision within him. Such men differ widely in moral and intellectual quality, and, like forces of nature, do both good and harm in the world. To this type belong Garibaldi, Trotsky, Parnell, de Gaulle, perhaps Lenin too – the distinction I am drawing is not a moral one, not one of value but one of type. There are great benefactors, like Wilson, as well as fearful evil-doers, like Hitler, within this category.

The other kind of effective statesman is a naturally political being, as the simple hero is often explicitly anti-political and comes to rescue men, at least ostensibly, from the subtleties and frauds of political life. Politicians of this second type possess antennae of the greatest possible delicacy, which convey to them, in ways difficult or impossible to analyse, the perpetually changing contours of events and feelings and human activities round them – they are gifted with a peculiar, political sense fed on a capacity to take in minute impressions, to integrate a vast multitude of small evanescent unseizable detail, such as artists possess in relation to their material. Statesmen of this type know what to do and when to do it, if they are to achieve their ends, which themselves are usually

not born within some private world of inner thought, or intro-
verted feeling, but are the crystallisation, the raising to great
intensity and clarity, of what a large number of their fellow citizens
are thinking and feeling in some dim, inarticulate, but nevertheless
persistent fashion. In virtue of this capacity to judge their material,
very much as a sculptor knows what can be moulded out of wood
and what out of marble, and how and when, they resemble doctors
who have a natural gift for curing, which does not directly depend
upon that knowledge of scientific anatomy which can be learned
only by observation or experiment, or from the experiences of
others, though it could not exist without it. This instinctive, or at
any rate incommunicable, knowledge of where to look for what
one needs, the power of divining where the treasure lies, is
something common to many types of genius, to scientists and
mathematicians no less than to businessmen and administrators and
politicians. Such men, when they are statesmen, are acutely aware
of which way the thoughts and feelings of human beings are
flowing, and where life presses on them most heavily, and they
convey to these human beings a sense of understanding their inner
needs, of responding to their own deepest impulses, above all of
being alone capable of organising the world along lines which the
masses are instinctively groping for. To this type of statesman
belonged Bismarck and Abraham Lincoln, Lloyd George and
Thomas Masaryk, perhaps to some extent Gladstone, and to a
minor degree Walpole. Roosevelt was a magnificent virtuoso of
this type, and he was the most benevolent as well as the greatest
master of his craft in modern times. He really did desire a better life
for mankind. The great majorities which he obtained in the
elections in the United States during his four terms of office,
despite mounting hostility by the press, and perpetual prophecies
on their part that he had gone too far, and would fail to be re-
elected, were ultimately due to an obscure feeling on the part of the
majority of the citizens of the United States that he was on their
side, that he wished them well, and that he would do something for
them. And this feeling gradually spread over the entire civilised
world. He became a legendary hero – they themselves did not
know quite why – to the indigent and the oppressed, far beyond
the confines of the English-speaking world.

As I said before, he was, by some of his opponents, accused of
betraying his class, and so he had. When a man who retains the
manners, the style of life, the emotional texture and the charm of

the old order of some free aristocratic upbringing revolts against his milieu and adopts the ideas and aspirations of the new, socially revolted class, and adopts them not out of expediency but out of genuine moral conviction, or from love of life, inability to remain on the side of what seems to him narrow, mean, restrictive – the result is fascinating and attractive. This is what makes the figures of such men as Condorcet or Charles James Fox, or some of the Russian, Italian and Polish revolutionaries in the nineteenth century, so attractive; for all we know this may have been the secret also of Moses or Pericles or Julius Caesar. It was this gentlemanly quality together with the fact that they felt him to be deeply committed to their side in the struggle and in favour of their way of life, as well as his open and fearless lack of neutrality in the war against the Nazis and the Fascists, that endeared him so deeply to the British people during the war years. I remember well how excited most people were in London, in November 1940, about the result of the Presidential election in the United States. In theory they should not have worried. Willkie, the Republican candidate, had expressed himself forcibly and sincerely as a supporter of the democracies. Yet it was absurd to say that the people of Britain were neutral in their feelings *vis-à-vis* the two candidates. They felt in their bones that Roosevelt was their lifelong friend, that he hated the Nazis as deeply as they did, that he wanted democracy and civilisation, in the sense in which they believed in it, to prevail, and that he knew what he wanted, and that his goal resembled their own ideals more than it did those of all his opponents. They felt that his heart was in the right place, and they did not, therefore, if they gave it a thought, care whether his political appointments were made under the influence of bosses or for personal reasons, or thoughtlessly; or whether his economic doctrines were heretical or whether he had a sufficiently scrupulous regard for the opinion of the Senate or the House of Representatives, or the prescriptions of the United States Constitution, or for the opinions of the Supreme Court. These matters were very remote from them. They knew that he would, to the extent of his enormous energy and ability, see them through. There is no such thing as long-lived mass hypnotism; the masses know what it is that they like, what genuinely appeals to them. What the Germans thought Hitler to be, Hitler, in fact, largely was, and what free men in Europe and in America and in Asia and in Africa and in Australia, and wherever else the rudiments of political thought stirred at all – what all these felt

Roosevelt to be, he in fact was. He was the greatest leader of democracy, the greatest champion of social progress in the twentieth century.

His enemies accused him of plotting to get America into the War. I do not wish to discuss this controversial issue, but it seems to me that the evidence for it is lacking. I think that when he promised to keep America at peace he meant to try as hard as he could to do so, compatibly with helping to promote the victory of the democracies. He must at one period have thought that he could win the War without entering it, and so, at the end of it, be in the unique position, hitherto achieved by no one, of being the arbiter of the world's fate without needing to placate those bitter forces which involvement in a war inevitably brings about, and which are an obstacle to reason and humanity in the making of the peace. He no doubt too often trusted in his own magical power of improvisation. Doubtless he made many political mistakes, some of them difficult to remedy: some would say about Stalin and his intentions, and the nature of the Soviet State; others might justly point to his coolness to the Free French movement, his cavalier intentions with regard to the Supreme Court of Justice in the United States, his errors about a good many other issues. He irritated his staunchest supporters and faithful servants because he did not tell them what he was doing; his government was highly personal and it maddened tidy-minded officials and humiliated those who thought the policy should be conducted in consultation with and through them. He sometimes exasperated his allies, but when these last bethought them of who his ill-wishers were in the USA and in the world outside, and what *their* motives were, their respect, affection and loyalty tended to return. No man made more public enemies, yet no man had a right to take greater pride in the quality and the motives of some of those enemies. He could justly call himself the friend of the people, and although his opponents accused him of being a demagogue, this charge seems to me unjust. He did not sacrifice fundamental political principles to a desire to retain power; he did not whip up evil passions merely in order to avenge himself upon those whom he disliked or wished to crush, or because it was an atmosphere in which he found it convenient to operate; he saw to it that his administration was in the van of public opinion and drew it on instead of being dragged by it; he made the majority of his fellow citizens prouder to be Americans than they had been before. He raised their status in their own eyes – immensely in those of the rest of the world.

It was an extraordinary transformation of an individual. Perhaps it was largely brought about by the collapse of his health in the early 1920s and his marvellous triumph over his disabilities. For he began life as a well-born, polite, not particularly gifted young man, something of a prig, liked but not greatly admired by his contemporaries at Groton and at Harvard, a competent Assistant Secretary of the Navy in the First World War; in short, he seemed embarked on the routine career of an American patrician with moderate political ambitions. His illness and the support and encouragement and political qualities of his wife – whose greatness of character and goodness of heart history will duly record – seemed to transform his public personality into that strong and beneficent champion who became the father of his people, in an altogether unique fashion. He did more than this: it is not too much to say that he altered the fundamental concept of government and its obligations to the governed. The Welfare State, so much denounced, has obviously come to stay: the direct moral responsibility for minimum standards of living and social services, which it took for granted, are today accepted almost without a murmur by the most conservative politicians in the Western democracies; the Republican Party victorious in 1952 made no effort to upset the basic principles – which seemed Utopian in the 1920s – of Roosevelt's social legislation.

But Roosevelt's greatest service to mankind (after ensuring the victory against the enemies of freedom) consists in the fact that he showed that it is possible to be politically effective and yet benevolent and human: that the fierce left- and right-wing propaganda of the 1930s, according to which the conquest and retention of political power is not compatible with human qualities, but necessarily demands from those who pursue it seriously the sacrifice of their lives upon the altar of some ruthless ideology, or the practice of despotism – this propaganda, which filled the art and talk of the day, was simply untrue. Roosevelt's example strengthened democracy everywhere, that is to say the view that the promotion of social justice and individual liberty does not necessarily mean the end of all efficient government; that power and order are not identical with a strait-jacket of doctrine, whether economic or political; that it is possible to reconcile individual liberty – a loose texture of society – with the indispensable minimum of organising and authority; and in this belief lies what Roosevelt's greatest predecessor once described as 'the last best hope of earth'.[1]

[1] Abraham Lincoln, Annual Message to Congress, 1 December 1862: p. 537 in *The Collected Works of Abraham Lincoln*, ed. R. P. Basler (New Brunswick, 1953), vol. 5.

CHAIM WEIZMANN

CHAIM WEIZMANN's achievement – and the details of his public life – are too well documented to need description or analysis from me. His personal characteristics are less well known. He was the only statesman of genius whom I have ever had the good fortune of knowing intimately, and I would like to try to convey something of the quality of that genius. Something: no more than a small part of a character and a life unique in our time.

To know – to enjoy the friendship of – a great man must permanently transform one's ideas of what human beings can be or do. Social theorists of various schools sometimes try to convince us that the concept of greatness is a romantic illusion – a vulgar notion exploited by politicians or propagandists, and one which a deeper study of the facts will always dispel. There is no way of finally refuting this deflationary theory save by coming face to face with an authentic instance of greatness and its works. Greatness is not a specifically moral attribute. It is not one of the private virtues. It does not belong to the realm of personal relations. A great man need not be morally good, or upright, or kind, or sensitive, or delightful, or possess artistic or scientific talent. To call someone a great man is to claim that he has intentionally taken (or perhaps could have taken) a large step, one far beyond the normal capacities of men, in satisfying, or materially affecting, central human interests. A great thinker or artist (and by this I do not necessarily mean a man of genius) must, to deserve this title, advance a society, to an exceptional degree, towards some intellectual or aesthetic goal, for which it is already, in some sense, groping; or else alter its ways of thinking or feeling to a degree that would not, until he had performed his task, have been conceived as being within the powers of a single individual. Sometimes such an achievement is felt as a great act of liberation by those upon whom such a man binds his spell, sometimes as an enslavement, sometimes as a peculiar mixture or succession of both. Similarly, in the realm of action, the great man seems able, almost alone and single-handed, to transform one form of life into another; or – what in the end comes to the same – permanently and radically alters the outlook and values of a significant body of human beings. The transformation he effects, if he is truly to deserve his title, must be such as those best qualified to judge consider to be antecedently improbable – something unlikely to be brought about by the mere force of events, by the 'trends' or 'tendencies' already working at the time – that is to say, something unlikely to occur without the intervention, difficult or impossible to discount in advance, of the man who for this very reason deserves to be described as great. At any rate that is how the situation will look in retrospect. Whether this is a vast mistake – whether, in fact, human beings (as Marx, or Tolstoy, for instance, believed) overestimate the importance of some of their own number – whether some more impersonal view of history that does not admit the possibility of heroes is in fact correct, cannot be discussed here. If the notion of the hero who makes or breaks a nation's life springs from an illusion, it is, despite all the weighty arguments produced against it, a very persistent, obsessive and universal illusion, to which the experience of our own time has given powerful support. At any rate, I propose, for my present purpose, to assume that it is not delusive, but a true view of society and history. And thence I should like to embark only on the comparatively modest proposition that if great men – heroes – have ever existed, and more particularly if individuals can in any sense be said to be the authors of revolutions that permanently and deeply alter many human lives – then Chaim Weizmann was, in the sense which I have tried to explain, a man of this order.

I have said that one of the distinguishing characteristics of a great man is that his active intervention makes what seemed highly improbable in fact happen. It is surely difficult to deny that the actions which culminated in the creation of the State of Israel were of this improbable or surprising kind. When Theodor Herzl began to preach that it was both desirable and possible to set up a sovereign Jewish State of a modern type by means of a formal, public act of recognition by the great powers, most sane, sensible, reasonable people, both Jews and Gentiles, who heard of this plan regarded it as quite insane. Indeed, it is difficult to see how they could have thought otherwise.

In the nineteenth century the Jews presented an exceedingly

anomalous spectacle. Scattered among the nations of the world, they constituted something which it was hard or perhaps impossible to define in terms of such concepts as nation, race, association, religion or the other terms in which coherent groups of a hereditary or traditional type were commonly described. The Jews were clearly not a nation in any normal sense of the word: they occupied no fixed territory of which they constituted the majority of the population; they could not even be described as a minority in the sense in which the ethnic or national minorities of multinational empires – the Austro-Hungarian, or Russian, or British Empires – were so denoted; they occupied no stretch of country which could be called their native territory in the sense in which Welshmen, or Slovaks, or Ruthenians, or Zulus, or Tartars, or even Red Indians or Australian aborigines – compact continuous groups living on their ancestral soil – patently did so. The Jews certainly had a religion of their own, although a good many of them did not appear to profess it in any clearly recognisable sense; but they could not be defined as a solely religious body; when in modern times Jews were discriminated against or persecuted, it was, for the most part, not their religious observances that were in the first place abhorred; when Jews who had left their faith and had become converted to Christianity – like Disraeli or Karl Marx or Heine – were thought of, the fact that they were still looked upon as Jews, or as being of Jewish origin, certainly did not imply merely that their ancestors had practised a religion different from that of the surrounding populations. Nobody, after all, spoke of persons of Presbyterian, or Roman Catholic, or even Muslim origin or descent; a man might be of Turkish or Indian origin – but hardly of Muslim descent or of Muslim race.

What, then, were the Jews? Were they a race? The word 'race' was, and is still, felt to carry somewhat disreputable associations. Vague historical notions such as those of Indo-European or Mongol race were at times used by ethnologists. Groups of languages were occasionally classified as Aryan or Hamitic or Semitic, but these were at most technical terms for defining the culture of those who spoke them. The idea of race as a political description was not, towards the end of the last century, one which intellectually respectable persons held with; it was felt to be connected with the undesirable attitudes of national or cultural chauvinism. Indeed it was its lurid propagandist colour that made the word itself, whatever its context, seem a strong appeal to prejudice. Competent ethnologists, anthropologists and sociologists vied with each other in proving that there were no 'pure' races, that the notion was hopelessly vague and confused.

But if the Jews were not a race, what were they? A culture, or 'way of life'? Apart from the fact that they participated, at any rate in the countries of the West, in the civilisation of their surroundings, this seemed a very thin notion in terms of which to define something so immediately recognisable, a group of persons towards whom feelings were as strong and definite as they quite clearly were in respect of the Jews. For there undoubtedly existed certain cardinal differences in outlook and behaviour, and to a large degree in outward physical characteristics, that appeared to be persistent, hereditary and easily recognisable both by the Jews themselves and by non-Jews. So much seemed clear to any honest man who was not either too embarrassed or too polite to face the obvious facts. The martyrdom of the Jews in the Christian world was so painful and notorious, the wounds which it had inflicted on both persecutors and persecuted were so deep, that there was a natural temptation on the part of enlightened and civilised people to try to ignore the problem altogether, or to insist that it had been much exaggerated, and might, if only it was not so frequently discussed and mentioned, with luck perhaps soon vanish altogether.

This was an attitude which a good many Jews themselves were only too anxious to adopt. The more optimistic 'assimilationists' among them fondly supposed that with the general spread of education and liberal culture the Jews would peacefully melt into their surroundings so that, if the Jewish religion continued to exist, those who practised it would come to be thought of by their Christian fellow citizens as being neither less nor more different than, let us say, Presbyterians or Anglicans or, at the most, Unitarians or Quakers in countries with Roman Catholic majorities. To some degree this process was, in fact, already taking place in the countries of the West; not, to be sure, to a great degree as yet, but from small beginnings great consequences sometimes issued. At any rate, the notion that the Jews were in some sense a nation, as the Italians or, at least, the Armenians were a nation, and had just claims – could, indeed, be conceived as having any claims at all – to a territorial existence as a nation organised in the form of a State, seemed a wild absurdity to the vast majority of those who gave the matter any thought. It was very well for isolated romantics with strong imaginations – Napoleon or Fichte, for example, or the Russian Decembrist revolutionary Pestel' – to suggest that the Jews were in fact a nation, though certainly a very odd, scattered one, and should be returned to Palestine, there to create some sort of State of their own. These remained idle fancies which no one, not even their authors, took very seriously. So also later in the century, when benevolent Christians like Laurence Oliphant in England or Ernest Laharanne in France, or Jewish publicists like Salvador or Moses Hess, or the rabbi Hirsch Kalischer, advocated a return to the Holy Land, this was regarded as mere eccentricity, sometimes dangerous perversity. When novelists – Disraeli or George Eliot – played with romantic nostalgia of this kind, this could be written off as a sophisticated version of the visions of an idealised past that Chateaubriand and Scott and the German romantics had made fashionable – exotic fruit of the new historical imagination, of possible religious or aesthetic or psychological significance, but with no possible relevance to political practice. As for the fact that pious Jews everywhere thrice daily prayed to be returned to Zion, that was, again quite naturally, regarded as an expression of the longing for the coming of the Messiah, for the end of the world of evil and pain, and for the coming of the reign of God on earth, and wholly remote from secular ideas about political self-determination. Even when the growth among the Jews of Eastern Europe of secular education, with the nationalist and socialist ideas which it brought with it, had caused a sufficient ferment among the poorer Russian Jews to cause some of them (especially after the wave of pogroms in Russia that followed the assassination of the Emperor Alexander II) to found small, idealistic, agricultural settlements in Palestine; even after Baron Edmond de Rothschild in Paris had, by a unique act of imaginative generosity, saved these colonies from extinction and made possible a considerable degree of agricultural develop-ment; all this still seemed nothing more than a Utopian experiment, queer, noble, moving, but a sentimental gesture rather than real life.

When finally the idea of a Jewish State began to be seriously bruited, and reached Western countries, and caught the imagina-tion of such serious and effective statesmen as Joseph Chamberlain and Milner, and when it stirred the enthusiasm of so temperate, sagacious and deeply responsible a man as Herbert Samuel, need we be surprised that some solid and respectable Western Jews could scarcely credit this? The most characteristic reaction was that of Samuel's political colleague and kinsman Edwin Montagu, at that time himself a member of Asquith's (and subsequently Lloyd George's) Cabinet, who felt personally traduced. The late Lord Norwich once told me that Montagu used to address his colleagues with anger and indignation, declaring that the Jews did not wish – and did not think they deserved – to be sent back to the ghetto; and buttonholed his friends in various drawing-rooms in London, and asked them vehemently whether they regarded him as an oriental alien and wanted to see him 'repatriated' to the eastern Mediterranean. Other sober and public-spirited British Jews felt no less upset and bitter; similar feelings were expressed in corresponding circles in Paris and Berlin.[1]

All this is perfectly intelligible in terms of the life led by the Jews of the Western world, even of the great twentieth-century Jewish settlement in the United States. Whatever the truth about the status of the Jews in these countries – whether one was to call them a race, a religion, a community, a national minority, or invent some unique term to cover their anomalous attributes – a new nation and State could not be constructed out of them; neither they nor their leaders conceived this as a real possibility; and this remains true of them still. For, despite all the social friction, discomfort, even humiliation and, in bad times, persecution that they have had to suffer, they were and are, by and large, too deeply involved in the life of the societies of which they form a part, and have in the process lost too great a part of their original, undiluted national personality to have retained the will to build a totally new life on new foundations. Even Hitler's onslaught did not seem to stir within the majority of the German Jews a feeling of specific Jewish nationalism, but mainly bewilderment, indignation, horror, individual heroism or despair. Jewish nationalism was given reality almost entirely by the Jews of the Russian Empire and to some degree of the Muslim East.[2]

Assimilation, integration, Russification, Polonisation had, of course, to some degree also occurred among the Jews of Russia and Poland. Nevertheless the bulk of them lived under their own dispensation. Herded by the Russian government into the so-called

---

[1] 'To be a Zionist it is not perhaps absolutely necessary to be slightly mad,' Weizmann is reported to have said, 'but it helps.'

[2] This was predicted over a hundred years ago with unparalleled prescience by Moses Hess in his most remarkable book, *Rome and Jerusalem* (Leipzig, 1862), to this day the most telling analysis and indictment of 'emancipated' Jewish society.

Pale of Settlement, bound by their own traditional religious and social organisation, they constituted a kind of survival of medieval society, in which the secular and the sacred were not divided, as they had been (at any rate since the Renaissance) among the middle and upper classes in Western Europe. Speaking their own language, largely isolated from the surrounding peasant population, trading with them, but confined within their own world by a wall of reciprocal distrust and suspicion, this vast Jewish community formed a geographically continuous enclave that inevitably developed its own institutions, and thereby, as time went on, came to resemble more and more an authentic national minority settled upon its own ancestral soil.

There are times when imagination is stronger than so-called objective reality. Subjective feeling plays a great part in communal development, and the Yiddish-speaking Jews of the Russian Empire came to feel themselves a coherent ethnic group: anomalous indeed, subject to unheard-of persecution, remote from the alien world in which their lives were cast, but, simply in virtue of the fact that they were densely congregated within the same relatively small territory, tending to resemble, say, the Armenians in Turkey: a recognisably separate, semi-national community. In their involuntary confinement they developed a certain independence of outlook, and the problems which affected and sometimes tormented many of their co-religionists in the West – in particular the central question of their status – were not crucial for them. The Jews of Germany, Austria, Hungary, France, America, England tended to ask themselves whether they were Jews, and if so, in what sense, and what this entailed; whether the view of them held by the surrounding population was true or false, just or unjust, and, if distorted, whether any steps could be taken to correct it without too much damage to their own self-esteem; whether they should 'appease' and assimilate at the risk of losing their identity, and perhaps of the guilt that comes of the feeling of having 'betrayed' their ancestral values; or, on the contrary, resist at the risk of incurring unpopularity and even persecution. These problems affected the Russian Jews to a far smaller degree, relatively secure as they were – morally and psychologically – within their own vast, insulated ghetto. Their imprisonment, for all the economic, cultural and social injustice and poverty that it entailed, brought with it one immense advantage – namely that the spirit of the inmates remained unbroken, and that they were not as powerfully tempted to seek escape by adopting false positions as their socially more exposed and precariously established brethren without. The majority of the Jews of Russia and Poland lived in conditions of squalor and oppression, but they did not feel outcast or rootless; their relations with each other and with the outside world suffered from no systematic ambivalence. They were what they were; they might dislike their condition, they might seek to escape from it, or revolt against it, but they did not deceive themselves or others, nor did they make efforts to conceal from themselves their own most characteristic attributes that were patent to all – particularly their neighbours – to see. Their moral and spiritual integrity was greater than that of their more prosperous and civilised and altogether grander brothers in the West; their lives were bound up with religious observance, and their minds and hearts were filled with the images and symbolism of Jewish history and religion to a degree scarcely intelligible in Western Europe since the waning of the Middle Ages.

When Herzl with his magnificent appearance and visionary gaze appeared like a prophet from a distant land, many of them were dazzled by the very strangeness and distance which divided them from this Messianic messenger from another world, who could not speak to them in their own language – a remoteness which made him and his message all the more magical and magnetic. But when their leader seemed prepared to accept the compromise solution, offered by the British Colonial Secretary, Joseph Chamberlain, of a settlement in Uganda in place of the unattainable Palestine, many of them were shocked and alienated. Herzl's talent for heroic over-simplification is one that fanatics, possessed by a single idea, often exhibit – indeed it is one of the qualities that make them exceptionally, dangerously effective – and Herzl ignored difficul-ties, cut Gordian knots, electrified the Jewish masses in Eastern Europe, developed his ideas before politicians and important personages in the Western world with logic, simplicity, imagina-tion and great fire. The Jewish masses followed him uncompre-hending, but aware that here at last was a path towards the light. Like many visionaries Herzl understood issues but not human beings: least of all the culture and feelings of his devoted Eastern European followers. Paris was surely worth a mass; the Jewish problem was urgent and desperate; he was prepared, for the sake of a concrete territory waiting for immigration, to disregard, at least for the time being, the saturation of Jewish thought and feeling

with the image and symbol of Zion and Palestine, its preoccupation, its obsession by the actual words of the Prayer Book and the
Bible. Never has any people lived so much by the written word:
not to have realised the crucial importance of this was a measure of
the distance of the West from the East. The Russian Zionist leaders
did not require to be taught this truth: they grew up with it, and
took it for granted. The prospect of nationhood without the land
which was the oldest root, the only goal of all their faith, was
virtually meaningless for most of them; it could be accepted only
by the more rational, but more exhausted – the thinner-blooded –
Jews of the West, who in any case were not the stuff from which a
new society could be moulded overnight. If the Jews of Russia had
not existed, neither the case for, nor the possibility of realising,
Zionism could have arisen in any serious form.

There is a sense in which no social problem arose for the Jews so
long as rigid religious orthodoxy insulated them from the external
world. Until then, poor, downtrodden and oppressed as they
might be, and clinging to each other for warmth and shelter, the
Jews of Eastern Europe put all their faith in God and concentrated
all their hope either upon individual salvation – immortality in the
sight of God – or upon the coming of the Messiah whose approach
no worldly force could accelerate or retard. It was when this great
frozen mass began to melt that the social and political problem
arose. Once the Enlightenment – secular learning and the possibility of a freer mode of life – began at first to seep, and then to flood,
into the Jewish townlets and villages of the Pale, a generation grew
up no longer content to sit by the waters of Babylon and sing the
songs of Zion in exile. Some, in search of a wider life, renounced
the religion of their fathers and became baptised and earned
positions of eminence and distinction in Russian society. Some did
so in Western Europe. Some believed that the injustice done to
their people was only a part of the larger injustice constituted by
tsarist despotism, or by the capitalist system, and became radicals,
or socialists, or members of other social movements which claimed
that the peculiar anomalies of the Jewish situation would disappear
as part of the general solution of all political and economic
problems. Some among these radicals and socialists and believers in
'Russification' or 'Europeanisation' desired the total dissolution of
the Jews as a closely knit group among their neighbours. Others,
infected by the 'populism' of that time (an idealistic movement of
the 'conscience-stricken' sons and daughters of the Russian gentry,

seeking to improve the lot of the peasants), conceived in vague and sentimental terms of semi-autonomous Jewish communities, speaking their own Yiddish language and creating in it works of art and science, as one among a family of free communities, constituting, between them, some kind of decentralised, semi-socialist, free federation of peoples within the Russian Empire. Again there were those who, still faithful to the ancient religion, were resolved to keep out the menace of secularism by raising the walls of the ghetto still higher, and devoted themselves with an even more rigid and fanatical faith to the preservation of every jot and tittle of Jewish law and tradition, viewing all Western movements – whether nationalist or socialist, conservative or radical – with equal detestation or horror. But the vast majority of the younger generation of the Russian Jews in the 1880s and '90s joined none of these movements. Affected and, indeed, fascinated by the general ideas then afloat they might be; but they remained bourgeois Jews, semi-emancipated from the shackles of their fathers, aware of – discontented by, but not ashamed of – their anomalous status, with a mild but uninhibited devotion to the traditional ways of life in which they were brought up, neither conscious heretics, nor in the least degree renegades, neither zealots nor reformers but normal human beings, irked by their legal and social inferiority, seeking to lead the most natural and unbroken lives that they could, without worrying overmuch about ultimate ends or fundamental principles. They were devoted to their families, to their traditional culture, their professional pursuits. Faced with persecution, they preserved their closely knit social texture (often by means of bizarre subterfuges and stratagems) with astonishing optimism, tenacity, skill and even gaiety, in circumstances of unexampled difficulty.

To this generation, and to this solid milieu, Weizmann belonged, and he became its fullest, most gifted, and most effective representative. When he spoke, it was to these people, whom he knew best, that his words were addressed; to the end of his days he was happiest among them. When he thought of the Jews, he thought of them; his language was theirs, and their view of life was his. Out of them he created the foundations of the new State, and it is their character, ideals, habits, way of life that have, more than any other single set of factors, imposed themselves on the State of Israel. For this reason, it is perhaps the most faithful nineteenth-century democracy at present extant in the modern world.

II

Chaim Weizmann was born and bred in a completely Jewish milieu near the city of Pinsk, in western Russia. His father was a timber-merchant of small means, a typical member of a lively and devout community, and developed in his many children his own energetic and hopeful attitude to life; in particular, respect for education, for fully formed personality, for solid achievement in every sphere, together with a clear-eyed, concrete – and, at times, irreverent – approach to all issues, combined with a belief that with effort, honesty, faith and a critical faculty a good life can be lived on earth. Realism, optimism, self-confidence, admiration for human achievement, and above all an insatiable appetite for life as such, whatever it might bring, accompanied by the conviction that all that comes (or nearly all) can, late or soon, be turned to positive advantage – a vigorously extroverted attitude, rooted in a sense of belonging to the unbroken historical continuity of Jewish tradition, as something too strong to be dissolved or abolished by either man or circumstance – these are the characteristics most prominent, it seems to me, in the outlook of this most constructive man. He was, moreover, of a monolithic solidity of character, incapable of self-pity and self-deception, and absolutely fearless. There is no evidence that he was ever prey to agonising doubts about moral or political issues. The traditional framework in which he was born was too secure.

Early in life he accepted the proposition that the ills of the Jews were caused principally by the abnormality of their social situation; and that so long as they remained everywhere a semi-helot population, relegated to an inferior and dependent status, which produced in them the virtues and vices of slaves, their neuroses, both individual and collective, were not curable. Some might bear this fate with dignity, others were broken by it, or betrayed by their principles and played false roles because they found the burden too heavy. Personal integrity and strength were not enough: unless their social and political position was somehow altered – made normal – brought into line with that of other peoples, the vast majority of Jews would remain permanently liable to become morally and socially crippled, objects of compassion to the kindly, and of deep distaste to the fastidious. For this there was no remedy save a revolution – a total social transformation, a mass emancipation.

Others had reached this conclusion before him: indeed it formed the substance of the most celebrated of all the pre-Zionist pamphlets – Leo Pinsker's *Auto-Emancipation* – and animated the colonising efforts of the early pioneers of the settlement in Palestine. Herzl translated it into Western terms and gave it coherent and eloquent political shape. Weizmann was not an intellectual innovator: his originality lay in the exceptionally convincing, wholly concrete content which he poured into ideas he received from others. His political, no less than his scientific, genius lay in applied, not in pure, theory. Like his contemporary Lenin, he translated doctrine into reality, and like him he transformed both. But unlike Lenin he had a harmonious nature, free from that streak of bigoted rationalism which breeds belief in final solutions for which no price – in terms of human suffering and death – can be too high. He was above all things an empiricist, who looked on ideas primarily as tools of practical judgement, and he was endowed with a very strong and vivid sense of reality and the allied faculty of historical imagination – that is to say, with an almost infallible sense of what cannot be true, of what cannot be done.

Weizmann and his generation assumed without question that if Jews were to be emancipated, they must live in freedom in their own land, that there alone they would no longer be compelled to extort elementary human rights by that repellent mixture of constant cunning, obsequiousness and occasional arrogance which is forced on all dependants and clients and slaves; and finally that this land must – could only – be Palestine. In his milieu scarcely anyone who was convinced of the main thesis seriously conceived of other possibilities. Spiritual ties rightly seemed to them more real than any other; economic and political factors appeared less decisive by comparison. If a people has lived and survived against unbelievable odds by purely ideal resources, material considerations will not, for good or ill, divert it from its vision. At the centre of this vision was the Holy Land. Herzl, Israel Zangwill, others who were born or bred in the West might need convincing of this: in Russia it was taken for granted by most of those who accepted the fundamental promise – that the Jews could neither assimilate and melt away, nor remain segregated. If this was sound, the rest followed.

Weizmann shared other unspoken assumptions with his milieu: he was not troubled by the problem of what the government of the future State would or should be: whether, for example, it should be religious or secular, socialist or bourgeois. His notions of justice, equality, communal organisation, were non-sectarian and pre-Marxist; he was no more concerned to graft on to his simple, moderate, instinctive, democratic nationalism this or that precisely formulated political or social doctrine than were Garibaldi or Kossuth or other great nineteenth-century nationalist leaders, who believed in, and promoted, the renaissance of their peoples not as a policy founded on a particular doctrine, but as a movement which they accepted naturally and without question. Such men – from Moses to Nehru – create or lead movements primarily because, finding themselves naturally bound up with the aspirations of their society, and passionately convinced of the injustice of the order by which they are kept down, they know themselves to be stronger, more imaginative, more effective fighters against it than the majority of their fellow victims. Such men are not, as a rule, theorists: they are sometimes doctrinaire, but more often adapt current ideas to their needs. Little that Weizmann believed throughout his life came to him from books, from the beliefs of this or that social or political teacher, or from any other source than the community that he knew best, from its common stock of ideas, from the very air that he breathed. In this sense, if in no other, he was a very true representative of his people. All his life he instinctively recoiled from *outré* or extremist tendencies within his own movement. He was one of those human beings who (as someone once said of an eminent Russian critic)[1] stood near the centre of the consciousness of his people, and not on its periphery; his ideas and his feelings were, as it were, naturally attuned to the often unspoken, but always central, hopes, fears, modes of feeling of the vast majority of the Jewish masses, with which he felt himself, all his life, in deep and complete natural sympathy. His genius largely consisted in making articulate, and finding avenues for the realisation of, these aspirations and longings; and he did this without exaggerating them in any direction, or forcing them into a preconceived social or political scheme, or driving them towards some privately conceived goal of his own, but always along the grain.

For this reason, although he was not a great popular orator, practised no false humility, often behaved in a detached, ironical

---

[1] Vissarion Belinsky.

and contemptuous fashion, was proud, imperious, impatient, and an utterly independent commander of his troops, without the least inclination to demagogy, or talent for it, he never, despite all this, lost the confidence of the vast majority of his people. He was not sentimental, said biting and unpopular things, and addressed himself always to the reason and never to the passions. In spite of this, the masses instinctively felt that he understood them, knew what was in their hearts, and wanted this himself. They trusted and, therefore, followed him. They trusted him because he seemed to them an exceptionally powerful, self-confident, solid champion of their deepest interests. Moreover he was both fearless and understanding. He understood their past and their present, but above all was not frightened of the future.

This last quality is rare enough anywhere; but is, for obvious reasons, particularly seldom found among the crushed and the oppressed. Like the other great leaders of democracies in our time, like Lloyd George and the two Roosevelts, Weizmann had an unconquerable belief that whatever the future brought could be made grist to his, and his people's, mill. He never abandoned hope, he remained balanced, confident, representative. He never disappeared from the view of his followers into private fantasies or egomaniacal dreams. He was a man of immense natural authority, dignity and strength. He was calm, paternal, imperturbable, certain of himself. He never drifted with the current. He was always in control. He accepted full responsibility. He was indifferent to praise and blame. He possessed tact and charm to a degree exceeded by no statesman of modern days. But what held the Jewish masses to him until the very last phase of his long life was not possession of these qualities alone, dazzling as they were, but the fact that although outwardly he had become an eminent Western scientist (which made him financially and therefore politically independent), and mingled easily with the remote and unapproachable masters of the Western world, his fundamental personality and outlook remained unchanged. His language, his images, his turns of phrase were rooted in Jewish tradition and piety and learning. His tastes, his physical movements, the manner in which he walked and stood, got up and sat down, his gestures, the features of his exceedingly expressive face, and above all his tone of voice, the accent, the inflexion, the extraordinary variety of his humour, were identical with theirs – were their own. In this sense he was flesh of their flesh, a man of the people. He knew this.

But in his dealings with his own people he behaved without any self-consciousness. He did not exaggerate or play up even his own characteristics. He was not an actor. He dramatised neither himself nor his interlocutors. He cultivated no idiosyncrasies. His unshakeable authority derived from his natural qualities, from his combination of creative and critical power, his self-control, his calm, from the fact that he was a man of wide horizons, obsessed by nothing, not even his own ideals, and therefore never blinded by passion or prejudice to any relevant factor in his own Jewish world.

The failures of the Zionist movement – and they were many – did not embitter him; its successes did not drive him into unrealistic assessments. He combined an acute and highly ironical awareness of the shortcomings and absurdities of the Jewish character – it was a subject on which he was seldom silent – with a devoted affection for it, and a determination at all costs to rescue his people from the humiliating or perilous predicaments in which it landed them. To this end he directed all his extraordinary resources. He believed in long-term strategy; he distrusted improvisation; he was a master of manoeuvre, but despite all that his critics have alleged, he was not in the least machiavellian. He was not prepared to justify wrongdoing by appeals to historical or political necessity. He did not attempt to save his people by violence or cunning – to beat them into shape, if need be with the utmost brutality, like Lenin, or to deceive them for their own good, like Bismarck, or to turn their heads with promises of blessings awaiting them in some remote future which could be shaped to anyone's fantasy. He never called upon the Jews to make terrible sacrifices, or offer their lives, or commit crimes, or condone the crimes of others, for the sake of some felicity to be realised at some unspecified date, as the Marxists did; nor did he play upon their feelings unscrupulously, or try deliberately to exacerbate them against this or that real, or imaginary, enemy, as extremists in his own movement have frequently tried to do. He wished to make his nation free and happy,[1] but not at the price of sinning against any human value in which he and they believed. He wished to lead

---

[1] Hermann Cohen, the philosopher, is said to have remarked, with the scorn of an old Stoic sage, to Franz Rosenzweig, who tried to convince him of the merits of Zionism, 'Oho! So the gang now wants to be happy, does it?' Weizmann wanted exactly that; he could not see why this was thought a shameful act of surrender.

them out of exile into a land where they could live a life worthy of human beings, without betraying their own ideals or trampling on those of others.

Like Cavour, whom politically he much resembled in his hatred of violence and his reliance on words as his sole political weapons, he was prepared to use every possible stratagem, to expend his immense charm upon cajoling this or that British or American statesman, or cardinal, or millionaire, into providing the means he needed for his ends. He was prepared to conceal facts, to work in secret, to fascinate, and enslave, individuals, to use his personal followers, or anyone who appeared to him to be useful, as a means for limited ends – only to lose all interest in them, to their bewildered indignation (which was at times exceeding articulate and bitter), once the need for them was at an end. But he was not prepared to compromise with his own central moral and political principles, and never did so. He was not afraid of making enemies, nor of public or private opinion, nor, in the least degree, of the judgement of posterity. He understood human beings and took an interest in them; he enjoyed his power of casting his spell over them; he liked political flirtation; he was, indeed, in addition to his gifts as a statesman, a political virtuoso of the highest, most inspired order.

These qualities carried their defects with them. They entailed a certain disregard for the wills and attitudes – perhaps rights – of others. He was at times too little concerned with the purposes and characters of those with whom he did not sympathise, and they complained of neglect or heartless exploitation or despotism. He was, in a sense, too fearless, he was too confident that his cause and his friends must triumph, and often underestimated the violence and sincerity of the convictions held by his opponents, both in his own party and in the world at large. This was both a strength and a weakness; it added immeasurably to his feeling of inner security and his optimism, and it liberated his creative energies; but it blinded him to the effects of the fears and the implacable hostility he was bound to encounter among those men outside his own community whom Zionism offended or upset – anti-Semites open and concealed, Arabs and their champions, British Government officials, churchmen of many faiths, the respectable and established in general. It seemed a necessary element in his positive, unswerving, vigorous, almost too uncompromising constructive temper to ignore individual human weaknesses – envy, fear, prejudice, vanity, small acts of cowardice or spite or treachery, in particular obstructive tactics on the part of the feeble, or stupid, or timid, or ill-disposed officials, which more, perhaps, than major decisions cumulatively blocked his path, and, in the end, as everyone knows, led to bloodshed.

Similarly he tended to ignore his opponents and enemies, personal and ideological. These he had in plenty, not least in his own nation. The fanatically religious Jews saw him as an impious would-be usurper of the position of the divine Messiah. Tremulous Jews in important positions in Western countries, especially those prosperous or prominent figures who had at last attained to what they conceived as secure positions in modern society, achieved after much wandering and at great expense, regarded him as a dangerous troublemaker likely to open wounds that they had taken much trouble to bandage and conceal; at best they treated him with nervous respect, as a highly compromising ally. Socialists, radicals, internationalists of many hues – but especially of course the Marxists – regarded him as a reactionary nineteenth-century nationalist, seeking to lead the Jews back from the broad and sunlit uplands of the world-wide society of their dreams to the stifling confines of a petty little nationality exiled to a backward region of the eastern Mediterranean – a grotesque anachronism destined to be swept aside by the inexorable impersonal forces of history. Then there were the Jewish populists in Russia or America who believed in a kind of local or regional Jewish popular culture – a kind of quasi-nationality in exile – Yiddish-speaking, plebeian, unpolitical, a parody of the Russian populism of the time. These looked on Weizmann as a snob, a calculating politician, an enemy to their programmes of warm-hearted social welfare, embellished by amiable and unpretentious arts and crafts and the preservation of carefully protected centres of old-fashioned Jewish life in an unsympathetic and unsentimental Gentile world. And finally there were sceptics and scoffers, sane and ironical, or bitter and cynical, who looked on Zionism as nothing but a foolish dream. He paid little attention to his opponents; but he felt sure that he knew what was strong and what was weak in them – as they did not – and felt sufficiently superior to them morally and intellectually to be determined to save them from themselves (humility, as I said before, was not one of his characteristics). He did not hate them as they hated him – save only the Communists, whom all his life he genuinely feared and detested as swarms of political locusts who, whatever their professions, always destroyed far more than they created. So far as he took notice of them at all, he looked on his opponents as so many sheep that he must attempt to rescue from the inevitable slaughter towards which they seemed to be moving with such fatal eagerness. Consequently he regarded the Russian socialist leaders, with whom he used to argue (and with whom, at least once, before the First World War, he formally debated in a public hall in Switzerland), simply as so many rival fishers of souls, likely to detach from the movement of Jewish liberation and drive to their doom some of the ablest and most constructively minded sons of his people. It is a pity that these debates[1] are not extant. Never can two movements have come into sharper or more articulate collision than in these acrimonious and uniquely interesting controversies between the leaders of the two conceptions of life destined to divide the modern world – communism and nationalism. It is a historical irony that this crucial debate was conducted on the small and obscure platform of the specifically Jewish needs and issues of the time.

Weizmann believed that he would win – he never doubted this – not because of any overwhelming faith in his own powers, great though these were; not from *naïveté* – although, in some respects, he did possess the deep simplicity and trustfulness of a certain type of great man, especially in his dealings with Englishmen – but because he was convinced that the tendencies in Jewish life which he represented were central and indestructible, while the case of his opponents was built on the shifting sands of history, rested on smaller areas of experience, and arose out of issues more personal and factional, and therefore ephemeral, than the great, overmastering human desire for individual liberty, national equality and a tolerable life that he felt that he himself represented. He derived great moral strength from his belief in the central ends, the deepest interests, of mankind, that could not for ever be thwarted, that alone justified and guaranteed the ultimate success of great and revolutionary undertakings. He did not, I am sure, distinguish his personal sentiments from the values for which he stood, the historical position that he felt himself to occupy.

When biographers come to consider his disagreements with the

---

[1] Plekhanov, Lenin, Trotsky, Radek are the names that, to the best of my recollection, he mentioned to me as being among those who debated against him in Berne and elsewhere at this time. I do not know whether any record of this has been found.

founder of the movement, Theodor Herzl, his duels with Justice Louis Brandeis, and with the leader of the extreme right-wing Zionists, Vladimir Jabotinsky; or, for that matter, his differences with such genuine supporters of his own moderate policies as Sokolow, or Ben-Gurion, and many a lesser figure, they will[1] – they inevitably must – ask how much of this was due to personal ambition, love of power, underestimation of opponents, impatient autocracy of temper; and how much was principle, devotion to ideas, rational conviction of what was right or expedient. When this question is posed, I do not believe that it will find any very clear answer: perhaps no answer at all. For in this case, as in that of virtually every statesman, personal motives were inextricably connected with, at the lowest, conceptions of political expediency and, at the highest, a pure and disinterested public ideal. Weizmann committed none of those enormities for which men of action, and later their biographers, claim justification, on the ground of what is called *raison d'état* – the notorious reasons of State which permit politicians caught in some major crisis to sacrifice the accepted standards and principles of private morality to the superior claims of State, or society, or Church, or party. Weizmann, despite his reputation as a master of *realpolitik*, forged no telegrams, massacred no minorities, executed and incarcerated no political opponents. When Jewish terrorism broke out in Palestine he felt and behaved much as Russian liberals did when reactionary tsarist ministers were assassinated by idealistic revolutionaries. He did not support it; in private he condemned it very vehemently. But he did not think it morally decent to denounce either the acts or their perpetrators in public. He genuinely detested violence: and he was too civilised and too humane to believe in its efficacy, mistakenly perhaps. But he did not propose to speak out against acts, criminal as he thought them, which sprang from the tormented minds of men driven to desperation, and ready to give up their lives to save their brothers from what, he and they were equally convinced, was a betrayal and a destruction cynically prepared for them by the foreign offices of the Western powers.

Bevin's Palestine policy had finally caused Weizmann to wonder whether his own lifelong admiration for, and loyalty to, England and British governments had perhaps cost his people too dear. His devotion to his cause was deeper than to any personal issue. And

[1] This was written in 1958.

since he was neither vain, nor constitutionally obstinate, he was not blinded to the possibility of error on his own part. He did not literally give up hope; he believed that it would take more than ministers and civil servants to defeat the Jewish settlement fighting for its very survival. He kept saying about the Foreign and Colonial Offices, as he paced up and down his hotel room in London, and listened to reports about this or that post-war anti-Zionist move by Whitehall, 'It is too late. It will not help them.' But he wondered whether his own earlier trust in England had not gratuitously lengthened the birth-pangs of the new Jewish State. He was not convinced that a Jewish State might not be premature; he would have preferred dominion status. The Peel Commission's partition scheme of 1936 had marked the highest point of fruitful collaboration between the British Government and himself, and he regarded those who had wrecked this scheme, especially in the Foreign Office, as responsible for the calamities that followed. He knew that he had himself been removed from his office because he trusted these men too much. But his own lifelong reputation as an Anglophile, as a moderate, as a statesman, was now to him as nothing in the face of the struggle for life of the Jewish settlement in Palestine. He had moments of black pessimism; but he believed that men fighting in a just cause must, when the worst came to the worst, sell their lives as dearly as possible – if need be – like Samson in the temple of the Philistines. And he held this to be no less true for nations than individuals.

When the Arab–Jewish war broke out his conscience was clear. He was not a pacifist, and the war was – no Jew doubted this – one of self-defence. All his life he believed in, and practised, a policy of accommodation; he had politically suffered for it, and the war was not one of his making.

Like the late Justice Holmes, Weizmann had all his life believed that when great public issues are joined one must above all take sides; whatever one did, one must not remain neutral or uncommitted, one must always – as an absolute duty – identify oneself with some living force in the world, and take part in the world's affairs with all the risk of blame and misrepresentation and misunderstanding of one's motives and character which this almost invariably entails. Consequently, in the Jewish war of independence he called for no compromise, and he denounced those who did. He regarded with contempt the withdrawal from life on the part of those to whom their personal integrity, or peace of mind, or purity of ideal, mattered more than the work upon which they were engaged and to which they were committed, the artistic, or scientific, or social, or political, or purely personal enterprises in which all men are willy-nilly involved. He did not condone the abandonment of ultimate principles before the claims of expediency or of anything else; but political monasticism – a search for some private cave of Adullam to avoid being disappointed or tarnished, the taking up of consciously Utopian or politically impossible positions in order to remain true to some inner voice, or some unbreakable principle too pure for the wicked public world – that seemed to him a mixture of weakness and self-conceit, foolish and despicable. He did not disguise his lack of respect for purists of this type. He did not always treat them fairly; and his point of view is one which has, of course, been opposed, and indeed detested, by men of the greatest courage and integrity; but I should be less than candid if I did not confess that it is a point of view that seems to me superior to its opposite. However that may be, it was of a piece with all that he believed and was.

Weizmann lived a rich inner life, but he did not escape into it to avoid the second-best realities of the outside universe. He loved the external world. He loved whatever seemed to him likely to contribute to a broad, full, generous tide of life in which the full resources of individuals could be developed to their richest and most diversified extent. Best of all he liked positive human gifts: intelligence, imagination, beauty, strength, generosity, steadfastness, integrity of character, and especially nobility of style, that inner elegance and natural breadth and sweep and confidence which only old and stable cultures, free from calculation, narrowness and neurotic self-preoccupation, seemed to him to possess. England seemed to him to display these qualities most richly, and he remained devoted to her until the end of his days. This fidelity, which was not unreciprocated, at first sustained, and then broke, his political life. He loved her independence, freedom, dignity, style. These were free men's virtues, and them, above all, he desired the Jews to acquire and develop and possess.

The connection of England with the Zionist experiment, and in particular with Weizmann's part in the securing of the Balfour declaration and the mandate over Palestine, is usually regarded as a somewhat fortuitous one. It is sometimes asserted that, had he not happened to obtain a post in the University of Manchester, he might never have settled in England, and would then scarcely have met Arthur Balfour in the early years of the century, and, in that case, would certainly have been in no position to influence either him or Lloyd George or any of the other British statesmen whose voice was decisive in the establishment of the Jewish settlement. This is true, and is, perhaps, a characteristic case of the influence of accident in history. But then one may begin to wonder if it is altogether an accident that it was to England that Weizmann migrated from the continent of Europe. For to him, as to so many Jews of his background and upbringing in Eastern Europe, England, above all other lands, stood for settled democracy, humane and peaceful civilisation, civil liberty, legal equality, stability, toleration, respect for individual rights, and a religious tradition founded as much on the Old Testament as on the New. She embodied all those free middle-class virtues that made for Anglomania in France in the last century of the *ancien régime*, and in Eastern Europe, for much the same reasons, in the nineteenth century. She was, above all, a country in which the Jews enjoyed a secure and peaceful and progressive existence, in full possession of the rights of men and citizens – everything, in short, that the more educated among them craved for most of all, and lacked most deeply in their own midst. This was the atmosphere in which Weizmann was brought up, and he therefore arrived in England with a preconceived respect bred in him by the attitude of his entire milieu.[1] His long and fascinated flirtation with Lord Balfour, from which so much in his life and that of the Zionist movement sprang, is not intelligible unless it is realised that in Balfour he met what, at all times, he found most attractive: aristocratic attributes in their finest and most fastidious form.

Weizmann was a celebrated and, indeed, when he set himself to it, an irresistible political seducer, but he did not offer himself except to those whom he truly admired, and he was not prepared to enter into a personal relationship for the sake of mere political expediency with those who morally or politically – and, at times indeed, aesthetically – repelled him. Perhaps he would have been wiser not to quarrel with Justice Brandeis, not to despair of 'building a bridge between Pinsk and Washington'; not to ignore

[1] It is a significant fact that in a letter written in Hebrew before he was twelve to his former schoolmaster, he speaks of England as the good and free country which will help the Jews to establish their own State. I owe this fascinating piece of information to Boris Guriel, who did so much to preserve the record of Weizmann's life and activity.

Arab leaders, or dignitaries of the Roman Church; not to react so strongly to the brutal ill-humour of Ernest Bevin; but he could not break his own temperament. He liked only large, imaginative and generous natures, and he believed that the future of his people was bound up with what they alone could give, that agreement could be reached only with such men, and that marriages of pure political convenience were bound to fail. His opponents condemned this as mere romanticism, mistakenly as I believe. He believed that lasting agreement required a large measure of genuine harmony of interests, principles and outlook between negotiators, and came to believe that this affinity obtained between the Jews and the English to a unique degree. This last, like most generalisations of this type, may have been a sentimental error, and one for which both sides have paid dearly, but it was an interesting and attractive error, and one that deeply influenced the character of the new State.

Perhaps Weizmann was carried away too far by his personal tastes. He liked the English almost too well: he liked the concreteness of English life, language, ideals; the moderation, the civilised disdain of extremes, the whole tone of public life, the lack of cruelty, of excitement, of shoddiness. He liked still more the wayward imagination, the love of the odd and the idiosyncratic, the taste for eccentricity, the quality of independence. He was a great charmer, as Disraeli had been before him; and the English like to be charmed. They might be conscious, as Queen Victoria perhaps knew when Disraeli wrote or spoke to her, that they were being enticed; but they were not – until their bad days – suspicious of it; they did not think that the power to delight, the play of fancy, gay and often mordant humour, bold ideas moderately expressed, political romanticism conveyed in a mixture of vivid similes, sober, temperate language and perpetual reference to intelligible material achievement were necessarily insincere or wicked, or constituted a danger to themselves. They were secure themselves and, therefore, they were courteous; they listened, and they welcomed opportunities of being fascinated. No French statesman, no American (not to speak of the Germans whom Herzl tried to address) would have let himself be as deeply and, above all, as willingly influenced by Weizmann's political imagination and historical memories as Balfour or Lloyd George or Churchill, and many a soldier, many a politician and professor and journalist, gladly allowed themselves to be. They were not merely beguiled by a clever and delightful talker; the values of the foreign chemist and his English hosts did in fact largely coincide. They did not find it difficult to think of the world in the terms in which he spoke, or at any rate were quite ready to see it so, and were grateful to anyone who lifted them to that level. And in fact they were right, and those who dismissed his talk as full of cunning or deliberate exoticism were morally and politically unperceptive. For it turned out that history conformed to Weizmann's vision, compounded of hard-headed common sense and deep historical emotion, and not to the normal categories of the 'realists' in the government departments of Britain, France and the United States. What he advocated was nearly always practicable. What his opponents urged was for the most part falsified by events.

I have said that his words were addressed to reason rather than feeling. His method of argument was, as a rule, neither a demonstration founded on statistical or other carefully docu-mented evidence, nor emotional rhetoric, nor a sermon addressed to the passions; it consisted in painting a very vivid, detailed, coherent, concrete picture of a given situation or course of events; and his interlocutors, as a rule, felt that this picture, in fact, coincided with reality and conformed to their own experience of what men and events were like, of what had happened, or might happen, or, on the contrary, could not happen; of what could and what could not be done. The moral, historical, economic, social and personal factors were blended in Weizmann's remarkable, unrecorded expositions much as they combine in life (thus he spoke most effectively face to face, in private, and not before an audience). He was not an analytic but a synthetic thinker, and presented a pattern or amalgam of elements, not the essence of each separate component isolated, taken apart and looked at by itself. There was no country in which such concreteness was a more habitual form of thought than in England, and the natural sympathy which his mode of thought and action found here caused him to invest – invest irretrievably – far more of his emotional capital in his friendship for England than, I think, he realised. And an element in the opposition to him and to his ideas, whether by his own followers or from outside his movement, derived from the instinctive revulsion from English values on the part of those who found themselves in greater sympathy with other outlooks or forms of life.

I must be forgiven for reverting again to the theme of his passion for England; it was very central in him, and in his ideal, for he wanted the new Jewish society – the new State – to be a political child of English – almost exclusively English – experience. He valued especially the tendency toward instinctive compromise, whereby sharp edges are not indeed planed away, but largely ignored by both sides in a dispute if they threaten to disrupt the social texture too widely, and break down the minimum conditions for common life. Moreover he believed profoundly in the application of scientific method to human life, in which England once led the world; his interest in pure science was very limited; but he was a magnificent inventor, and wanted invention to respond to basic human needs and create new, more civilised ones – he believed in the unlimited transforming powers of natural science. This was at the heart of his optimism, of his hope and faith in the future; and he liked to think of this view as characteristically British. It was therefore one of the bitterest disappointments of his life when, in the later 1930s, and during the Second World War, his services as a scientist were virtually ignored by the British government departments.

When war broke out in 1939, he offered to lay aside some of his political preoccupations, in order once more to try to be of service to his adopted country, as he had been with his celebrated invention in the First World War. He met with lack of response. He complained of dullness, timidity, pettiness, conservatism, fear of the future on the part of most of the British officials with whom he discussed these matters, of their total inability to grasp the economic position of their country, still less the dangers and opportunities in the world that was bound to come. Throughout the War he reverted to this fact with melancholy incredulity; he found it difficult to accept that as a scientist he had, in fact, met with a far readier response in America. He wondered whether British imagination and appetite for life were dying. It seemed to him that one and the same negative attitude – a symptom of exhaustion and defeat – was palpably present in the fears of the new world and the desperate attempts to cling to an outworn conception of the world political order that he found in Whitehall, and in the squalid efforts to back out of British commitments to the Jews in Palestine. It all seemed to him part and parcel of the general retreat from moral and political principles, beginning with the condoning of Arab violence in Palestine, of Japanese aggression in Manchuria, of Mussolini in Abyssinia, of Franco in Spain, and, above all, of course, of Hitler. And when, speaking of anti-

Zionists, he said to the Prime Minister, Winston Churchill, in 1940 or 1941, with characteristic boldness, 'Remember, sir, our enemies are also yours', this is certainly part of what he meant. Political appeasement, weakness, nervous fears, blindness to distasteful facts, seemed to him merely an aspect of one and the same gloomy condition of decline, which blinded the eyes of British economic planners to the possibility – to the necessity, indeed – of recouping the slipping British position by one of the main devices which, he felt sure, could still help to save it – the imaginative application of the resources of the African empire to the creation of a great new synthetic materials industry; it was a field about which he himself, as a chemist, knew a great deal, and one he had done much to develop. Since he thought in vast, synoptic terms, he saw the Jewish establishment in Palestine in these same scientific terms. As he reflected on the poverty of the land and its lack of natural resources, he placed his hope upon turning the one kind of capital that the Jews did seem to possess – technical skills, ingenuity, energy, desperation – to the production of miracles in scientific technology that would contribute to the building of the new world, and especially the new, post-Chamberlain Britain. He believed that the British would understand this, and was depressed by finding that this seemed no longer so. He felt rebuffed, he no longer recognised the nation he had loved so steadfastly and disinterestedly.

He felt he had a right to complain. On the two principal occasions when he suffered public defeat at the hands of his own followers, the principal cause of it lay in what seemed to them his fanatical reliance on the good faith of British governments. He was compelled to resign in 1931 as a protest against the policy of concessions to Arab violence at the expense of its victims, begun by the Labour Government with the Passfield White Paper, and continued by its successors. In 1946 a very similar situation once again arose; and it could plausibly be argued that Weizmann's policy of accommodation with Britain, which had led to a total betrayal of the Jewish position in 1938–9, must, if persisted in (he was then advocating acceptance of what was called the Morrison Plan), lead to a further series of promises broken and hopes destroyed. In the end he began, with painful reluctance, to think that this might be true. He could not bring himself to admit this publicly; but in private he spoke with bitter scorn about what seemed to him the complacent stupidity of post-Churchillian statesmanship. When some of his English friends (Lord Keynes for example) tried to say to him that England was too tired and too poor to carry the burden of its incompatible promises to the Jews and the Arabs any longer, and consequently must abandon both parties to their own devices, he rejected this doctrine with scorn and fury, as craven, unworthy of the men who urged it, and above all a false analysis and a suicidal policy for any great power.

His own position became increasingly unenviable. His followers in Palestine and elsewhere looked on his Anglophile policy as bankrupt, and on him as too deeply committed to it – and with it to a world that had vanished – to be anything but a dignified but obsolete mammoth of an earlier age. No member of the government in England or America was anxious to see him. He was a tragic, formidable and politically embarrassing figure. It had always been a somewhat daunting, not to say punishing, experience both for ministers and their officials to meet the full impact of Weizmann's terrifying indignation. This was now no longer necessary. The relief was almost audible. The Colonial Office treated him with icy politeness. He was systematically snubbed by the Foreign Office, as often as not by junior officials, who took their cue from their superiors, or perhaps felt that they could with impunity allow their own solidly pro-Arab sentiments free expression. He was treated with brutal rudeness by Bevin, who conceived for him, and for the entire Zionist movement, a notorious personal hostility which nothing staunched. And yet he could not give up his oldest political love. England meant more to him than all other countries put together.

When I stayed with him in Palestine, as it still was, in 1947, during the height of Jewish military and terrorist activity against the British forces stationed in that country, his fondness for, and delight in seeing, the British commander of his district and other British officers continued unabated, to the mounting scandal of his followers. He felt betrayed, and he could not, despite all his realism and his tough-minded approach to politics, understand what had happened. The romantic, somewhat Churchillian, image of England as moved, in the last resort, by her moral imagination, and not by a short view of her self-interest or passing emotion, would not leave him. The England which had stood alone against barbarism and evil, the England for which his son had lost his life, was scarcely less real to him than his vision of the Jewish past and future. He tried to close his eyes. He fell back on his scientific work. He often said that nothing had a morally more purifying effect, after the unavoidable contaminations of public life, than the impersonal work of a researcher in his laboratory, where the truth could not be cheated, and the vices and follies of men played little part. He busied himself in his work in the Institute at Rehovot that bears his name.[1] But the remedy was not wholly effective. He had put his faith in British statesmen and had rendered his followers into their hands; every shipload of immigrants turned away by Bevin and Sir Harold McMichael brought his part in the betrayal home to him. From it he never fully recovered.

The British Government – in particular the Labour Government – had wounded him as no one else ever could; least of all the Jews. He did not ask, and did not expect, gratitude from his own people. The fate of Moses seemed to him natural and perhaps deserved. To his own close followers he seemed, if anything, altogether too invulnerable: especially when he behaved toward them (as he often did) with casual offhandedness, or ill-concealed contempt, or, from time to time, the sudden ruthlessness of a great man of action. Yet their personal loyalty survived most of the shocks which he administered. For his personal magnetism was quite unique. Men crossed great distances to visit him, knowing or suspecting that he had completely forgotten why he had sent for them, and that when they arrived he would be genuinely puzzled by their appearance, at best agreeably surprised, and would dismiss them with a few careless, gay and friendly sentences. His relationship to his immediate followers was, in some ways, not unlike that of Parnell to the Irish party in the House of Commons. And they treated him with much the same mixture of adoration, nervous respect, resentment, worship, envy, pride, irritation, and almost always, in the end, the overwhelming realisation that before them stood someone of more than human size, a powerful, sometimes terrifying, leader of newly liberated prisoners in terms of whose thoughts and activities their own history was largely made. They might revolt, but in the end they always – most of them – submitted to the force of his intellect and personality.

---

[1] The Institute was the deepest love of his old age. He always spoke of it, and of all his colleagues and, indeed, everyone connected with its work, with immense personal pride and affection, and derived from it a feeling of satisfaction that nothing else gave him to an equal degree. The flourishing state of this great establishment is evidence of the lasting vitality that he communicated to all that he truly believed in.

It was otherwise with England. His preoccupation – it grew at times to an obsession (perhaps his only *idée fixe*) – with Anglo-Zionist relations blinded him to too many other factors in the situation: the attitude of other powers, especially in Europe, of the Arab rulers, of social and political forces within the Palestine settlement itself. The collapse of the Anglo-Zionist connection was not only intertwined for him with his own personal failure to retain real power in the movement that was his life; it also seemed to support the claims of those who said that against Britain only violence paid – that nothing would save the Jewish settlement but methods of terrorism – a view that he abhorred and rejected passionately with his whole being, then and all his life. But there was something far greater at stake even than that. He could not bear the thought that the State that he had desired to establish, and which he desired to place under the protection of Great Britain, would now perhaps never acquire those moral and political attributes which he had so long and steadfastly admired as peculiarly English and which, he now gloomily began to wonder, were disappearing everywhere – even from this island where he had spent his happiest years.

He was in due course elected President of the State of Israel, a position of splendid symbolic value, but little power. He accepted it, fully realising what it meant and what it did not mean, amid the acclamation of Jews and their well-wishers everywhere. He understood the extent of his own achievement and never spoke of it; he was one of those rare human beings who estimate themselves at their true worth, and see themselves in the true perspective in which they see others. His autobiography, particularly in its earlier chapters, is an astonishingly objective and lifelike narrative, without a trace of dramatisation, exaggeration, vanity, self-pity, self-justification; it conveys his authentic, richly and evenly developed, autonomous, proud, firmly built, somewhat ironical nature, free from inner conflict, in deep, instinctive harmony with the forces of nature and society, and therefore possessed of natural wisdom, dignity and authority.

His unhappiness came from without, hardly ever from within; he remained inwardly tranquil to the end of his days. He knew well that his achievement was without parallel. He knew that, unlike any man in modern history, he had created a nation and a State out of the flotsam and jetsam of the Diaspora, and had lived to see it develop an independent, unpredictable life of its own. This worried him. Freedom and independence were not enough. Like the ancient prophet that Western statesmen sometimes saw in him, he craved for virtue. He disliked certain elements in Jewish life, and wondered uneasily whether they would emerge uppermost. Obsessed and lop-sided natures repelled him; he was contemptuous of addiction to doctrine and theory without constant concrete contact with empirical reality. He did not value the achievements of the unaided intellect for their own sake, and admired them only when they made some contribution to human life. He liked solidity, practical judgement, vitality, gaiety, understanding of life, dependability, courage, stoutness of heart, practical achievement. Martyrs, failures, casualties, victims of circumstance or of their own absurdities – the stock subjects of the mocking, sceptical Jewish sense of humour – filled him with distress and disgust. The central purpose of the entire Zionist experiment, the settlement in Palestine, was designed to cure the Jews of precisely these wounds and neuroses that only their enforced rootlessness had bred in them. He therefore particularly disliked the mixture of avant-garde sophistication, political fanaticism, cynicism, vulgarity, cleverness, *humeur noire*, knowingness and occasional bitter insight with which able, typically Central European, Jewish journalists were filling the pages of the world's Press. Even more he hated stupidity, and he did not trouble to conceal this. In his last years, when he was living in peace and great honour in his home in Rehovot, a figure respected by the entire world, he was occasionally haunted by nightmare visions of the future of the State of Israel. He saw it jeopardised by just such a combination of stupidity – innocent, fearless, but blind – with the corrupt and destructive cleverness of slaves, the aimless, feckless, nihilistic restlessness inherited from too long a sojourn in the ghetto. Yet he also saw that this might not happen; and then the thought that the dream had come true against all the overwhelming odds of his youth and manhood, that he was actually living among Jews, a free nation in their own country, would fill him with incredible happiness.

He was not a religiously orthodox Jew, but he lived the full life of a Jew. He had no love for clericalism, but he possessed an affectionate familiarity with every detail of the rich, traditional life of the devout and observant Jewish communities, as it was lived in his childhood, in the villages and small towns of Eastern Europe. I cannot speak of his religious beliefs; I can only testify to his profound natural piety. I was present on more than one occasion, towards the end of his life, when he celebrated the Seder service of the Passover with a moving dignity and nobility, like the Jewish patriarch that he had become. In this sense he had always lived in close contact with the life of the Jewish masses, and his optimism had its source in the belief which they shared – that their cause was just, their sufferings could not last for ever, that somewhere on earth a corner must exist in which their claim to human rights – their deepest desires and hopes – would find satisfaction at last. Neither he nor they would accept the proposition that the mass of mankind could remain for ever indifferent to the cry for justice and equality even on the part of the weakest and most wretched minority on earth. Men must themselves work and fight to secure their basic rights. This was the first prerequisite. Then, if these claims were recognised as valid in the great court of justice that was the public conscience of mankind, they would, soon or late, obtain their due. Neither force nor cunning could help. Only faith and work, founded on real needs. 'Miracles do happen,' he said to me once, 'but one has to work very hard for them.'

He believed that he would succeed – he never doubted it – because he felt the pressure of millions behind him. He believed that what so many desired so passionately and so justifiably could not for ever be denied; that moral force, if it was competently organised, always defeated mere material power. It was this serene and absolute conviction that made it possible for him to create the strange illusion among the statesmen of the world that he was himself a world statesman, representing a government in exile, behind which stood a large, coherent, powerful, articulate community. Nothing was – in the literal sense – less true, and both sides knew it well. And yet both sides behaved – negotiated – as if it were true, as if they were equals. If he did not cause the embarrassment that suppliants so often engender, it was because he was very dignified, and quite free. He could be very intimidating; he uttered, in his day, some very memorable insults. Ministers were known to shrink nervously from the mere prospect of an approaching visit from this formidable emissary of a non-existent power, because they feared that the interview might prove altogether too much of a moral experience: and that, no matter how well briefed by their officials, they would end, for reasons which they themselves could not subsequently explain or under-stand, by making some crucial concession to their inexorable guest. But whatever the nature of the extraordinary magic that he exercised, the one element signally absent from it was pathos. Chaim Weizmann was the first totally free Jew of the modern world, and the State of Israel was constructed, whether or not it knows it, in his image. No man has ever had a comparable monument built to him in his own lifetime.

EINSTEIN AND ISRAEL

ALBERT EINSTEIN's chief title to immortal fame is his transcendent scientific genius, about which, like the vast majority of mankind, I am totally incompetent to speak. Einstein was universally revered as the most revolutionary innovator in the field of physics since Newton. The exceptional respect and attention that were everywhere paid to his person and to his opinions on other topics sprang from this fact. He knew this himself: and although he was a genuinely modest man, embarrassed by the adulation which he excited, and disliked publicity, he expressed pleasure at the thought that, if homage was to be paid to individuals at all, it should go to those who could claim achievement in fields of intellect and culture rather than of power and conquest. Indeed, that a mathematical physicist should have become a great world figure is a remarkable fact and a credit to mankind.

If the impact of Einstein's ideas outside the realms of theoretical physics and, perhaps, of the philosophy of physics is compared to that made by the ideas of other great scientific pioneers, an odd conclusion seems to emerge. Galileo's method, to go no further back, and his naturalism, played a crucial role in the development of seventeenth-century thought, and extended far beyond technical philosophy. The impact of Newton's ideas was immense: whether they were correctly understood or not, the entire programme of the Enlightenment, especially in France, was consciously founded on Newton's principles and methods, and derived its confidence and its vast influence from his spectacular achievements. And this, in due course, transformed – indeed, largely created – some of the central concepts and directions of modern culture in the West, moral, political, technological, historical, social. No sphere of thought or life escaped the consequences of this cultural mutation.

This is true to a lesser extent of Darwin – the concept of

evolution affected many fields of thought outside biology: it upset the theologians, it influenced the historical sciences, ethics, politics, sociology, anthropology. Social Darwinism, founded on a misapplication of Darwin's and Huxley's views, with its eugenic and sometimes racist implications, did social and political harm. I should perhaps hesitate to refer to Freud as a natural scientist; but there is no doubt that his teaching, too, affected fields far outside psychology – history, biography, aesthetics, sociology, education.

But Einstein? His scientific achievement touched on the philosophy of science; his own views – his early acceptance of Mach's phenomenalism, and his subsequent abandonment of that view – show that he possessed the gifts of a philosopher, and so, indeed, did his views of the central doctrines of Spinoza, Hume, Kant, Russell. In this respect, Einstein and Planck were virtually unique among the outstanding physicists of our century. But his influence on the general ideas of his time? On educated opinion? Certainly he presented a heroic image of a man of pure heart, noble mind, unusual moral and political courage, engaged in unswerving pursuit of the truth, who believed in individual liberty and social equality, a man sympathetic to socialism, who hated nationalism, militarism, oppression, violence, the materialistic view of life. But apart from embodying a combination of human goodness with a passion for social justice and unique intellectual power, in a society in which many seemed to live by the opposite values – apart, that is, from his exemplary life, from being, and being seen to be, one of the most civilised, honourable and humane men of his time – what impact did Einstein have?

It is true that the word 'relativity' has been, to this day, widely misinterpreted as meaning relativism, the denial of, or doubt about, the objectivity of truth or of moral and other values. But this is a very old and familiar heresy. Relativism in the sense in which Greek Sophists, Roman Sceptics, French and British subjectivists, German romantics and nationalists professed it, and in which theologians and historians and ordinary men have, in modern times, been tormented by it – this was the opposite of what Einstein believed. He was a man of simple and absolute moral convictions, which were expressed in all he was and did. His conception of external nature was that of a scientifically analysable, rational order or system; the goal of the sciences was objective knowledge of an independently existent reality, even though the concepts in which it was to be analysed and described were free, arbitrary human creations.

What general impact did his doctrines have? Modern theoretical physics cannot, has not, even in its most general outlines, thus far been successfully rendered in popular language as Newton's central doctrines were, for example, by Voltaire. High-minded public men in England like Haldane and Herbert Samuel tried to derive general metaphysical or theological truths, usually somewhat trite ones, from the general theory of relativity, but this only showed that their gifts lay in other spheres.

But if the impact of Einstein's scientific thought on the general ideas of his time is in some doubt, there can be none about the relevance of his non-scientific views to one of the most positive political phenomena of our time. Einstein lent the *prestige mondial* of his great name, and in fact gave his heart, to the movement which created the State of Israel. Men and nations owe a debt to those who help to transform their realistic self-image for the better. No Zionist with the least degree of self-esteem can refuse to pay him homage if the opportunity of doing so is offered to him. Einstein's support of the Zionist movement and his interest in the Hebrew University were lifelong. He quarrelled with Weizmann more than once; he was highly critical of the Hebrew University and, in particular, of its first President; he deplored the shortcomings of Zionist policy towards the Arabs; but he never abandoned his belief in the central principles of Zionism. If young people (or others) today, whether Jews or Gentiles, who, like the young Einstein, abhor nationalism and sectarianism and seek social justice and believe in universal human values – if such people wish to know why he, a child of assimilated German Jews, supported the return of the Jews to Palestine, Zionism and the Jewish State, not uncritically nor without the anguish which any decent and sensitive man cannot but feel about acts done in the name of his people which seem to him wrong or unwise, but nevertheless steadily, to the end of his life – if they wish to understand this, then they should read his writings on the subject. With his customary lucidity and gift for penetrating to the central core of any issue, whether in science or in life, Einstein said what had to be said with simplicity and truth. Let me recall some of the things he said and did, and in particular the path which led toward them.

He was born in Ulm, the child of irreligious parents. He was educated in Munich, where he seems to have encountered no discrimination; if he reacted strongly against his school and suffered something approaching a nervous breakdown, this does not seem to have been due to anti-Jewish feeling. What he reacted against was, perhaps, the quasi-military discipline and nationalist fervour of German education in the 1890s. He studied intermittently in Milan and Zurich, taught in Zurich, obtained a post in the Patent Office in Bern, then held university chairs in Prague and Zurich, and in 1913 was persuaded by Nernst and Haber, as well as Planck, whose reputations were then at their peak, to accept a research post in Berlin.

I do not need to describe the atmosphere of Prussia on the eve of the First World War. In a letter written in 1929 to a German Minister of State, Einstein said, 'When I came to Germany fifteen years ago [that is, in 1914] I discovered for the first time that I was a Jew. I owe this discovery more to Gentiles than Jews.'[1] Nevertheless, the influence of some early German Zionists, in particular Kurt Blumenfeld, the apostle to the German Jews, played a significant part in this – and Einstein remained on terms of warm friendship with him for the rest of his life. But, as in the case of Herzl, the decisive factor in his awakening as a Jew was not so much encounter with an unfamiliar doctrine (he had met adherents of it in Prague but apparently took no interest in it then) as the chauvinism and xenophobia of leading circles, in this case in Berlin, which led him to a realisation of the precarious predicament of the Jewish community even in the civilised West. 'The best in man can only flourish', he declared, 'when he loses himself in a community. Hence the moral danger of the Jew who has lost touch with his own people and is regarded as a foreigner by the people of his adoption.'[2] 'The tragedy of the Jews is ... that they lack the support of a community to keep them together. The result is a want of solid foundations in the individual which in its extreme form amounts to moral instability.'[3]

The only remedy, he argued, is to develop a close connection with a living society which would enable individual Jews to bear the hatred and humiliation to which they are often exposed by the rest of mankind. Herzl is to be admired, Einstein tells us, for saying

[1] Albert Einstein, *Ideas and Opinions* (based on *Mein Weltbild*, ed. Carl Seeling, and other sources), new translations and revisions by Sonja Bargmann (London and New York, 1954), p. 171. All subsequent references for quotations from Einstein are to this volume, by page number alone.
[2] p. 184.   [3] p. 171.

'at the top of his voice' that only the establishment of a national home in Palestine can cure this evil. It cannot be removed by assimilation. The Jews of the old German ghettos were poor, deprived of civic and political rights, insulated from European progress. Yet

> these obscure, humble people had one great advantage over us: each of them belonged in every fibre of his being to a community in which he was completely absorbed, in which he felt himself a fully privileged member, and which demanded nothing of him that was contrary to his natural habit of thought. Our forefathers in those days were pretty poor specimens intellectually and physically, but socially speaking they enjoyed an enviable spiritual equilibrium.[1]

Then came emancipation; rapid adaptation to the new open world; eager efforts to don clothes made to fit others, involving loss of identity, the prospect of disappearance as a group. But this was not to be:

> However much the Jews adapted themselves, in language, manners, and to a great extent even in the forms of religion, to the European peoples among whom they lived, the feeling of strangeness between the Jews and their hosts never disappeared. This spontaneous feeling is the ultimate cause of anti-Semitism, which is, therefore, not to be got rid of by well-meaning propaganda. Nationalities want to pursue their own path, not to blend.[2]

To ignore, or argue against, emotional prejudice or open hostility, Einstein declared, is wholly futile; the baptised Jewish *Geheimrat* was to him merely pathetic. National frontiers, armies he regarded as evil, but not national existence as such: the life of peaceful nations, with reciprocal respect for one another and toleration of each other's differences, was civilised and just. There follows a statement of Zionism not unlike the reaction to a similar predicament of another internationalist and socialist, Moses Hess, in the 1860s. Let me quote Einstein's words in 1933: 'It is not enough for us to play a part as individuals in the cultural development of the human race, we must also tackle tasks which only nations as a whole can perform. Only so can the Jews regain social health.'[3] Consequently: 'Palestine is not primarily a place of

---

[1] p. 181.   [2] p. 182.   [3] p. ibid.

refuge for the Jews of Eastern Europe but the embodiment of the re-awakening corporate spirit of the whole Jewish nation.'[1]

This seems to me a classical formulation of the Zionist creed, with an affinity to the unpolitical cultural nationalism of Ahad Ha'am: what Einstein was advocating was, in essence, the creation of a social and spiritual centre. But when British policy and Arab resistance, in his judgement, made the State inevitable, he accepted it, and the use of force to avoid annihilation, as being, perhaps, something of a necessary evil, but nevertheless as a burden and a duty to be borne with dignity and tact, without arrogance. Like all decent Zionists he was increasingly worried about the relationship with the Arabs of Palestine. He wished for a State in which Jews and Arabs could fully co-operate. But he realised, sadly, that events made this unlikely for the time being. He remained a consistent supporter of the Jewish State of Israel; here Jewish ideals must be pursued, especially three of them: 'the pursuit of knowledge for its own sake, an almost fanatical love of justice, and the desire for personal independence'.[2]

I need hardly say how sharply this differed from the general attitude of the educated German Jews of his milieu, not to speak of men of similar origin and social and intellectual formation elsewhere in Western Europe. When one remembers Einstein's earlier life, remote from Jewish affairs, his lifelong idealistic internationalism, his hatred of all that divided men, it seems to me to argue a remarkable degree of insight, realism and moral courage, of which his fellow Jews today have good reason to feel proud. After all, other eminent German-Jewish scientists, honourable men of unimpeachable personal integrity, Fritz Haber, Max Born, James Franck, reacted very differently. So did writers and artists like Schnitzler, Stefan Zweig, Mahler, Karl Kraus or Werfel, who were all too familiar with anti-Semitism in Vienna.

I do not wish to imply that Einstein necessarily condemned assimilation to the culture of the majority as always ignoble or doomed to failure. It was plainly possible for children of Jewish parents to find themselves so remote from their community and its traditions that, even if they considered it, they were unable psychologically to re-establish genuine links with it. He was clear that in a civilised society every man must be free to pursue his own path in the manner that seemed to him best, provided that this did

---

[1] p. 181.   [2] p. 183.

not do positive harm to others. He did not accuse these scientists and writers and artists of dishonourable or craven motives; their human dignity was not, for him, in question, only their degree of self-understanding.

It was his incapacity for self-deception or evasion, his readiness to face the truth, and – if the facts demanded it – to go against the current of received ideas, that marked Einstein's bold rejection of the central elements in the Newtonian system, and it was this independence that characterised his behaviour in other spheres. He rejected conventional wisdom: 'Common sense', he once said, 'is the deposit of prejudice laid down in the mind before the age of eighteen.' If something did not seem to him to fit, morally or politically, no less than mathematically, he would not ignore, escape, forget it; adjust, arrange, add a patch or two in the hope that it would last his time; he would not wait for the Messiah – the world revolution – the universal reign of reason and justice – to dissolve the difficulty. If the shoe does not fit, it is no use saying that time and wear will make it less uncomfortable, or that the shape of the foot should be altered, or that the pain is an illusion – that reality is harmonious, and that therefore conflict, injustice, barbarism belong to the order of appearances, which superior spirits should rise above. If his philosophical mentors, Hume and Mach, were right, there was only one world, the world of human experience; it alone was real; beyond it there might be mystery; indeed, he regarded the fact, of which he was totally convinced, that the universe was comprehensible as the greatest of mysteries; yet no theory was valid which ignored any part of direct human experience, in which he included imaginative insight, arrived at by paths often far from conscious.

It was this sense of reality that saved him, despite his deep convictions, from being doctrinaire. When what he knew, understood directly, was in conflict with doctrinal orthodoxy, he did not ignore the immediate evidence of his moral, social or political sense. He was a convinced pacifist; during the First World War he made himself unpopular in Germany by denouncing it. But in 1933 he accepted the necessity of resisting Hitler and the Nazis, if need be by force, which horrified his pacifist allies. He was an egalitarian, a democrat, with an inclination towards socialism. Yet his sense of the need to protect individuals from the State was so strong that he believed that Bills of Rights would be trampled on unless an élite of educated and experienced persons in authority at times effectively resisted the wishes of majorities. He praised the American Constitution, and in particular the balance of power between the President, Congress and public opinion (his early political mentor, the Austrian socialist Fritz Adler, would scarcely have approved). He hated walls between human beings, exclusiveness. But when Jewish students were being hounded by nationalist students in German or Polish universities, he declared that Weizmann was right; liberal and socialist resolutions were useless; the Jews must act, and create their own university in Jerusalem.

He hated nationalism all his life. But he recognised the acute need of the Jews for some form of national existence; above all, he did not regard a sense of national identity and nationalism as being one and the same thing. It is clear that he took political allegiance seriously. He renounced his German nationality twice. He would not, as a young man, have chosen to adopt Swiss or, after Hitler, American citizenship, had he not felt that he could give his full allegiance to these democratic countries when, for obvious reasons, he found it unbearable to retain his German passport. It was this combination of social sensitiveness and concrete insight into what it is that men live by that saved him from doctrinaire fanaticism; it was this that made him morally convincing.

He was an innocent man, and sometimes, I should think, taken in by fools and knaves. But innocence has its own modes of perception: it sometimes sees through its own eyes, not those of the spectacles provided by conventional wisdom or some uncriticised dogma. The very same independence which caused him to reject the accepted notions of physical space-time, and boldly offer the hypothesis of gravitational waves and light quanta against the resistance of physicists and philosophers, also liberated him morally and politically.

Consequently this man who sought privacy, who remained wholly uncorrupted by adulation and unparalleled fame in five continents, who believed in salvation by work and more work to unravel the secrets of nature – secrets miraculously amenable to analysis and solution by human reason – this gentle, shy and modest man displeased many establishments: German nationalists, Germanophobe Frenchmen, absolute pacifists, Jewish assimilationists, Orthodox rabbis, Soviet Marxists, as well as defenders of absolute moral values in which, in fact, he firmly believed.

He was neither a subjectivist nor a sceptic. He believed that the concepts and theories of science are free creations of the human imagination, not, as Bacon or Mill or Mach thought, themselves abstracted from the data of experience; but what the scientist seeks to analyse or describe by means of these theories and concepts is itself an objective structure of which men, viewed scientifically, are themselves a part. Moral and aesthetic values, rules, standards, principles cannot be derived from the sciences, which deal with what is, not with what should be; but neither are they, for Einstein, generated or conditioned by differences of class or culture or race. No less than the laws of nature, from which they cannot be derived, they are universal, true for all men at all times, discovered by moral or aesthetic insight common to all men, and embodied in the basic principles (not the mythology) of the great world religions.

Like Spinoza, he thought that those who deny this are merely blinded by the passions; indeed, he felt Spinoza to be a kindred spirit. Like Spinoza, he conceived God as reason embodied in nature, as being, in a literal sense, a divine harmony, *deus sive natura*; and, again like Spinoza, he showed no bitterness towards his detractors, nor did he compromise with them – he remained serene and reasonable, humane, tolerant, undogmatic. He did not wish to dominate, and did not demand blind fidelity from his followers. He supported any movement – say, the League of Nations or left-wing groups in America – if he thought that on the whole it did good, or at least more good than harm.

So with Jewish Palestine. He hated the chauvinists; he was critical, at times to an unrealistic degree, of the attitude of the Zionist leadership towards the Arabs, but this did not make him lean over backward occasionally as it did others; he denounced the Eisenhower Administration for seeking to please the Arab States at the expense of Israel, a policy which he attributed to American imperialism. He was critical of some of the Hebrew University's policies: for instance, he thought that, among the academic refugees from Fascist Europe, young scholars, not the old and famous, should be offered appointments. But his loyalties remained unimpaired. He was not prepared to abandon the Zionist movement because of the deficiencies of some of its leaders. His Zionism was grounded in the belief that basic human needs create a right to their satisfaction: men have an inalienable right to freedom from hunger, nakedness, insecurity, injustice, and from homelessness too.

He was somewhat homeless himself. In a letter to his friend Max Born he wrote that he had no roots; that he was a stranger everywhere. He was, on his own admission, a lonely man who instinctively avoided intimacy. He was a solitary thinker, not easy to know as a human being. His deep humanity and sympathy with the victims of political oppression, social discrimination, economic exploitation, were central to his outlook and need no special explanation; they were in part, perhaps, a compensation for his difficulty in forming close personal relationships.

Like many physicists connected in some way with the production of the atom bomb, he was, in his later years, oppressed by a sense of the responsibility of scientists for introducing a terrible new means of destruction into the world; and he condemned the use of it made by his adopted country, which seemed to him bent on a dangerously imperialist course. His hatred of the cruelty and barbarity of reactionaries and Fascists at times led him to believe that there were no enemies on the left – an illusion of many decent and generous people, some of whom have paid for it with their lives.

Perhaps his very gifts as a scientist led him to schematise, to oversimplify practical problems, including complex political and cultural ones, which allow of no clear-cut solutions, to be too sweeping and to ignore the wrinkles and unevennesses of daily life, insusceptible as they are to exact quantitative analysis. For it seems to me that there may exist a certain difference between the gifts of scientists and humanists. It has often been pointed out that major discoveries and inventions – as opposed to demonstrations of their validity – require great imaginative power and an intuitive sense, not rationally analysable, of where the right solution must lie, and that this is not dissimilar from the vision of artists or the sympathetic insight into the past of gifted historians or scholars. This may well be true. Yet those who deal with human beings and their affairs need some awareness of the essential nature of all human experience and activity, a sense of the limits of what it is possible for men and women to be or to do; without some such awareness of the limits imposed by nature there is no criterion for dismissing an infinity of logically possible but wildly improbable or absurd historical or psychological hypotheses.

About what makes men rational Aristotle and Kant and Voltaire and Hume may well be right: on this sense of what can, and what clearly cannot, be the case in human affairs, on the normal association of ideas, on such basic concepts as those of past, future, things, persons, causal sequence, logical relations – a closely woven network of categories and concepts – human rationality, perhaps even sanity, in practice, depends. Departure from these, as attempted, for example, by surrealist painters or poets, or aleatory composers, may be interesting, but it is deliberately counter-rational.

But in mathematics or theoretical physics this sense of reality does not necessarily seem to be required. Indeed, something close to the opposite may, at times, be needed. In the case of seminal discoveries – say, of imaginary numbers, or non-Euclidean geometry, or the quantum theory – it is precisely dissociation of commonly associated ideas, that is, departure from some categories indispensable to normal human experience, that seems to be required, namely a gift for conceiving what cannot in principle be imagined, nor expressed in ordinary language, which is concerned with day-to-day communication, with the facts and needs of human life. It is this detachment from, even flouting of, everyday reality that leads to the popular image of the abstract thinker – Thales who falls into a well, the absent-minded professor who boils his watch in place of an egg.

This kind of escape into abstractions – an ideal world of pure forms expressed in a specially invented symbolism free from the irregularities and untidiness, or even the basic assumptions, of ordinary experience – may possibly, at times, be connected with a psychic disturbance, some kind of displacement in early life. Einstein's breakdown as a schoolboy in Munich is paralleled by similar childhood experiences of Newton and Darwin, who also remained somewhat inaccessible emotionally. These thinkers, too, spoke of a type of experience which Einstein described as a deeply religious feeling before a vision of the divinity revealed in the all-embracing unity and rational harmony of the rigorously causal structure of nature. This was a vision of reality which nothing could shake: consequently Einstein remained an unyielding determinist, and never accepted the uncertainty principle as an ultimate category of natural knowledge, or as an attribute of objective nature – only as part of our provisional and incomplete analysis of it.

Such addiction to pure abstraction and generalisation may, at times, be connected with an incapacity for close personal relationships with others, a full social life; this appears to me to be a plausible hypothesis. It may well have been so with Albert Einstein. What he withheld from private life he gave to the world. Not only the fame of his achievement, but his figure, his face, are known to millions of men and women. His appearance became a visible symbol, a stereotype, of what people supposed a scientist of genius should look like, much as an idealised Beethoven became a commercialised image of the inspired artist. How many people know what other scientists of genius – Planck, Bohr, Rutherford – looked like? Or, for that matter, Newton or Galileo, or even Darwin? Einstein's features, with their simple, kindly, bemused, melancholy expression, moved men's hearts everywhere. He was very famous, virtually a folk hero, and his appearance was as familiar and as widely loved as Charlie Chaplin's, long before he was portrayed on American stamps or Israeli banknotes.

Let me return briefly, in conclusion, to the State of Israel. The Zionist movement, like the State of Israel, has often been attacked, today more than ever, both by countries outside its borders and from within; sometimes with, more often without, reason or justice. That Einstein, who tolerated no deviation from human decency, above all on the part of his own people – that he believed in this movement and this State and stood by it through thick and thin, to the end of his life, however critical he was at times of particular men or policies – this fact is perhaps among the highest moral testimonials on which any State or any movement in this century can pride itself. Unswerving public support by an utterly good (and reasonably well-informed) man, against a virtually complete lack of sympathy for it on the part of the members of his social and intellectual milieu (whose general moral and political views he largely shared), may not by itself be enough to justify a doctrine or a policy, but neither can it be dismissed; it counts for something; in this case for a great deal.

YITZHAK SADEH

YITZHAK SADEH is today chiefly known as one of the heroes of the Israeli War of Independence. This is doubtless his chief claim to immortality, but his earlier life was so unusual and filled with such peculiar contrasts that its claim on our interest is scarcely smaller.

His father, Jacob Landoberg, was a rich merchant, a man of considerable charm, vitality and sense of pleasure, and a deeply sensual nature, which made the confines of an orthodox Jewish marriage intolerable to him, with the result that he left his wife Rebecca, the handsome, opulent-looking daughter of one of the most celebrated and saintly rabbis of his time, idolised by his community in the city of Lublin in Russian Poland, and led a feckless, unhappy but not uninteresting life, in the course of which he scattered his originally considerable fortune, and, it is said, died in poverty and illness.

His son was somewhat spoilt in childhood, grew up as a rich, good-looking, physically well-developed, precocious boy, adored by his mother, and determined, as soon as he reached maturity, to break away from the suffocating atmosphere of philistine respectability and conventional religion in which prosperous middle-class Jewish families then lived, and their deeply provincial outlook: against these restrictions he spoke with vehemence for the rest of his life.

Isaac was a wayward, obstinate, strikingly handsome young man. He obtained a normal Russian school education, but refused to go to university, which appeared to him to be a waste of his talents.[1] In sharp reaction against what was in effect the vast ghetto in which the Jews of Russia were then confined, he

[1] He did have a thirst for knowledge – he liked reading and study – and indeed became a student during his army days in the civil war: in 1918–20, at the University of Simferopol in the Crimea, he studied philosophy and linguistics, of all subjects.

developed a fanatical passion for physical self-improvement. He became a boxer, a wrestler and, what was very rare indeed in Russia at the turn of the century, a passionate footballer, who played the game as often as he could, taught it to others, and became a notable sporting figure in his (and my) native city of Riga.

Riga at this time was a city largely dominated by German culture, which derived both from the Baltic barons, who owned vast estates and formed a solid and fanatical caste of servants of the Russian monarchy, and the solid German middle class, which in Riga created an outpost of German nineteenth-century culture, a German opera, a German theatre, and a nationalist outlook directed against all efforts at assimilation by its Russian overlords. At the bottom of the social hierarchy were the original natives of the country – the Letts, a severe, industrious, oppressed population of Lutheran peasants, who at this time began to generate the beginnings of an intelligentsia, and were making strides particularly in the graphic and plastic arts. In the interstices of this social structure was to be found the small official Russian establishment which governed the Baltic provinces, and finally the Jews, who were divided into the upper stratum of those whose language and habit were German (together with some surviving descendants of the community of pre-Petrine Swedish times) and the lower stratum of the mainly Yiddish-speaking Russian Jews, whose children spoke Russian and were moving in the main directions which divided Russian Jewry at that period: liberal bourgeois, socialist and Zionist.

Isaac Landoberg, we are told by his nearest relations, looked upon all these movements and strata of population with equal contempt. He was filled with the romantic ideal of personal self-realisation: this took, in the first place, the form of physical self-perfection; that once achieved, he turned towards moral and intellectual self-education. He cut himself off from his parents, who were by this time divorced – he despised his mother's second husband, Isaac Ginzburg, and hardly ever spoke of him – and with such money as his father had left him, determined to make his own life and career. An expert in nothing save boxing, wrestling and football, he was too lazy and too bohemian by nature to wish to acquire any kind of professional skill. Consequently he decided to become an art dealer – this would shock his milieu, and afford him an opportunity, as he supposed, of a free and imaginative life, meeting painters and sculptors and other free spirits and living an independent, gay and, above all, Gentile life, free from the cramped, over-intellectual, orthodox life of the Jewish merchants and scholars of whom his family was composed.

His mode of life was extraordinary: his shop remained closed in the mornings, which he devoted to boxing, organising football matches, wrestling and posing as a model for painters and sculptors. He was proud of his appearance, and the fact that his well-built body at times attracted the interest of some of the young naturalistic painters and sculptors who were then to be found in Riga flattered him greatly, and he took pleasure in the thought of how profoundly outraged his mother and relations would be by accounts of this pagan activity. He had read Nietzsche and determined to cultivate the Dionysiac side of his nature. Sexually he seems to have been perfectly continent at this period, although later he was to become a lover celebrated for his infidelities.

In 1912 he married my father's sister Evgenia (Zhenya) Berlin, his first cousin: their mothers were sisters.[1] This lady, the very opposite of Landoberg in every respect, a socialist who proposed to devote her life to the improvement of the lives of workers and peasants, a graduate of two faculties, humourless, earnest, respectable, idealistic, without any feminine attainments, exceedingly plain, with a cast in one of her eyes which gave her a peculiarly governessy appearance, fell passionately in love with the splendid savage whom Landoberg delighted to impersonate. He did not reciprocate her passion, but was impressed by her intellectual attainments, by the fact that she had braved the anger of her parents and respectable friends by taking part in the revolutionary activities of 1905, that she was sought after by the police for two years; consequently he permitted her to marry him. The wedding, which relieved their common relatives by its respectability, was celebrated in the best bourgeois style at an immense party at which the bridegroom became somewhat intoxicated, to the mingled horror and pride of the bride. The life of boxing, wrestling, art dealing continued until 1914.

As soon as war broke out Landoberg immediately volunteered for service in the army. As he was an only son and a married man it

---

[1] I was taken to his wedding, but I am told that there were so many guests and the music was so loud that I burst into tears and said 'I hate this screaming music' and had to be removed. I never saw him on that occasion.

was not legally necessary for him to become a soldier: his rich relations promptly bought him out of the army. He allowed himself to be brought back to his doting wife and child, a daughter called Asia; after a few weeks of tranquillity he deserted his wife and secretly joined the army again. He was 'bought back' again. He did this for a third time and disappeared – his relatives were discouraged by the two earlier flights and ceased to trouble about him.

In 1917 he appeared in Petrograd as a member of the Socialist Revolutionary Party, dedicated to the peasants' cause, armed with an enormous Mauser revolver and an arm-band proclaiming him to be a member of the People's Militia. He was at this stage filled with revolutionary zeal and childish pride in his new uniform, his pistol and the intoxication of the Revolution. He appeared in the Petrograd flat of his very respectable brother-in-law and cousin, Mendel Berlin, and his wife Marie – my parents – and boasted about his revolutionary exploits with such innocence and charm, such infantile delight in the violent upheaval then in progress, that he enchanted us all. His hostess, also a cousin, took his revolver away and plunged it in a bath of cold water as if it was a bomb which might go off. He allowed himself to be disarmed and sat in our flat till three or four in the morning regaling his goggling relations with his own and his comrades' exploits as heroes of the Revolution, under the ultimate command of Pinchas (in those days Petr) Rutenberg, whose view of Lenin and Trotsky he shared: he told us, I remember, that they were a couple of dangerous fanatics and should be suppressed. His wife took a more serious view of events, but allowed herself to be carried away by his exuberance and his utter unconcern and irresponsibility.

He was a man of considerable temperament, a gifted actor, and a great wooer of others, particularly women. He was followed by adoring ladies and addressed revolutionary meetings, although those who heard him could never remember anything in particular that he said. He was a natural orator, fiery, convinced, rhetorical and inspiring: with this went a quality of gay and cynical frivolity, not unlike that of the greatest of all Russian revolutionary tribunes, Mikhail Bakunin, in the nineteenth century. Like Bakunin, Landoberg was fundamentally a pleasure-loving anarchist, irked by all ties and frontiers, heartless, as innocent children are heartless, in pursuit of some goal on which he has fixed his fancy, but, like a child, naïve, transparent and affectionate.

He stormed round Petrograd in 1917, and probably effected nothing. After the Bolshevik Revolution he disappeared again. For some months his wife had no idea where he was and had to be supported by her relations. He left her with no means of subsistence and appeared to take not the slightest interest in either her or his child. He was subsequently discovered to have joined the Red Guard – simply from love of action, as he later told me – and to have wandered about with his detachment in Central and then Southern Russia. Then he reappeared in Petrograd, went to see his wife in Moscow, where by this time she was living with her brothers; she was overjoyed to see him and asked no questions – he showed concern about his child's illness, but almost at once disappeared again, promising to come back very soon. He duly deserted the Red Guard, whom he found too violent and too brutal, and somewhere joined a detachment of Whites at the beginning of 1919. His mother, meanwhile, had died, but this appeared a matter of no concern to him. One of his half-brothers had been shot for commercial speculation, and another had become a member of the Cheka or secret police. Neither of these facts caused him the slightest anxiety; he communicated with neither brother and wandered about with merry unconcern, proclaiming the evils of Communism. With a White regiment he reached the outskirts of Theodosia, on the shores of the Black Sea.

At this point his wife, who had with the greatest difficulty traced his movements, joined him with their child. He expressed delight at seeing them and managed to get the White commander to quarter them in one of the unused flats deserted by the inhabitants in the port town. The little girl was visibly worse, and was in fact dying of the croup. Her mother, who had no eyes but for her husband, nursed her as well as a distracted, unpractical bluestocking could, torn between thoughts of revolution, the peasantry, the workers, the rival claims of Marxism and anti-Marxism, and her husband's peculiar tergiversations between Reds and Whites. They discussed the possibility of joining the Green armies – wild marauding bands of peasants who belonged to an anarchist movement directed equally against Whites and Reds – and in the course of these discussions Asia, his daughter, died. Her mother was broken by this, but Landoberg appeared to feel little.

He developed an immense passion for music at this time, and when not marching or counter-marching listened to an amateur quartet, in which Nicolas Nabokov, later an eminent composer and writer on music, took part. Nabokov remembered him well as one of the small informal audience which gathered to listen to this quartet in the midst of the civil war on the shores of the Black Sea, and recollects that he was a man of irresistible spontaneity, warmth and charm.

Landoberg took part in several indecisive battles between Reds and Whites. Then one night, as he sat near a camp fire with a small group of White officers, he listened to one of the staple themes of White soldiers – their hatred of the Jews as members of an international conspiracy, sworn to destroy Russia, murderers of the Tsar, to be exterminated at all costs, both in the immediate future and when victory was finally achieved over the forces of darkness.

This frightened him: there and then he determined to get away from these dangerous allies, and collecting his wife he bluffed his way into a ship carrying refugees from ports in the Black Sea to Turkey. It is not clear how he managed to make his way into a ship of this type without the necessary documents: but he was a man of infinite resource, and his artless charm, then and later, evidently melted the hearts of those in charge.

He determined to go to Palestine. He had never been a Zionist: indeed he had regarded that as a typical piece of bourgeois Jewish folly, an attempt on the part of victims to create a respectable liberal State or community, of the stuffiest, most Victorian type, and to perpetuate all the most philistine and socially mean and iniquitous characteristics of their oppressors. Nevertheless he suddenly decided that a new world was opening in Palestine for the Jews, rediscovered his Jewish origins and emotions, and joined the Zionist pioneer group Hechalutz in the Crimea. Inevitably, he became its leader after the celebrated soldier, Joseph Trumpeldor, who had organised Jewish self-defence against pogrom-makers in Russia, had left the Crimea for Palestine.

He landed in Jaffa at the head of a group of thirty-one pioneers, at the beginning of 1920, with his wife and a small bundle of luggage, and two devalued Russian roubles in his pocket. They travelled with a collective visa granted by the British authorities. He later said that they represented themselves as returning refugees from Palestine; when asked how long they had been refugees, they replied 'two thousand years'. This was very much in the spirit of Russian Zionists of those days.

In common with other immigrants they were taken to a Zionist reception camp. They were kindly treated and he was asked what profession he wished to choose. He indicated that physical labour was what he preferred. This wish was granted. He became a navvy engaged in breaking stones in a quarry. He is next heard of as taking part in the anti-British riots in Jaffa, together with the followers of the revisionist Jewish leader, Jabotinsky, whose by this time violent romantic nationalism was the very opposite of what Landoberg and his wife believed. However, where there was violence, thither he was irresistibly attracted. The British stood for all that was moderate, limited, dull, official, pompous and dead. Moreover they were for the most part pro-Arab and attracted by Middle Eastern semi-feudalism. The revisionists belonged to the extreme right wing of Zionism and stood for passion, militancy, resistance, self-assertion, pride and a nationalist mystique. He never actually joined the revisionists, and remained identified with the Haganah.

Landoberg was a man not permanently wedded to any ideal or any person. He changed his views, his mode of life, everything about himself, easily, with pleasure, delighting in everything new, exulting in his own capacity for beating any drum, wearing any suit of clothes, provided they were sufficiently gaudy – life was a carnival in which one changed one's disguise to raise one's own spirits and those of other people. He was duly arrested for taking part in the riots, and found himself in prison. Lady Samuel, the wife of the then High Commissioner of Palestine, Sir Herbert Samuel, was a prison visitor, and asked him what he had done. 'I am Lady Samuel,' she began. 'I am Isaac Landoberg,' he answered at once, and glared at her with amiable insolence. 'What is your crime?' she asked. 'I fight for liberty everywhere,' he answered. 'All officials are my enemies. I fought with the Reds against the Whites, I fought with the Whites against the Reds, I fight with the Jews against the British. I am prepared to conceive that one day I may fight with the Arabs against the Jews, or anyone else.' This was held to be inexcusable insolence. His sentence was doubled.

After his release from prison he broke stones to such effect that he was soon appointed manager of one of the quarries of the Jewish co-operative enterprise, Solel Boneh. His family had heard nothing about him. In 1924 he wrote a letter to my father, who by this time was living in London, saying that he was a happy, patriotic Zionist, with a bright future before him, urging all the members of his family to settle in this new and splendid land, where equality, fraternity and, one day, liberty would reign – a small country in which it was possible to do things impossible in larger, more unwieldy territories.

In the same year he appeared as the representative of the Palestine Jews in the Palestine pavilion at the Wembley Empire Exhibition in London. He was in the happiest possible mood. He visited my father and presented me, then a schoolboy, with a text of Ovid, whom he loved (Latin was among his few, curious scholastic attainments), and a book by Warde Fowler entitled *Social Life in Rome in the Time of Cicero*, which he thought a good book for a schoolboy to read. He was full of vitality, of wonderful talk; he had tremendous gusto and great charm; he was gay, insouciant and the most delightful company in the world. He taught us the latest Hebrew songs. He taught me a new tune for the song 'B'tzet Yisrael Mimitzraim' ('De exitu Israel de Aegypto', which has also been set by Mendelssohn in a very different fashion) and other new Hebrew songs, pre- and post-war. He talked with immense life and imagination, in the richest possible Russian, about a vast variety of subjects. I was completely charmed, and have remained so for the rest of my life. He invited the family to see the Palestine pavilion in Wembley. There we found him seated cross-legged on the stone relief map of Palestine – watched with fascination and horror by the representatives of the Palestine Arabs, who uncomfortably shared the pavilion with the Jews – eating sandwiches composed of Palestine produce, and drinking bottle after bottle of wine.

Unlike most of the Jews of his generation, he was a boon companion with an infectious wit and a most amiable disposition. His wife, gloomy, aware that her husband's eye was straying elsewhere, not convinced of the value of Zionism, inasmuch as it was a nationalistic patriotic conception, not allied to the social-democratic ideals for which she had suffered in 1905 and which she still carried in her heart, tried to enter his moods of unrestrained gaiety, but did not succeed. This irritated him. He complained to my father about the arid, unimaginative, doctrinaire character of his sister, and said that if this situation continued, he would be forced, in the interests of his duty to his new country, which he must serve with all his heart, to leave her; unable to fly herself, she clipped his wings. My father reasoned with him, fearing what would happen to his sister if she were abandoned; she continued to love her husband with a most violent and ever-increasing passion, despite his lack of interest in her and complaints about her lack of *joie de vivre*.

After Wembley he returned to Palestine and continued in his quarries. In due course he abandoned his wife and took up with a number of other ladies who were only too delighted with the companionship of this attractive, unbridled, romantic figure of more than ordinary human size. His feeling about the Jews was, in a sense, wholly external; although he was one by birth and education, his behaviour was that of a happy fellow-traveller, whom pure accident had brought to an unfamiliar shore, who found the people and their ideals sympathetic, so that although he did not feel bound to them by any profound emotion, despite the ties of blood, he was ready to collaborate with them and forward their ends with the greatest good will.

All this may have been transformed by the years during which no certain information about his psychological state can be obtained. His qualities of leadership, his reckless, lion-hearted courage, the total absence of any physical or any other fear (despite his flight from the Whites, which indicated that he had some self-protective instinct), his rich imagination and love of his fellows, his very childlikeness endeared him to many. Dr Weizmann, when he visited Palestine in 1936, had him assigned to himself as bodyguard, and found him an agreeable, lively and intelligent Russian, a welcome relief from the tense and worried faces he saw round him, and from the political problems and political intrigue to which he was normally condemned. They remained friends until the end. Not so David Ben-Gurion, who looked on him, mistakenly it seems to me, as a dangerous power-seeker.

His wife, despairing of recapturing his affection, returned to Moscow to her brothers, where she duly wore herself out in good works and faded towards an untimely death. His relations found it difficult to forgive Landoberg for abandoning her; judging him in terms of their own morality, they showed, as might be expected, blindness to his heroic attributes. He was a guerrilla by nature, and the rules of settled, non-nomadic populations did not apply to him. In the 1930s, when self-defence units among the Jews gradually coalesced into the Haganah – the underground Jewish army – he was a natural recruit and became its principal trainer in shock tactics. He was a chief architect of the Palmach – the *force de frappe*, the successor in 1941 of earlier units – which he saw as the heart of resistance, battling against alien rule. I imagine that the Arabs entered his mind no more than they did that of the Yishuv.

He became one of the principal leaders of the Haganah. At the outbreak of war he fought with the British Army (with which the Haganah was allied), was called 'Big Isaac', and fought the Vichy forces in Lebanon and Syria. After the War was over, he grew a beard, went into hiding, and took part in the Jewish resistance to the Mandatory British authorities. A price was put on his head, but he was never caught.

I had tried to find him when I went to Palestine for the first time, in 1934, but no one I knew could tell me where he was. He was presumably at this time engaged in creating the beginning of what later became the Palmach, but of that I was to know nothing at that time. I next met him in 1947, while I was staying with Dr Weizmann at Rehovot. Somehow the conversation turned on my relatives in Russia. I mentioned Yitzhak Sadeh (he had begun to use this name in 1938), and Weizmann said he knew him, and was greatly taken by him: he referred to him, with a smile, as 'Reb Yitzhok'. The fact that Reb Yitzhok did not greatly care for David Ben-Gurion did not distress Weizmann too deeply. He said he thought he could find out where my uncle and cousin was. It was not too easy, because the Palestine police were looking for him. But I succeeded in meeting him clandestinely in the back of a café in Tel Aviv, and had a very good two hours with him. He was in the best of spirits. He told me about his exploits with the British Army. He assured me that no one would inform on him to the authorities. He proved right.

As for his relations to the British, he said that he had no feeling against them, he liked some of them and greatly admired their qualities; but since their policies were what they were, there was no alternative – they had to be fought tooth and nail. Submission to the Arabs – which the Colonial Office plainly wanted – was unthinkable. He said that the Palestine administration in the 1920s and 1930s really was too much for him: the officials, even when well-meaning and not overtly anti-Jewish or anti-Zionist, were too mean-minded, too pedantic, too narrow. Above all they were philistine; they lacked what he called genuine culture; with few exceptions, it was impossible to talk to them about books, ideas, music, history, particularly the long Jewish tradition with consciousness of which the Jews, of course, were filled. There was no contact: it was never and could never be a marriage, the sooner there was complete divorce the better – perhaps relations would improve after that.

When I first knew Sadeh, he was slender, elegant and had a certain pride in his appearance: now he was plump, had grown a beard, his clothes were ragged, and he plainly did not care what he looked like – he was totally uninterested in the amenities of life, what he adored was action – he enjoyed his hunted existence quite enormously. He was certainly a happy man when I met him in this café, with no sign of the slightest nervousness, fear or real concern about the future – every day brought its own problems, every day brought its own pleasures – he simply went from adventure to adventure with the greatest appetite for life.

In 1948, after the British left Palestine, he became a commander of a mobile unit, and captured Egyptian fortresses, and took prisoners. His method, as we learn from those under his command (for example, a grandson of the very Lady Samuel to whom he was so insolent), simply consisted of rushing Egyptian outposts with a grenade in each hand, shouting loudly and telling his men to do likewise. The Egyptians duly fled, leaving their shoes behind. Little blood was shed. He gathered up whatever weapons caught his eye.

The trophies he collected – guns, daggers, yataghans – afterwards proudly adorned his house in Jaffa. I met him there after the War of Independence. By this time he was something of a national hero. He showed me a great many photographs of himself in action against Egyptian troops and strongholds. When I told him that he was a kind of Jewish Garibaldi – the famous Italian national hero who fought the Austrians in the nineteenth century – he was delighted.

He turned out to know all about Garibaldi: his life and campaigns had always fascinated him, he said, and in the postcard he wrote me shortly afterwards he signed himself 'Garibaldi'. He kept a goat tethered to a tree in the garden, not because he needed its milk, but simply because this was forbidden by the new Israeli laws, and he believed in defying idiotic regulations. He seemed to me totally unchanged. His by this time considerable fame had not gone to his head; he remained simple, informal, with an undiminished gaiety and verve, above all vitality, a love of life in all its phases, a love of action, a love of change, events, a love of whatever might happen, a hatred of peace and quiet and boredom and a settled life. He had a large bottle of vodka on the table – 'I keep that for the Soviet Ambassador,' he said.

His part in Israeli politics had exactly the same quality of insouciance and irresponsibility as everything else that he did. Adoring children gazed at him rapturously in the streets. Fellow-travellers and Communists gathered in his Sabbath salon. He drank with members of the Soviet Embassy and wondered if he ought to pay a visit to Moscow to see what had happened in his absence. He explained his pro-Soviet attitude by his conviction that the Americans and British would never bomb Israel, but the Russians might: hence the need to keep in with them – he disclaimed ideological sympathies. He said to me in Jaffa: 'The Russians would like a large Arab federation to include our little State – but that is impossible – we shall never be Communists. The Israeli Communist Party is a ridiculous party, and the Arabs will not be Communists either, whatever they may say. Good relations with the Soviet Union are possible, Communism never. Our problem is not political, our problem is relations with the Arabs, which is a moral and personal problem. At one time I believed in the possibility of a bi-national State of Jews and Arabs, but I see it is impossible – they hate us too much, and I quite understand that. We must live separate lives. Of course, we shall try to treat our Arab minority as well as possible, but I am afraid that will not reconcile them. Still, one never knows – the future is the future, all kinds of things can happen, one must not give up hope, above all one must not be afraid, one must simply regard everything as material out of which to build one's life, and make it as rich and full as possible.'

He took particular pride in his friendship with his disciples, as he thought of them, Moshe Dayan and Yigal Allon, both of whom he adored – there is a famous photograph, at one time on public sale, showing him with his arms round the shoulders of the two warriors. He was determined not to be taken altogether seriously. He adored telling of his exploits, like a retired revolutionary Mexican general – but even there he displayed qualities of vanity so simple, and so attractive, that no one was moved to jealousy.

He was by this time happily married to a well-known partisan lady, having abandoned many others in his victorious course. He enquired tenderly, when I visited him, after his family, and regaled me with stories of his magnificent past. In a country filled with tensions and anxiety and earnest purpose, as all pioneering communities must be, this huge child introduced an element of total freedom, unquenchable gaiety, ease, charm and a natural elegance, half bohemian, half aristocratic, too much of which would ruin any possibility of order, but an element of which is something which no society should lack if it is to be free or worthy of survival.

He was one of life's irregulars, wonderful in wars and revolutions and bored with peaceful, orderly, unexciting existence. Trotsky once said that those who wanted a quiet life did badly to be born into the twentieth century. Yitzhak Sadeh certainly did not want a quiet life. He enjoyed himself enormously, and communicated his enjoyment to others, and inspired them and excited them and delighted them. I liked him very much.

His exploits – his training of, and friendship with, other Israeli soldiers, his emergence as a legendary hero – are not part of this story: they belong to the history of the War of Independence and the foundation of the State of Israel. All I have attempted to do is to present some recollections of my close relation, and some facts about his early life. He was a generous and adventurous man who played his part in the history of his nation, whose weaknesses attracted me at least as much as his virtues, and to whose memory I dedicate this modest and deeply affectionate memorial. *Zikhrono livrakha.*[1]

---

[1] 'May his memory be blessed.'

L. B. NAMIER

THIS ACCOUNT of Lewis Namier is based upon no research and is composed purely from memory. Namier was one of the most distinguished historians of our time, a man of fame and influence. His achievement as a historian, still more his decisive influence on English historical research and writing, as well as his extraordinary life, deserve full and detailed study. For this task I am not qualified. My sole purpose is to describe to the best of my ability the character and some of the opinions of one of the most remarkable men that I have ever known. I was not at any time one of his intimate friends; but his immediate intellectual and moral impact was such that even those who, like myself, met him infrequently but regularly, and spoke with him, or rather were addressed by him, on matters in which he was interested, are unlikely to forget it. It is this impression that I should like to record for the benefit of those who did not know him and may be curious about the kind of man that he was.

I first came across his name as an undergraduate at Oxford, in, I think, 1929. Someone showed me an article by him in the *New Statesman* on the condition of the Jews of modern Europe.[1] It was the best and most arresting piece on that subject that I or, I suspect, anyone had ever read. Much was being written on that topic then; for the most part it was competent journalism: a combination of intellectual power, historical sweep and capacity for writing clear and vigorous prose was seldom, if ever, to be found among the writers on this subject, whether Jews or Christians. This essay was of an altogether higher quality. In reading it one had the sensation – for which there is no substitute –

---

[1] 'Zionism', *New Statesman*, 5 November 1927, 103–4; reprinted in *Skyscrapers and Other Essays* (London, 1931). Cf. 'The Jews', *The Nineteenth Century and After* 130 (July–December 1941), 270–7; reprinted in *Conflicts* (London, 1942).

of suddenly sailing in first-class waters. Namier compared the Jews of Eastern Europe to a glacier, part of which remained frozen; part of which had evaporated under the influence of the rays of the Enlightenment; while the rest had melted and formed violent nationalist or socialist-nationalist torrents. He developed this thesis with incomparable imagination and a power of incisive historical generalisation that was at once factually concrete and had great historical sweep, with no attempt to play down disturbing implications. I wondered who the author might be. I was told that he was a historian whose work had caused some stir in the world of learning, at most a respected specialist, but not a scholar of the same order as Tout or Barker or Fisher, not to speak of Halévy or Trevelyan. That was that: the author was a minor historical expert with a fairly high reputation in his own profession. I heard no more until 1932 when I was elected to All Souls.

There I found that a higher opinion of Namier was entertained by my new historical colleagues – G. N. Clark, Richard Pares, A. L. Rowse and others. From them I learnt something of Namier's real achievement. My election to All Souls had evidently intrigued Namier, who had failed to secure election himself some years before the First World War.[1] I received a note in which, in huge majuscule letters, the author informed me that he proposed to call on me one afternoon in the following week and hoped that I would be free to receive him. The letter was signed 'L. B. Namier'. When he arrived, he said in his slow, deliberate, ponderous voice that he wished to see me because his friend Richard Pares had told him that I was interested in Karl Marx, of whom he held a low opinion. He wished to know why I was engaged in writing a book about him. He had some respect for the Fellows of All Souls. He believed them, for the most part, with certain exceptions which he did not wish to mention, to be intellectually qualified to do genuine research work. Marx appeared to him unworthy of such attention: he was a poor historian and a poor economist, blinded by hatred. Why was I not writing about Freud? Freud's importance for historical and biographical science had still been insufficiently appreciated. Freud's books were, unlike those of Marx, works of genius, and far better written. Besides which, Freud was still alive

---

[1] 'I have always had a certain grudge against Grant Robertson, who, as examiner, had preferred Cruttwell to myself,' Namier said to me in the late 1930s, 'but when I think of what he has done for the German-Jewish refugees – I forgive him.'

and could be interviewed. Marx, fortunately, was not; his followers, especially in Russia, which was now intellectually dead, had
used up far too much printer's ink, and were comparable in this
respect with German philosophers, who suffered from an equal
lack of sense of proportion and of literary talent and taste.

He stood in the middle of my room and spoke his words in a
slow, somewhat hypnotic voice, with great emphasis and in a
continuous unbroken drone, with few intervals between the
sentences, a strongly Central European accent and a frozen
expression. He kept his eyes immovably upon me, frowning now
and then, and producing (I realised later that this was how he drew
his breath without seeming to do so) a curious mooing sound
which blocked the gaps between his sentences and made interrup-
tion literally impossible. Not that I dreamt of interrupting: the
entire phenomenon was too strange, the intensity of the utterance
too great; I felt that I was being eyed by a stern and heavy
headmaster who knew precisely what I was at, disapproved, and
was determined to set me right and to get his instructions obeyed.
Finally he stopped and glared in silence. I begged him to sit down.
He did so, and went on glaring. I made a halting defence of what I
was, in fact, doing. He scarcely listened. 'Marx! Marx!' he kept
intoning, 'a typical Jewish half-charlatan, who got hold of quite a
good idea and then ran it to death just to spite the Gentiles.' I asked
whether Marx's origin seemed to him relevant to his views. This
turned out to be the stimulus that he needed to plunge into his own
autobiography. The next two hours were full of interest. He spoke
almost continuously.

He told me that he was born the son of a man called Bernstein
(or Bernsztajn), the Jewish administrator of a large Polish estate,
and that his father had been converted to the Roman Catholic faith,
which, he said, was common enough in his family's class and
circumstances. He had himself been given the education of a young
Polish squire, for his parents believed that assimilation to a Polish
Catholic pattern was a feasible and desirable process if one wanted
it strongly enough. They supposed that the only barrier between
Jews and Gentiles was the difference of religion, that if this were
abolished, the social and cultural obstacles which it had historically
brought about would fall with it. Conversion could bring about
the total integration of the Jews into the prevailing social texture,
and would put an end to the insulation, ambiguous status and,
indeed, persecution of Jews sensible enough to follow this rational

course. His parents' theory was essentially the same as that which had moved Börne and Heine, as well as Heinrich Marx and Isaac d'Israeli – two fathers of famous sons – to embrace Christianity. The hypothesis was, in his view, baseless and degrading; and he, Ludwik Bernsztajn as he then was, came to understand this when he was still quite young, sixteen or seventeen. He felt himself in a false position, and realised that the converted Jews in his circle lived in an unreal world – had abandoned the traditional misery of their ancestors only to find themselves in a no man's land between the two camps, welcome to neither. His father's conventional, bourgeois outlook repelled him in any case. He decided to return to the Jewish community – at any rate in his own mind – partly because he believed that to attempt to cut oneself off from one's own past was self-destructive and shameful, and in any case impracticable; partly because he wished to show his contempt for his family and their unworthy ideals. His father thought him ungrateful, foolish and perverse, and refused to support him. He went to England, which to him as to many Central and Eastern European Jews appeared the most civilised and humane society in the world, as well as one respectful of traditions, including his own. As part of his general revolt against his father's way of life, which was in his mind associated with the mixture of corruption, hypocrisy and oppression by which the Austro-Hungarian Empire was governed, he was attracted to socialism. The false and humiliating lives lived by his parents and their society seemed to him largely due to systematic delusion about themselves and their position, and, in particular, the attitude towards them of the Poles, whether Austrianised or nationalist, among whom they lived. Marxism was the leading philosophy which attempted to explain away and to refute such liberal fantasies as so many disguises intended to conceal an irrational and unjust social order, and one based on ignorance or misinterpretation of the real (largely economic) facts.

When he arrived in London, he became a student at the London School of Economics, then dominated by the Webbs, Graham Wallas and their followers, who, if not Marxists, were socialists and militantly anti-Liberal. However, in due course he realised that he had simply left one set of delusive ideologies for another. The principles and generalisations of socialism were as silly and unrealistic as those it sought to supplant. The only reality was to be found in the individual and his basic desires – conscious and unconscious, particularly the latter, which were repressed and rationalised by a series of intellectual subterfuges, which Marxism had detected, but for which it had substituted illusions of its own. Individual psychology, not sociology, was the key. Human action – and social reality in general – could be explained only by fearless and dispassionate scientific examination of the roots of individual human behaviour – basic drives, permanent human cravings for food, shelter, power, sexual satisfaction, social recognition and so on. Nor was human history, and in particular political history, to be explained in any other way.

He was not disappointed in England. It took, as he had supposed, a humane, civilised and, above all, sober, undramatised, empirical view of life. Englishmen seemed to him to take account, more than most men, of the real ends of human life – pleasure, justice, power, freedom, glory, the sense of human solidarity which underlay both patriotism and adherence to tradition; above all they loathed abstract principles and general theories. Human motives could be illuminated by attention to unexamined, occult causes which Freud and other psychologists had begun to investigate. Nevertheless, even such overt considerations as were present to the mind of an average Englishman, far more than to that of, say, an average German or an average Pole, accounted for a great deal of human behaviour – a far larger sector of it than had been explained by the 'ideologists'. At some point in this discourse, delivered with a kind of controlled ferocity, Namier spoke – as he often later spoke – of the absurdity of those who attempted to account for human behaviour by invoking the influence of ideas. Ideas were mere interpretations by the mind of deep-seated drives and motives which it was too cowardly, or too conventionally brought up, to face. Historians of ideas were the least useful kind of historians. 'Do you remember', he asked me, 'what Lueger, the anti-Semitic Mayor of Vienna, once said to the municipality of Vienna when a subsidy for the natural sciences was asked for? "Science? That is what one Jew cribs from another."[1] That is what *I* say about *Ideengeschichte*, history of ideas.' Perhaps he saw a discontented expression on my face, for I well remember that he repeated all this

---

[1] He quoted this with much relish in German: 'was ein Jud' vom andern Juden abschreibt'. But for once he appears to have been inaccurate. The real author, I have since learnt, appears to have been Hermann Bielohlawek, a member of Lueger's Christian-Social party in the Austrian parliament, of Czech origin, who apparently once said 'Literatur ist was ein Jud' vom andern abschreibt.'

again in still more formidable accents, and emphasised it over and over again in a slow, heavy, drawling voice, as he often did on later occasions.

The London School of Economics was not the England that he had admired from afar, and he felt this still more strongly when he met it face to face. It was a pathetic offshoot of the worst continental nonsense. He migrated to Balliol College, Oxford, and was there taught history by A. L. Smith and others. Oxford (he continued) had less truck with ideologies: here he could freely profess what he thought to be the deepest factor in modern history – the historically grounded sense of nationality. The notion that rational men, Jews or Gentiles, could live full lives either by dedication to a religion (organised falsification – rabbis were worse than priests, and lived on and by deception), or by abandoning their religion, or by emigrating to lands beyond the sea, or by any means other than those by which all other human communities had done so, that is, by organising themselves into political units and acquiring a soil of their own – all such notions were sheer nonsense. Self-understanding was everything, both in history and in individual life; and this could be achieved only by scrupulous empiricism, the continuous adaptation of one's hypotheses to the twisted and obscure windings of individual and social lives. Hence his respect for Freud and other psychological theorists – including graphologists, in whom his faith was very strong – and his lack of respect for Marx, who had, indeed, correctly diagnosed the disease, but then had offered a charlatan's nostrum. Still, that was better than Burke or Bentham, who peddled mere ideas rooted in nothing, and were rightly distrusted by sensible, practical politicians.

He returned to his autobiography: he had not been too well treated by England. He deserved a permanent post in Oxford, which he had not obtained. Scant recognition had been shown him by many established scholars, because they knew that he could 'show them up'. Nevertheless, it was the only country to live in. It was less fanatical and closer to empirical reality than other nations, and there was in its political tradition a certain realism – some called it cynicism – which was worth all the vapid idealism and idiotic liberalism of the Continent. There were Englishmen who were taken in by continental '-isms' – here followed names of some eminent contemporaries – but they were relatively few and not too influential: the majority wisely went by habit and well-tried

Winston Churchill on his way to 10 Downing Street, 1940

Franklin D. Roosevelt

Chaim Weizmann in 1945

Albert Einstein in Christ Church Meadow, Oxford, 1932

Yitzhak Sadeh

L. B. Namier

Felix Frankfurter in his office in the Supreme Court
George James/NYT Pictures

Richard Pares

Hubert Henderson

J. L. Austin in 1952

John Plamenatz

Maurice Bowra in Oxford, 1950

Lord David Cecil and the author in the cloisters, New College, Oxford, 1950

Virginia Woolf

Edmund Wilson, *c.*1953

Auberon Herbert in the garden at
Pixton, his home in Somerset

Aldous Huxley

Anna Akhmatova and Boris Pasternak at a public reading in Moscow, 1946

practical rules and kept clear of theory, thereby avoiding much nonsense in their ideas and brutality in their action. He could not talk to English Jews about Zionism. The Jews of England were victims of pathetic illusions – ostriches with their heads in some very inferior sands – foolish, ridiculous creatures not worth saving. But Englishmen understood its appeal and its justification. The only Jew he had ever met who in this respect could be compared to an Englishman was Weizmann – indeed, he was the only Zionist for whom he had complete respect. Upon this note he ended, and having, as must be supposed, diagnosed me sufficiently – although he took not the slightest notice of my occasional queries – he marched out of my room to tea with Kenneth Bell of Balliol, 'whose family is very fond of me', he added.

I felt flattered by his visit, as well as deeply impressed and slightly bewildered by his lecture. In the five or so years before the War I met him more than once. He spoke bitterly about the policy of appeasement. He felt that their sense of reality and their empiricism had evidently deserted the ruling classes in England: not to understand that Hitler meant everything he said – that *Mein Kampf* was to be taken literally, that Hitler had a plan for a war of conquest – was self-deception worthy of Germans or Jews. The Cecils were 'all right', they understood reality, they stood for what was most characteristic of England. So was Winston Churchill. The men who opposed Zionism were the same as those who were against Churchill and the policy of national resistance – Geoffrey Dawson, the editor of *The Times*, Chamberlain, Halifax, Toynbee, the officials of the Foreign Office, Archbishop Lang, the bulk of the Conservative Party, most trade unionists. The Cecils, Churchill, true aristocracy, pride, respect for human dignity, traditional virtues, resistance, Zionism, personal grandeur, no-nonsense realism, these were fused into one amalgam in his mind. Pro-Germans and pro-Arabs were one gang.

He spoke a good deal about Zionism to me, no doubt because he thought (rightly) that I was sympathetic. Gradually I became convinced that this was the deepest strain in him: and that he was fundamentally driven into it by sheer pride. He found the position of the Jews to be humiliating: he disliked those who put up with this or pretended that it did not exist. He wanted a free and dignified existence. He was intelligent enough to realise that to shed his Judaism, to assume protective colouring and disappear into the Gentile world, was not feasible, and a pathetic form of self-deception. If he was not to sink to the level of the majority of his brethren (whom on the whole he despised), if he had to remain one of them, as was historically inevitable, then there was only one way out – they must be pulled up to his own level. If this could not be achieved by slow, gradual, peaceful, kindly means, then it must be achieved by rapid and, if need be, somewhat drastic ones. He had not believed this to be wholly possible until he had met Weizmann, whom he admired to the point of hero-worship: here at least was a Jew whom he did not find it embarrassing to associate with, indeed, even to follow. But the other Zionist leaders appeared nonentities to him and he did not trouble to conceal this. He called them 'the rabbis' and said that they were no better than priests and clergymen – to him, then, terms of abuse. His Zionist colleagues valued his gifts but could scarcely be expected to enjoy his open and highly articulate contempt. Despite Weizmann's favour, he was never made a permanent member of the World Zionist Executive – a fact that rankled with him for the rest of his life. Despite all his talk of realism and his historical method, he had the temperament of a political romantic. I am not sure that he did not indulge in day-dreams in which he saw himself as a kind of Zionist d'Annunzio riding on a white horse to capture some Trans-Jordanian Fiume. He saw the Jewish national movement as a Risorgimento; if he was not to be its Garibaldi, he would serve as the adviser and champion of its Cavour – the sagacious, realistic, dignified, Europeanised, the almost English Weizmann.

Privately I used to think that in character, if not in ideas, Namier was not wholly unlike his *bête noire*, Karl Marx. Namier too was an intellectually formidable, at times aggressive, politically minded intellectual – and his hatred of doctrine was held with a doctrinaire tenacity. Like Marx, he was vain, proud, contemptuous, intolerant, quick to give and take offence, master of his craft, confident of his own powers, not without a strain of pathos and self-pity. Like Marx, he hated all forms of weakness, sentimentality, idealistic liberalism; most of all he hated servility. Like Marx, he fascinated his interlocutors and oppressed them too. If you happened to be interested in the topic which he was discussing (Polish documents relating to the revolution of 1848, or English country houses), you were fortunate, for it was not likely that you would again hear the subject expounded with such learning, brilliance and originality. If, however, you were not interested, you could not escape. Hence those who met him were divided into some who looked on him as a man of genius and a dazzling talker and others who fled from him as an appalling bore. He was, in fact, both. He aroused admiration, enthusiasm and affection among his pupils and those who were sympathetic to his opinions; uneasy respect and embarrassed dislike among those who did not. If he came across latent anti-Semitism he stirred it into a flame; London clubmen (whom he often naïvely pursued) viewed him with distaste. Academics and civil servants, whom he bullied, loathed and denigrated him. Scholars looked on him as a man of prodigious powers and treated him with deep, if at times somewhat nervous, admiration.

I never experienced boredom in his company, not even when he was at his most ponderous. All the subjects that he discussed appeared to me, at any rate while he spoke about them, interesting and important; when in form he spoke marvellously. He spoke with sovereign, and often wholly unmitigated, contempt about other scholars, and indeed most other human beings. The only living persons wholly exempt from his disparagement were Winston Churchill, who could do no wrong; Weizmann, in whose presence Namier was simple, childlike, reverent, uncritical to the point of worship; and his great friend Blanche Dugdale, Balfour's niece. He was said to be transformed in her presence, but I never saw them together. Nor do I know how he felt and what he said in the country houses which he visited for the purpose of examining their muniments and family papers. His pleasure in staying in them was part of the romantic Anglomania which remained with him to the end of his days. The English aristocracy was for him bathed in a heavenly light. His interest in history is certainly not alone sufficient to explain this radiant vision. Rather it is probably the other way about: his interest in the history of individual members of the English Parliament during a time when many of them were members of (or closely connected with) a powerful and gifted Whig aristocracy was due to his idealisation of this style of life. He has, at times, been accused of being a snob. There is something in this; but Namier's snobbery was of the Proustian kind – peers, members of the aristocracy, rich, proud, self-possessed, independent, freedom-loving to the point of eccentricity – such Englishmen were for him works of art which he studied with devoted, indeed, fanatical attention and discrimination. He was not carried away by the fascination of this world, as Oscar Wilde, or even Henry James, appear to have been. He was content to remain an outsider. He gloried in his vision of the English national character, its strengths and its foibles, and remained a lifelong passionate addict to a single human species, to the analysis and, inevitably, celebration of which his life – for psychological reasons which Freud had certainly not helped him to understand – was devoted. He studied every detail in the life of the English governing class, as Marx studied the proletariat, not as an end in itself, as an object of fascinated observation, but as a social formation; in each case from an outside vantage-point, which neither bothered either to emphasise or to deny.

His origins obsessed him. His morbid hatred of obsequiousness, which may have had something to do with his memories of Poles and Jews in Galicia, often took ferocious forms. Meeting me in the corridor of a train, he said, apropros of nothing: 'I have been visiting Lord Derby. He said to me: "Namier, you are a Jew. Why do you write our English history? Why do you not write Jewish history?" I replied, "Derby! There *is* no modern Jewish history, only a Jewish martyrology, and that is not amusing enough for me." ' He spoke of Jews as 'my co-racials', and clearly enjoyed the embarrassing effect which this word produced on Jew and Gentile alike. In All Souls one afternoon someone in his presence – he was in the common room at tea as a guest – defended the German claim to colonies, a topic then much in the air. Namier rose, glared round the room, fixed a basilisk-like eye on one of his fellow-guests, whom he had, mistakenly as it turned out, assumed to be a German, and said loudly, 'Wir Juden und die anderen Farbigen denken anders.'[1] He savoured the effect of these startling words with great satisfaction. He was an out-and-out nationalist, and did not disguise his far from fraternal feelings towards the Arabs in Palestine, about whom his position was more intransigent than that of the majority of his fellow Zionists. I well recollect a meeting to interview candidates for a post in English in the University of Jerusalem, at which Namier would fix some timid lecturer from, say, Nottingham, with his baleful, annihilating glare, and say: 'Mr Levy, can you shoot?' – the candidate would mutter something – 'Because if you take this post, you will have to shoot. You will have to shoot our Arab cousins. Because if you do not shoot them, they will shoot you.' Stunned silence. 'Mr Levy, will you please

---

[1] 'We Jews and the other coloured peoples think otherwise.'

answer my question: can you shoot?' Some of the candidates withdrew. No appointment was made.

As the 1930s wore on and the position of the West steadily deteriorated, Namier grew steadily gloomier and more ferocious. He would visit me in All Souls, and later in New College, and say that as war was now inevitable, he proposed to sell his life as dearly as possible, and paint imaginary pictures involving the extermination of a good many Nazis by all kinds of diabolical means. The position of Zionism – one of the victims of British foreign policy at this time – depressed him further. The villains in his eyes were not so much the Conservative leaders – some of those were members of the aristocracy and as such enjoyed a certain degree of exemption from blame – but the Arab-loving 'pen-pushers of the Foreign Office' and the 'hypocritical idiots of the Colonial Office'. He would lie in wait for these – particularly the latter – in the Athenaeum. There he would drive some unsuspecting official into the corner of the smoking-room, where he would treat him to a terrifying homily which the victim would not soon forget, and which would probably increase his already violent antipathy to Zionism in general and Namier in particular.

Sir John Shuckburgh, then the Permanent Under-Secretary of the Colonial Office, was a not infrequent target for Namier when he was on the war-path. I was once present when Namier, in his soft but penetrating and remorseless voice, addressed Shuckburgh, who made every effort to escape; in vain. Namier followed him out of the room, on to the steps, into the street, and so on – down the Duke of York's Steps, probably to the door of the Colonial Office itself. Politically he was as great a liability to his party as he was an asset to it intellectually. His final and most savagely treated victim was Malcolm MacDonald, the Colonial Secretary himself. In 1939, after the Chamberlain government's White Paper on Palestine, which seemed to put an end to all Zionist hopes, Namier came to lunch with Reginald Coupland at All Souls. Coupland was the effective author of the Peel Report on Palestine, probably the most valuable document ever composed on that agonising subject. Coupland had spoken bitterly of the shameful betrayal of the Palestine Jews by the British Government, and said that he would write a letter to *The Times* pointing out the shortcomings of both Chamberlain and Malcolm MacDonald. Namier said that he had his own method of dealing with such cases. He had met Malcolm MacDonald somewhere in London. 'I spoke to him. I began with a jest. I said that in the eighteenth century peers made their tutors Under-Secretaries, whereas in the twentieth Under-Secretaries made their tutors peers. He did not seem to understand. I did not bother to explain.[1] Then I said something he would understand. I said to him, "Malcolm" – he is, you know, still Malcolm to me – I know him quite well – "I am writing a new book." He said, "What is it, Lewis?" I replied, "I will tell you what it is. I have called it *The Two MacDonalds: A Study in Treachery.*" ' I do not know whether Namier had actually said this; he supposed that he had and he was certainly capable of it. It was, again, not unlike Karl Marx at his most vindictive, and, like Marx's insults, was intended to draw blood. Yet he was surprised by the fact that he was feared and disliked so widely.

In 1941 I was employed by the Ministry of Information in New York, and there I met a man who threw a good deal of light on Namier's younger days. His name was Max Hammerling, and his father had been associated with Josef Bernsztajn, Namier's father, in the management of his estate near Lemberg in Galicia, long before the First World War. The younger Hammerling was a warm sympathiser with the British cause, and got in touch with me to offer his help at a time when Britain was fighting Hitler alone. In the course of general conversation he asked me if I knew a man called Professor Namier, and was surprised to hear that I did. He said that he used to see him in earlier years, but that since then the connection had ended and he was anxious to hear what had happened to the son of his father's associate. Hammerling Senior had, so his son told me, emigrated to America and acquired control of one or more of the foreign-language periodicals of New York in the years before the First World War. The young Namier first arrived in New York in 1913 with very little money – supplied by his father – to engage in research on the American War of Independence. Josef Bernsztajn had made an arrangement with his old associate under which Hammerling engaged Namier to write leading articles to be syndicated and translated for a section of his publications. Namier wrote these articles at night, and worked in the New York Public Library in the daytime, and in this way kept

---

[1] Only Namier would have supposed that the average educated Englishman (or Scotsman) would realise that he was referring to the fact that the philosopher Locke had been made an Under-Secretary by his ex-pupil, Lord Shaftesbury, and that Godfrey Elton, who had been Malcolm MacDonald's tutor at Queen's College, Oxford, had recently been elevated to the peerage.

body and soul together. According to Max Hammerling, Namier viewed the continued existence of the Dual Monarchy with extreme disfavour, and was a vigorous champion of the *Entente Cordiale*. Hammerling Senior had many Roman Catholic readers and had no great wish to alienate the Roman Church in the United States, which was on the whole pro-Austrian and isolationist. When Namier's articles became too violently interventionist, he was told to moderate them: he ignored hints and requests; matters came to a head, and his employment came to an end in the spring of 1914. It was then that Namier, without any obvious means of subsistence, returned to England and was given a grant by Balliol College which enabled him to continue his research. Namier told me that the news of the assassination of the Archduke Franz Ferdinand was brought to the editor of *The Times*, Geoffrey Dawson, in All Souls after dinner. Namier, who happened to be there too, announced to Dawson and his friends that war was now imminent. Dawson indicated that he did not believe this (he laboured under similar delusions in 1938–9) and turned to other topics.

When war was declared Namier volunteered for the British Army. He was evidently not a perfect soldier. Some intelligent person took him out of the army, and put him into the Foreign Office as adviser on Polish affairs attached to the Historical Adviser to the Foreign Office, Sir John Headlam-Morley. 'I remember', said Namier to me, 'the day in 1918 when the Emperor Karl sued for peace. I said to Headlam-Morley: "Wait." Headlam-Morley said to Balfour: "Wait." Balfour said to Lloyd George: "Wait." Lloyd George said to Wilson: "Wait." And while they waited, the Austro-Hungarian Empire disintegrated.[1] I may say that I pulled it to pieces with my own hands.'

Apart from feeling convinced that the Polish National Democratic Party was plotting his assassination, Namier enjoyed his work in the Foreign Office. The Foreign Office showed no desire to retain Namier on its staff after the War, nor did the Treasury, with which he also was temporarily connected. Nor did Balliol College, Oxford, which made him a temporary lecturer for a while – his most devoted Oxford pupils date from this period. Thereupon he left England for Vienna, and there made a few thousand

[1] Namier pronounced this word very slowly, syllable by syllable, which heightened the dramatic climax of his narrative.

pounds. In the early 1920s he came back to London with his exiguous capital. Here his extraordinary character showed itself at its fullest. He did not do what others might have been tempted to do: he did not try to spend as little as possible while looking for a means of subsistence; he knew that he had it in him to write an original and important book and decided to do so. He spoke of this to friends and allies (some of them connected with the Round Table group of Liberal Imperialists with whose ideas Namier had been in sympathy during the War). He told them that he needed money to write a book; he held out no promise of repayment: the money was to be regarded as an investment in learning and in that alone. Philip Kerr, who was among those approached, told me (in Washington in 1940 where he was by then Lord Lothian and British Ambassador) that he did not find Namier congenial company, but was overawed by his leonine personality and felt him to be a man of unusual intellectual power. He and his friends obtained a grant for him; he was also supported by at least one private person. Namier felt no false shame in accepting such patronage: this was usual enough in that best of all periods, the later years of the eighteenth century. He felt that he had as good a claim as Burke, or any other talented writer of the past, whom the rich and the powerful should be proud to support; and he bound his spell upon his 'patrons', who, as he had always known, had no cause to regret their generosity. The books that he wrote did what he wished them to do: they transformed the standards of historical scholarship (and to some degree the style of historical writing) in England for at least a quarter of a century.

Having discharged this intellectual obligation, Namier threw himself, in the later 1920s, with passion and ferocity into political work in the Zionist Organisation. This gave full play to his formidable gifts: his polemical skill, his sense of history, his pride, his nationalism, his passion for exposing weakness, cowardice, lies and unworthy motives. He derived deep satisfaction from these labours. In the course of them he managed to irritate and humiliate his less talented collaborators, to impress some members of the British intelligentsia, astonish and anger others, and permanently upset and infuriate a number of influential officials in the Foreign and Colonial Offices. After the Second World War, when it became plain that his unwavering and withering contempt for most of his Zionist colleagues had made it certain that if an independent Jewish establishment ever emerged he would not be amongst its guides, he turned his back upon Zionist politics, without changing his moral or political convictions. He returned to the study of history. He hoped and expected, not without reason, that he might yet be appointed to a post by his *alma mater*. This was not to be. Whenever a Chair in History (or International Relations, on which, too, he had made himself a leading expert) fell vacant, his name inevitably came up and was duly dismissed. Those responsible for such appointments in Oxford often said that it was a crying shame that some other group of electors had failed to appoint Namier to one or other of the three or four Chairs for which his distinction fitted him pre-eminently. But when their own turn came, such electors or advisers acted precisely like their predecessors. He was invariably passed over. Various reasons were adduced: that his field of specialisation was too narrow; that he was politically intemperate, as his Zionism or his low opinion of pre-war British foreign policy plainly showed; that he would be too arrogant to his colleagues or too exacting to his students; that he would be a terrible bore, intolerable at mealtimes to the Fellows of this or that college. The quality of his genius was not seriously disputed: but this was not regarded as a sufficiently weighty factor. He had made some implacable enemies. Yet, despite his acuteness, he was an unworldly man, and in personal matters clumsy, innocent and childlike. He was easily deceived: he took flattery for true coin. He often had no notion of who was covertly working against him: he was totally incapable of manoeuvre or intrigue. He achieved everything by the sheer weight of his huge intellectual armour. He misjudged motives and often could not tell friends from ill-wishers. He fell into traps and remained to his dying day unaware of this. He was an Othello who retained confidence in more than one minor academic Iago. His failure to obtain an Oxford Chair ate into his soul, as it has into those of others similarly treated. 'I will tell you how they make professors in Oxford,' he said bitterly to me during the period when he was delivering the Waynflete Lectures at Magdalen College shortly after the end of the Second World War. 'In the eighteenth century there was a club called the Koran Club. The qualification for membership was to have travelled in the East. Then it was found that there were various persons whom it was thought desirable to make members of the club and who had not travelled in the East. So the rules were changed from "travelling in the East" to "expressing a wish to travel in the East". That is how they make professors in Oxford. Do not', he added, 'let this story go too far.' He continued to teach at Manchester, but finally moved to London and was entrusted with the formidable enterprise of the History of Parliament, to be done in his own fashion – by means of detailed, microscopically examined lives of all who ever were members of it. Honours were showered upon him in England and abroad, but nothing made up for the Oxford disappointment. Balliol made him an Honorary Fellow. Two honorary doctorates were conferred upon him by the University. He delivered the Romanes Lecture. But although this pleased him, as did his knighthood, the old scar remained and troubled him.

It was at this period that he married for the second time (his first marriage had not lasted long – his wife is said to have been a Muslim and died during the Second World War). He was converted to the Anglican faith, and his marriage to Julia de Beausobre finally ended the period of acute loneliness and bitter personal unhappiness, mitigated by rare moments of pride and joy, which had begun for him after the First World War. Friedrich Waismann, an eminent Austrian philosopher whom he had met during his years in Vienna, told me that he had never in his life met an intellectually more gifted, penetrating and fascinating man, or one more deeply plunged in the most hopeless misery and solitude.

His conversion to Christianity cost him the friendship of Weizmann, who did not wish to examine the reasons for this step, but reacted instinctively, as his fathers would have done before him, to what he regarded as an act of apostasy for which no decent motive could exist. This, of course, hurt Namier deeply, but his marriage had created a new life for him and he bore such things more easily. He visited the State of Israel after Weizmann's death, was profoundly moved, but remained implacably opposed to the rabbis and complained of clerical tyranny. When I made light of this to him he turned upon me sternly and said 'You do not know rabbis and priests as I do – they can ruin any country. Clergymen are harmless. Nobody ever speaks of being in the hands of the clergymen as they do of the Jesuits and, I fear, now should do of the rabbis.' During this period I would receive occasional visits from him in Oxford. He had grown mellower with age; he was happier because his domestic life was serene, and because adequate recognition had been given him at last. He took criticism as painfully as ever: when his friend and disciple Alan Taylor wrote an insufficiently respectful review of a collection of his essays in the *Manchester Guardian*, he, like Marx, took this as a symptom of failing powers on the part of the critic.

He invested a great deal in his few personal relationships, and breaches were particularly painful to him. His relations with Taylor suffered further deterioration, in large part as a result of the role which Taylor believed him to have played in the choice of the successor to V. H. Galbraith as Regius Professor of History in Oxford. Taylor was not appointed; he blamed Namier for failing to support him sufficiently when he could have done so, and broke off relations. Namier was genuinely fond of him – fonder of him than of most men. He told me that some of his happiest hours had been spent at Taylor's house; that one must be careful – more careful than he had been – in one's human relations; but that Taylor, whose gifts were so extraordinary, had disappointed him by what he considered his addiction to popular journalism. 'And if I have hurt *your* feelings,' he said to me, 'I apologise also. I am not always too careful': this was a touching and handsome reference to the fact that I had sent him the printed version of a lecture on an abstract subject, which he had acknowledged with the words 'You must indeed be a very clever man to understand what you write.' This was a characteristic gibe aimed at the philosophy of history – a subject which he believed to be bogus, and which had been the subject of my lecture. I was delighted by his letter, which could not have been regarded as offensive by any normal person, still less by anyone who knew Namier and took pleasure in his prejudices and absurdities. E. H. Carr, who was a common friend, came to visit me on the day when I received it, and I read him Namier's letter with great relish. Shortly afterwards Namier's comment appeared in a gossip column of the *Daily Express*. Namier was horrified, and wrote to me immediately to explain that he had not, of course, meant to insult either me or the subject of my lecture. My reassurances did not convince him: he suspected Carr – quite baselessly, since Carr flatly denied this – of communicating the gibe to the *Daily Express*; serious journalism was, of course, another matter. How could such serious, learned, gifted men, Taylor, Carr, Fellows of the British Academy, who had it in them to give so much to historical study, compromise the dignity of their calling – and of academic life generally – by associating with the enemies of learning, however entertaining and informative? And in so public a fashion? At least Butterfield, than whom no one was more mistaken, did not dabble in this. Namier's suspicions were often (as in this case) without foundations; but he clung to them. My defence fell on deaf ears: an idealised image, which he had carried with him for the greater part of his life – the image of the scholar, and perhaps also of the Englishman – had in some way been damaged, and this was almost more painful than a personal attack.

He spoke often of the dignity of learning: of the need to keep scholarship pure, to protect it from its three greatest enemies: amateurism, journalistic prostitution, and obsession with doctrine. 'An amateur', he declared in one of his typical apophthegms, 'is a man who thinks more about himself than about his subject', and he mentioned a younger colleague whom he suspected of a wish to glitter. He passionately believed in professionalism in every field: he denounced fine writing, and, still more, a desire to startle or shock the reader, whether he was a member of the general public or of the world of scholars. He spoke with indignation about those who had accused him of wishing to reassess the character and historical influence of George III out of a desire to dish the Whigs and attack their values and their heroes. He would solemnly and with deep sincerity assure me that his sole purpose was to reconstruct the facts and explain them by the use of well-tested, severely empirical methods; that his only reason for distrusting party labels and professions of political ideals in the eighteenth century was his conviction – based on incontrovertible documentary and other factual evidence – that such labels and professions disguised the truth, often from the agents themselves. His own psychological tenets, on which these exposures were in part based, seemed to him confirmed over and over again by the historical evidence – the actual transactions of the politicians and their agents and their kinsfolk – which were susceptible of one and only one true explanation. Whether or not he was mistaken in this, he believed profoundly that he was guided not by theories but by the facts and by them alone. As for the question of what was a fact, what constituted evidence, this was a philosophical issue – something from which he shied with all the force of his whole abstraction-hating, anti-philosophical nature.

Journalism – the desire to *épater*, to entertain, to be brilliant – was, in a man of learning, mere irresponsibility. 'Irresponsible' was one of the most opprobrious terms in his vocabulary. His belief in the moral duties of historians and scholars generally was Kantian in its severity and genuineness. As for doctrinaire obsessions, that again appeared to him as a form of culpable self-indulgence – wanton escape from the duty of following minutely, wherever they led, the often complex, convoluted empirical paths constituted by the 'facts', into some symmetrical pattern invented by the historian to indulge his own metaphysical or moral predilection; alternatively it was a quasi-pathological intellectual obsession which rendered the historian literally incapable of seeing 'wie es eigentlich gewesen'. Hence Namier's distaste for, and ironies at the expense of, philosophical historians; and the emphasis on material factors and distrust of ideal ones. This was odd in a man who was himself governed by so many ideals and indeed prejudices: nationalism and national character, love of traditional 'roots', *la terre et les morts*, disbelief in the efficacy of intellectuals and theorisers, faith in individual psychology, even in graphology, as a key to character and action. But it was so.

It is not perhaps too extravagant to classify his essentially deflationary tendency – the desire to reduce both the general propositions and the impressionism of historians to hard pellet-like 'facts', to bring everything down to brass tacks – to regard this as part of the dominant intellectual trend of his age and milieu. It was in Vienna, after all, that Ernst Mach enunciated the principles of 'economy of thought' and tried to reduce physical phenomena to clusters of identifiable, almost isolable, sensations; that Freud looked for 'material', empirically testable causes of psychical phenomena; that the Vienna Circle of philosophers generated the verification principle as a weapon against vagueness, transcendentalism, theology, metaphysics; that the Bauhaus with its clear, rational lines had its origin in the ideas of Adolf Loos and his disciples. Vienna was the centre of the new anti-metaphysical and anti-impressionist positivism. Whether he knew this or not – and nobody could protest more vehemently against such ideological categorisation – this was the world from which Namier came. Its most original thinkers had reacted violently against German metaphysics and had found British empiricism sympathetic. In philosophy they achieved a celebrated and fruitful symbiosis with British thought. Namier was one of the boldest and most revolutionary pioneers of the application of this very method to history. The method – especially in the work of his followers – has been criticised as having gone too far – 'taken the mind out of history'. This kind of criticism has been levelled no less at the corresponding schools of philosophy, art, architecture, psychology. Whether the charge is just or not, even its sharpest critics can scarcely deny the value and importance of the early impact of the new method. It opened windows, let in air, revealed new horizons, made men see what they had not seen before. In this great constructive-destructive movement Namier was a major figure.

Namier's most striking personal characteristics were an unremittingly active intellectual power, independence, lack of fear, and an unswerving devotion to his chosen method. This method had yielded him rich fruit, and he would not modify it merely because it seemed to eclectics or philistines to be extreme or fanatical. Like Marx, like Darwin, like Freud, he was severely anti-eclectic. Nor did he believe in practising moderation or introducing qualifications simply in order to avoid charges of extremism, to please men of good sense. Indeed, anxiety to please in any fashion, still less appeasement of critics, was remote from his temperament. He believed that objective truth could be discovered, and that he had found a method of doing so in history; that this method consisted in a sort of *pointillisme*, 'the microscopic method', the splitting up of social facts into details of individual lives – atomic entities, the careers of which could be precisely verified; and that these atoms could then be integrated into greater wholes. This was the nearest to scientific method that was attainable in history, and he would adhere to it at whatever cost, in spite of all criticism, until and unless he became convinced by internal criteria of its inadequacy, because it had failed to produce results verified by research. This psychological Cartesianism was his weapon against impressionism and dilettantism of every kind. Kant had said that nature would yield up her secrets only under torture, only if specific questions were put to her. Namier believed this of history. The questions had to be formulated in such a way as to be answerable.

He was a child of a positivistic, deflationary, anti-romantic age, and his deep natural romanticism came out in other – political – directions. Dedicated historian that he was, he deliberately confined himself to his atomic data. He did indeed split up and reduce his material to tiny fragments, then he reintegrated them with a marvellous power of imaginative generalisation as great as that of any other historian of his time. He was not a narrative historian, and underestimated the importance and the influence of ideas. He admired individual greatness, and despised equality, mediocrity, stupidity. He worshipped political and personal liberty. His attitude to economic facts was at best ambivalent: and he was a very half-hearted determinist in his writing of history, whatever he may have said about it in his theoretical essays. Materialism, excessive determinism, were criticisms levelled against him, but they fit better those historians who, using the method without the genius, tend towards pedantry and timidity, where he was boldly constructive, intuitive and untrammelled. He thought in large terms. The care with which he examined and described the individual trees did not obscure his vision of the wood for the sake of which the huge accumulation and the minute analyses had been undertaken; the end, at any rate in the works of his best period, is never lost to view; the reader is not cluttered with detail, never feels that he is in the grasp of an avid fact-gatherer who cannot let anything go, a fanatical antiquary who can no longer distinguish between the trivial and the important. Perhaps, towards the end of his life, trees and even shrubs did begin to obscure his vision of the wood. But when he was at his best he might well have said, echoing Marx, for whom he had so little respect and by whose method he was in practice much influenced: 'Surtout, je ne suis pas namier-iste.'

FELIX FRANKFURTER AT OXFORD

I FIRST met Felix Frankfurter in, I think, the first or second week of the autumn term of 1933 at Oxford in the rooms of Roy Harrod in Christ Church, where I called one afternoon in October, in order to return a book. I was followed into the room by Sylvester Gates, then a lawyer in London, whom I knew; he was accompanied by a small, neat, dapper figure, who was introduced as Professor Frankfurter. His name, I am ashamed to say, was then scarcely familiar to me: I vaguely connected it with the New Deal and Roosevelt, though in no clear fashion; but this may merely be evidence of my own provincialism and lack of acquaintance with world affairs. I do not know whether the impending arrival of Felix Frankfurter as visiting Eastman Professor had caused a stir in the Law Faculty at Oxford, but I can testify to the fact that his visit was otherwise unheralded. Visits by eminent professors from foreign universities were not unusual at Oxford, then as now; and no matter how distinguished, such visitors were not, and are not, lionised; indeed, at times too little notice is taken of them. (Whatever the sociological explanation of this phenomenon, it is one that brings relief to some and much chagrin and disappointment to others.) At any rate, when I was introduced to Frankfurter, I wondered about his identity and attributes. I knew Gates to be a man of exceptionally fastidious taste – indeed, one of the cleverest, most intellectual, most civilised men I had ever met. He had brought a friend – a professor of law, doubtless distinguished in his own field – and that was all. Within five minutes, however, a conversation sprang up, about politics, personalities, Mr Stimson (whom the professor evidently knew well), Sir John Simon, Sacco and Vanzetti, the Manchurian invasion, President Lowell and his behaviour to Harold Laski, to all of which the unknown professor contributed with such vivacity, and so extraordinary and attractive a mixture of knowledge and fancy, that although I had not intended to stay, I listened (although I am, by nature, liable to interrupt) in a state of complete and silent fascination. After an hour or so an urgent appointment did finally force me to leave, without giving me an opportunity of enquiring about who this remarkable personage might be.

A few days later he dined at All Souls, which was my own college. His host on this occasion was, I think, Geoffrey Dawson, the editor of *The Times*, and one of the most influential political figures in England in his day. By this time I had discovered the identity of the remarkable stranger, nor was there, at All Souls, any way of avoiding this knowledge: Dawson and his circle (he had invited guests and got his friends to do so also) looked on Frankfurter, as I perceived, less as an academic figure than as a man of influence in Washington, an intimate friend and adviser of the President of the United States, and a man whom it was for obvious public reasons evidently desirable to cultivate. He responded to this treatment with the greatest naturalness and lack of self-consciousness. I do not suppose that he disliked being made an object of such attention – it was not surprising at All Souls, which, at that time particularly, was a meeting-place of a good many persons prominent in public life, among whom there were some very powerful men – but he did not display the slightest sign of grandeur, did not pontificate, did not speak in that measured and important fashion which often characterises the speech of one eminent person conscious of discussing affairs of State with other, equally weighty figures. He talked copiously, with an overflowing gaiety and spontaneity which conveyed the impression of great natural sweetness; his manner contrasted almost too sharply with the reserve, solemnity and, in places, vanity and self-importance of some of the highly placed persons who seated themselves round him and engaged his attention. He spoke easily, made his points sharply, stuck to all his guns, large and small, and showed no tendency to retreat from views and political verdicts some of which were plainly too radical for the more conservative of the public personages present; they were hailed with the greatest approval by the majority of our generation of fellows – then very young – who formed the outer circle of Frankfurter's audience, and were divided from most of their elders by irreconcilable differences of view on most of the political and social issues of that day – Manchuria, the 'Bankers' Ramp', Fascism, Hitler, unemployment, slumps, collective security (Abyssinia and Spain were still to come).

After something like two hours of talk on grave issues, Frankfurter cast a sharp look round the room and decided to make a break for freedom. Fidgeting visibly, he rose from his chair and made as if towards the table on which decanters of whisky and brandy and small chemist's bottles of seltzer water stood in rows. But long before he reached it – he was evidently in no need of artificial stimulation – he almost literally buttonholed a junior fellow who looked lively and sympathetic, and engaged him in frivolous conversation of some sort. Dawson, Simon, Lionel Curtis and other mandarins tried to bring him back to great Anglo-American issues. In vain. He would not be detached from this junior fellow – I think it was Penderel Moon, who was afterwards to play so original, fearless and admirable a part in India – and insisted on involving himself in some purely intellectual controversy that was clearly of no interest to the statesmen. Presently he drifted over into the corner of the room where the junior fellows were talking among themselves. Here he behaved with so gay, childlike and innocent a warmth of feeling, and talked with such enjoyment of, it seemed, everything, that the young men were charmed and exhilarated, and stayed up talking with him until the early hours of the morning.

Whenever I met him at dinner elsewhere in Oxford, I observed the same phenomenon: a certain amount of firm cultivation of him by those who felt it their right and duty to be talking to him as a representative of influential American circles in the law or government; the same polite but unenthusiastic response by the Eastman Professor; apparent unawareness on his part that some people were much more important than others; and affectionate familiarity in his dealings with everyone, which lightened the atmosphere in the most portentous milieux and delighted those who were young and observant.

Oxford in the 1920s and early '30s was stiffer, more class-conscious, hierarchical and self-centred than it is now (it may, of course, be only because I was young that I think so – but there is, I believe, a good deal of objective evidence for this too), and Felix Frankfurter had an uncommon capacity for melting reserve, breaking through inhibitions, and generally emancipating those with whom he came into contact. Only the genuinely self-important and pompous resented this, and they did so most deeply. I heard Maynard Keynes, who was himself a famous and merciless persecutor of pretentiousness and humbug, and a

considerable expert on the subject, accord recognition to Frankfurter as a master of this craft: indeed, he said that he placed him
first among Americans of his acquaintance in this respect, although
he supposed that Holmes had been even more formidable and less
inclined to mercy.

Indeed, Frankfurter had his blind spots. He was a genuine
Anglomaniac: the English, whatever he thought of their public
policies, individually could do little wrong in his eyes. It needed a
great deal of stupidity, wickedness or personal nastiness or
rudeness on an Englishman's part to arouse unfriendly sentiment
in Felix Frankfurter's breast. In general, he liked whatever could be
liked, omnivorously, and he greatly disliked having to dislike.
Everything delighted him: the relations of one ex-military fellow of
a college to another; C. K. Ogden's attitude to London restaurants;
unequal success in the wooing of their academic hosts achieved by
various German exiles then in England and the socially ludicrous
consequences of this; Salvemini's deflation of Harold Laski's
rhetorical homage to Burke; his own progress in London and
Oxford. His sense of the ridiculous was simple but acute, his
enjoyment of incongruities irrepressible. He was not what is
known as a good listener: he was too busy; like a bee, carrying
pollen from an unbelievable number of flowers (and what seemed
to some mere weeds), he distributed it and caused plants which had
never been seen to do so to burst into sudden bloom. The short
memoranda, several lines long, scribbled in pencil, and often
accompanied by cuttings or offprints, stirred pools that had not
been known to move before; this social gift he displayed to the
point of genius.

But to return to Oxford. Those who were sensitive to status, and
suffered from fears that their own might not be adequately
recognised, and dreaded irreverence in all its forms, complained of
the Eastman Professor's unseasonable frivolity, his lack of taste,
his noisy laughter, his childishness, his Americanisms, his immature
enthusiasm, his insensitivity to the unique qualities of Europe in
general, and Oxford in particular – a lack of *gravitas*, a deliberate
defiance of the genius of the place – and so on. These strictures
were certainly groundless: our guest did not practise irreverence
for its own sake. He admired Oxford, if anything, too deeply and
devotedly, and with a sensibility that exceeded that of his critics.
He understood what there was to understand. If he struck sharp
notes occasionally, he did so intentionally, and they were not

discordant in the ears of most of those who turned out, in the next quarter of a century, to be the bearers of the central traditions of Oxford, and of much of the intellectual life of England both before and after the Second World War. I do not know what impact he made on Oxford lawyers or the undergraduates who went to his lectures. So far as I and my friends were concerned, his genius resided in the golden shower of intellectual and emotional generosity that was poured forth before his friends, and liberated some among them who needed the unlocking of their chains. Whenever, during his first and subsequent visits, I met him at dinner in colleges or private houses, the same phenomenon was always to be observed: he was the centre, the life and soul of a circle of eager and delighted human beings, exuberant, endlessly appreciative, delighting in every manifestation of intelligence, imagination or life. He was (to use the phrase of a man he did not like) life-enhancing in the highest degree. No wonder that even the most frozen monsters in our midst responded to him and, in spite of themselves, found themselves on terms of both respect and affection with him. Only the vainest, and those most 'alienated' (a term then not in common use) from their fellow men, remained unaffected by his peculiar type of vitality or positively resented it. Attitudes towards him seemed to me a simple but not inadequate criterion of whether one was in favour of the forces of life or against them. I do not intend this as a moral judgement, or a judgement of value at all: there are moral, aesthetic and intellectual qualities of the rarest value which seem incompatible with a positive attitude to life; I mean this distinction only as a statement of fact.

He came to us twice again, once on a purely private visit, once to receive an honorary degree, and the welcome in each case from his friends and the friends of his friends was justifiably rapturous. I recollect no particularly memorable observations or epigrams by him, or about him, then or at any time, but two occasions stand out in my recollection as characteristic. One was a dinner party in Christ Church. I cannot now remember who was host – perhaps it was again Roy Harrod. All that I recollect is that a charade was acted by some of us after dinner, and such was the degree of vitality infused by the guest of honour that the acting (if I remember rightly, it had something to do with a jealous eighteenth-century French marquis and his peccant wife) became passionately expressive. I shall not reveal the identities of the actors; they have all attained to celebrity since. Felix applauded the performance and egged the actors on until the realism of the actors reached a maximum degree of intensity. I do not think I shall ever forget the expressions on the faces, the gestures, the inflections of voices on this extraordinary occasion. For Oxford dons – the most self-conscious, inhibited human beings in an already intensely self-conscious and inhibited society – to have broken out of their prisons to such a degree was something that only the most potent force could achieve – an elixir powerful enough to break through the most sacred spells. This liberating power seems to me evident in all Felix's dealings, from the most intimate to the most public, ever since the beginning of his career. Oxford, made by nature and art to be the greatest possible obstacle to this force, proved it indeed to be literally irresistible.

The second occasion is one that he mentions himself in his reminiscences: a dinner party held by him and his wife[1] at Eastman House, then situated in Parks Road, attended among others by Sylvester Gates, Freddie and Renée Ayer, Goronwy Rees, Maurice Bowra and one or two others, including, I think, the famous expatriate Guy Burgess, who was then staying in Oxford, and was pursuing a profession about which we were not clear – I think he published a city letter of financial advice, or something of the kind – at any rate, he was excellent company and, in those days, a friend of mine and of several of the others present.

It is always difficult to convey to others what it is about a particular occasion – particularly a private one – that makes it delightful or memorable. Nothing conveys less to the reader or (rightly) nauseates him more than such passages as 'How we laughed! Tears rolled down our cheeks', or 'His irresistible manner and his inimitable wit drew gusts of merry laughter from us all! How happy we were then, so young, so gay, such high spirits! How little did we see the shadows gathering over us all! How sad to reflect on the subsequent fate of X.Y.Z.! What a summer it was, etc.' The evening terminated, as Felix himself reports a little inaccurately, in a bet between Freddie Ayer and Sylvester Gates

---

[1] I have said nothing here of Marion Frankfurter. This is a deliberate omission: her distinction in every respect was too great to be treated in what would inevitably have been a marginal manner. That she deserves a full-length portrait to herself, none of those who were admitted to her friendship would, I think, deny. I have proceeded on the principle that a blank is better than an unworthy sketch.

about whether the sentence of the philosopher Ludwig Wittgenstein 'Whereof one may not speak, thereon one must preserve silence [*Wovon man nicht sprechen kann, darüber muß man schweigen*]' occurs once or twice in his *Tractatus Logico-Philosophicus*. Freddie said that he could have said it only once. He was then sent in a taxi to consult the text in his own flat in the High Street, and came back to report that Wittgenstein had indeed, as Gates maintained, said it twice, once in the preface[1] and once in the main body of the text, and paid ten shillings' forfeit.

Why was this so memorable? Only because the mixture of intellectual gaiety and general happiness generated at this and other dinner parties was too uncommon in so artificial an establishment as the University of Oxford – where self-consciousness is the inevitable concomitant of the occupations of its inhabitants – not to stand out as a peak of human feeling and of academic emancipation. Courage, candour, honesty, intelligence, love of intelligence in others, interest in ideas, lack of pretension, vitality, gaiety, a very sharp sense of the ridiculous, warmth of heart, generosity – intellectual as well as emotional – dislike for the pompous, the bogus, the self-important, the *bien-pensant*, for conformity and cowardice, especially in high places, where it is perhaps inevitable – where was such another combination to be found? And then there was the touching and enjoyable Anglomania – the childlike passion for England, English institutions, Englishmen – for all that was sane, refined, not shoddy, civilised, moderate, peaceful, the opposite of brutal, decent – for the liberal and constitutional traditions that before 1914 were so dear to the hearts and imaginations especially of those brought up in Eastern or Central Europe, more particularly to members of oppressed minorities, who felt the lack of them to an agonising degree, and looked to England and sometimes to America – those great citadels of the opposite qualities – for all that ensured the dignity and liberty of human beings. That which has sometimes been taken for snobbery in Felix Frankfurter – a profound possible misreading of his character – was, in fact, precisely this. His feeling for England was subjected to strain during the troubles in Palestine: he was a stout-hearted Zionist, and his conversations in Oxford on this topic with Reginald Coupland – the principal author of the Royal

---

[1] [Though here 'reden' appears in place of 'sprechen' at the end of the main text. I.B. took Ayer's side in the bet, and also paid a forfeit. Ed.]

Commission's report, which to this day is the best account of the Palestine issue of its time – are still unrecorded. Coupland frequently remarked that Frankfurter had taught him more on this subject than the officials instructed to brief him, and had doubtless made enemies by the courage and candour of his views. His part in this, like his contributions to the law, his influence on the policies of the New Deal, his work in United States government departments before he became professor, his advocacy of Sacco and Vanzetti, his public life and influence in general, may be worthier of comment and commendation than the personal qualities upon which I have dwelt here. But it is these last, and not the attributes which made him important to the leading political men in England by whom he was assiduously entertained, that made their deepest impact upon the academic community in Oxford.

No one had ever captivated so many unlikely and resistant members of an apparently forbidding fortress so swiftly. Obituaries often refer to the deceased's 'genius for friendship'. Not the dubious quality indicated by this cliché, but an unrivalled power of liberation of human beings imprisoned beneath an icy crust of custom or gloom or social terror – this seems to me to be Felix Frankfurter's rarest single personal gift. It was this that penetrated our defences – ramparts that have kept out and needlessly frustrated many a good and interested and intelligent and well-intentioned man.

RICHARD PARES

WHEN I first knew Richard Pares, in the early 1930s, he was an unmarried Research Fellow of All Souls, and lived an ordered life, governed by strict, self-imposed rules, dedicated to teaching and to scholarship. He looked much younger than his years, like a shy, distinguished, clever undergraduate; this alert and youthful look he retained to the end of his life. His intellect, clear, formidable and with a fine cutting edge, left no one in doubt of its elegance and power. With this he possessed charm of manner, a discriminating (at times almost feminine) love for whatever possessed style and form, and an ironical humour which alternately delighted and alarmed his more impressionable colleagues. He lived behind doors through which none but his intimate friends were permitted to enter; but his gifts, his distinction both as a scholar and as a human being, still more his uncompromising moral and intellectual principles, and his originality and strength of character, made him a natural leader of the younger, reforming party in All Souls. His moral influence upon his colleagues was very great. He talked very well: and his ascendancy was in part founded on his talent as a college orator. Few who heard it will forget the blend of original thought, caustic wit and controlled passion, expressed in apt and classically lucid sentences, that more than once altered the tone and direction of a college debate. I remember no one, old or young, who failed to respect his intelligence, his unsleeping integrity, or the combination of piety towards traditions and institutions with his own independent judgement which he brought to the defence of whatever he deeply believed in – historical scholarship, the sanctity of personal relations, the maintenance of rigorous stand-ards in the College or the University. Yet, with all his pride, his talent, his fastidious intellect and temper, he was kind, affectionate and gay. His moral feelings, which he did not trouble to conceal, did not make him censorious or priggish; they were allied to his deep and critical aesthetic sense. He chose the eighteenth century as his field of historical study, partly because he was attracted by order and formal beauty (he later occasionally complained that the human beings he found in it proved more brutal, coarse, bleak and repulsive than he had conceived possible). He read and reread Jane Austen, Emily Dickinson, Virginia Woolf; he adored Mozart, and this aesthetic sensibility and understanding entered into all his relationships.

With all this, he belonged to the central stream of Winchester and still more of Balliol: he had a tender social conscience; he respected earnestness and public spirit; he was very just; he was a willing and lifelong slave of self-imposed obligations; and in consequence wore himself out by his devotion to research, his pupils, and later his service to the State. But he was not dulled by this stern self-discipline; he liked to be amused and exhilarated; he delighted in every form of artistic and intellectual virtuosity. As is sometimes the case with delicate and slightly wintry natures, he needed, and was sustained by, the greater vitality of others, and rewarded it with grateful and lasting affection. He had a keen sense of pleasure, and, despite his Wykehamical piety towards estab- lished values and his careful judgement and sense of measure, he welcomed eagerly almost any kind of original gift, however extravagant or eccentric, if it raised his own at times somewhat melancholy spirits.

But he did not, I think, count on such moments; when they occurred, they were for him a kind of windfall; he did not hope for much. To his mediocre pupils, he remained a conscientious, acute, sympathetic and stimulating tutor. He never allowed himself to intimidate or pillory the weaker among them, or to ignore them, or treat them with disdain. He disliked only the idle and fraudulent. But to those among them who displayed exceptional gifts he responded beyond their expectations: they found the most sensi- tive understanding and wide encouragement to the freest play of their imagination. Imagination, but not ideas. His distaste for philosophy, which he acquired as an undergraduate reading for Greats, developed into distrust of all general ideas. He disliked speculation and preoccupation with questions capable of no clear answers. There was always a predictable limit beyond which he declined to move. His values were fixed by the good sense and the authority of the moral and social order in which he consciously believed. Attempts to raise fundamental issues, whether personal or historical, were stopped with a few dry words, and, if pressed, with growing impatience and even irritation.

He was perhaps the most admired and looked up to of the Oxford teachers of his generation. He was attached to his pupils, and followed their subsequent careers with sympathy. But he avoided intimacy and kept himself apart, surrounded by a reserve that few dared to violate. He did not seek to dominate, to form a school, to bask in the easily acquired worship of undergraduates. In the outer field of political or social views he was prepared to be influenced; in the inner citadel of personal life and scholarship he remained self-sufficient, untouched and proudly independent.

He had, in a full sense, belonged to the great decade that followed the First World War. When he was an undergraduate of Balliol he became a close friend of Francis Urquhart and a member of the celebrated group that met in his rooms in Balliol and in his Alpine chalet. In particular Humphrey Sumner, Roger Mynors, Tom Boase, Christopher Cox, John Maud became his friends. And Sligger's own disciplined life, his deep convictions and tolerance of others, made a lasting impression on him. At the same time he was on terms of intimacy with the leading *beaux esprits* of his generation: Cyril Connolly, Evelyn Waugh, John Sutro were his close friends, and indeed formed a society in his honour; and although he subsequently, by an act of will, turned away from these companions of his youth, to make himself an austere and dedicated scholar, his taste remained incurably and admirably sophisticated to the end of his days. He renounced what he had admired, even though he continued to admire what he had renounced. He fostered thoroughness, application, the disinterested pursuit of the truth; he told himself that there were no a priori reasons for supposing that the truth, when discovered, would necessarily prove interesting. He defended the duller virtues: he had always detested romantic rhetoric, ostentation, journalism. This became, to the point of pedantry, his conviction and his doctrine, but he was never solemn, was capable of moments of marvellous gaiety and high spirits, and had a strain of childlike innocence and fancy that went oddly but delightfully with the cultivated quality of his taste and intellect.

His lifelong belief in academic life and academic values was the faith of a convert; he wanted no recognition or reward outside its bounds. He was endowed by nature with a wide and generous vision, was very imaginative, and understood almost everything; it was therefore a deliberate self-narrowing – an act of self-imposed stoicism – by which he chose the life of a don, and adhered to it to the exclusion of many other interests. Universities were his home and his world. He was an excellent civil servant during the War; there, too, his colleagues regarded him with deep respect, admiration, and a liking not unmixed with awe. But he returned to academic life with relief. His professorial lectures at Edinburgh were, as always, fresh, first-hand, just; he earned the love and admiration of his pupils and colleagues there as everywhere. But when All Souls offered him the most distinguished research fellowship at its disposal, he resigned the professorship which his progressive paralysis made it hard for him to carry, and came back gladly. His academic distinctions – the Fellowship of the British Academy, the Ford Lectures, the honorary Fellowship of Balliol – gave him abiding pleasure. He was most happily married and delighted in his daughters. He took as full a part in the life of All Souls as his physical condition made possible. From his wheelchair he made pungent and effective speeches at college meetings, and carried all his old authority. His conversation was as clever and delightful as ever.

Great learning, tireless labours, unswerving pursuit of truth, even brilliant powers of exposition are qualities, if not frequently, yet sufficiently often found in combination not to constitute a unique claim. What was astonishing in Pares was the union of extreme refinement of mind and heart, an intellect of the first order, and rigorous self-discipline with acute perceptiveness and understanding of others, rare personal charm, an unflagging ironical pleasure in the comedy of life, and a disposition to gay and brilliant play of the imagination characteristic of a certain type of artistic genius. And with all this a sense of honour, greatness of soul, an unsullied purity of character, and a capacity for love and devotion which made his moral personality unique, and his example and his influence dominant in his generation.

Until the end he took a conscientious interest in public issues, but they were not central in his life. He was – so far as he had clearcut political views – a moderate socialist, somewhat right of centre; but his heart was not in politics. He lived his life within the frontiers of a deliberately circumscribed world, a formal garden which he could shape according to his own desire for order and unity, harmonious and enclosed: a universe that consisted of the study of history, of personal relations, and of his own full inner life. In this private world – perhaps the final flowering of Winchester and the Balliol of the 1920s – everything had its place, its own private name, its own particular relationship to himself. It was not an attempt on his part to protect his life against the chaos of the public world: within this *hortus inclusus* he demarcated carefully the realm of objective truth from that of his own sensibility and fancy.

His full height became revealed in the last year of his life, when he gradually lost control of his body, limb by limb, muscle by muscle, and, tended by, as he himself had called it, the loving-kindness of his wife, and by his children, he faced his end, which he knew to be near, with a noble serenity which no words of mine are fit to describe. He had not always been, but he died, a believing Christian. He was the best and most admirable man I have ever known.

HUBERT HENDERSON AT ALL SOULS

WHEN Hubert Henderson first came to All Souls in 1934 he was not known to many of its Fellows. D. H. Macgregor, the Drummond Professor, who, like Henderson, had come from Cambridge, had, I think, some acquaintance with him; R. H. (later Lord) Brand and Sir Arthur Salter knew him well, and one or two of the relatively senior Fellows had come into contact with him in the course of his public activities. But to the majority of the junior and academical Fellows who formed the bulk of the College he was virtually unknown. He appeared gentle, shy and a trifle vague. He was courteous, amiable, but reserved; and seemed a little bewildered. All Souls was, and still is, *sui generis*, and the effect it will have upon those who come to it in middle life is difficult to foretell. Henderson had been deeply involved in public life both as editor of the *Nation* and as Joint Secretary of the Economic Advisory Council. All Souls must have seemed to him a curious private world, exceedingly unlike either Cambridge or the larger world which he had inhabited. It took him a little time to assimilate, but when he did so he came to occupy a distinguished and unique position in the College. He liked conversation; he was interested in many topics and was glad to speak about them with anyone who responded to his own detached, disinterested, and essentially middle-road notions; he did not particularly expect or take pleasure in agreement. He was a man of deep convictions, which he held with clarity and a kind of tranquil passion; in argument he was eloquent, lucid and tenacious; and since he was free from solemnity and priggishness, and liked to discuss whatever interested him, he took equal pleasure in analysing personalities and in dissecting abstract topics or political issues, and treated them always in the same scrupulous, and sometimes animated, fashion. He talked well, and with a courtesy of manner which never abandoned him even in moments of acute provocation; nor were either his juniors or his seniors ever made to feel that he put them into any category or box, or that he was conscious of being in one himself. This made the experience of talking with him, whether *à deux* or in company, particularly delightful and profitable. Nobody, I think, felt about him that he belonged specially to any one section of the College, of the Senior Fellows, or of the Junior Fellows, or of academics or of 'Londoners', or of conservatives or of progressives. He had a genuinely independent personality, and held sharp ideas and opinions both about persons and about issues, and spoke about them without rancour, without self-consciousness, moderate in judgement, intellectually intense, and naturally civil.

I dwell upon the quality of his talk because All Souls has been, as long as anyone remembers, a college of talkers, and his own genuine love of conversation and debate caused him to fit into it without effort. He liked to talk an issue through and he liked argument; he wished to make his own views entirely clear to others and grasp theirs as fairly and as accurately as he could; and since he had an intellect of exceptional acuteness and integrity, and a genuine desire to establish the truth, and sincerely believed that this could sometimes be done by means of rational discussion, he used to argue on and on, with tenacity and absorption, and infectious spontaneity. His face would assume a puzzled, sometimes bewildered or incredulous expression when, as occasionally happened, his opponent seemed to him to advance opinions which no sane or well-informed person could conceivably hold. He would ruffle his hair, his voice would rise in pitch, he would make gestures of despair, but, whatever the hour, he would go on. He would never willingly let go. He would never grow angry, or rude, or waspish, no matter how maddening his opponent seemed to him to be. The hour would grow late, it would be past midnight, and the ashtray beside him would become filled and over-filled with the stubs of du Maurier cigarettes. If, as sometimes happened, the argument broke down under a hail of mere counter-assertions, he would simply grow silent and avert his thoughts; if the tone grew too sharp he would look at a newspaper or quietly leave the room. He was not at his ease save in an atmosphere of courtesy, intelligence, moderation, and a modicum of intellectual goodwill.

He had an acute sense of humour, and, in particular, of the ridiculous, which found free play in Oxford, together with a boyish sweetness of disposition, and a genuine hatred of all forms of sentimentality and humbug. For those younger than himself (of whom alone I can speak with confidence) he was easier to be with than almost any other of their seniors: he was not in the least pompous, not in the least vain, not in the least difficult; he had an open mind and a natural fund of sympathy and kindness. He treated all men as equals, and contact with him was direct and delightful. One was never reminded, by some unconscious phrase on his part, of his own eminence in the world of affairs, or of particular convictions or prejudices which it was not safe to touch upon. He liked to be amused, he was not censorious or disapproving of high spirits or gaiety or even of a degree of silliness and nonsense in others, and he was not put off by eccentricity; in short, he was in favour of the flow of life, he enhanced it and was a cause of it in others. What he liked above all was a combination of imaginative ideas and practical knowledge, and at All Souls he found these in sufficient quantity. On committees his good judgement, freedom from bias, clear principles, fearlessness and unruffled good temper (the high falsetto to which his voice rose in moments of excitement sometimes belied him) were a great asset, particularly at moments when these qualities seemed to be on the ebb; at college meetings he spoke with authority. All Souls is a large college, and to be effective at its meetings one must have a certain degree of oratorical power. This Henderson did not possess, but his speeches were listened to with respect because his impartiality and independence were evident and because he was widely liked and admired. I doubt whether he knew how widespread this feeling was until he was elected Warden: he was not a man who spent time on reflecting about other people's attitudes or feelings towards him; this went with his freedom from vanity and neurotic preoccupation with his own personality or status. He had, to everyone's sorrow, had a breakdown in health during the last war, but had seemed to make a complete recovery and continued to play his part in College, as a member of committees, and as a frequent assistant examiner in economics in the fellowship elections. His shrewd judgement as an examiner was always much trusted and has vindicated itself, so far as I remember, on all occasions.

After the untimely death of Warden Sumner in 1951 he was elected to succeed him in June of that year. He certainly did not seek the office. If ever there was a popular 'draft' of a reluctant candidate, this was an instance of it; for a long time he did not wish to be considered, and when in the end he allowed himself to be discussed, it was due not to ambition, nor even to a sense of duty (for I am sure he did not consider it anyone's particular duty to seek or hold such office), but because it was part of his inherent modesty not to resist too violently the pressure of his friends. I doubt if he asked himself whether he had much chance of being elected; I am sure that he did not care in the least how great or small it was. I remember very well his air after his election, which was, as so often in moments of crisis, slightly bewildered and incredulous; he was deeply moved by this token of corporate trust and affection.

He scarcely entered upon his reign. A few days after his election he had a heart attack in the Sheldonian Theatre, on the day of the Encaenia. I went to visit him at the Acland Nursing Home and he was, as always, charming and cheerful; with, as the Vice-Chancellor so well said of him in his commemorative remarks, 'his quiet gaiety and his transparent goodness'.[1] To goodness he added purity of character, distinction of intellect and of feeling, a sense of public duty, and a devotion to personal relations and private life, as well as, beneath his vagueness and gentleness, a foundation of Scottish granite which gave him an unsuspected strength of will. He possessed a blend of characteristics which All Souls, in the view of some, should aim at producing: he was intellectual – he was interested in general ideas – but he was neither woolly-minded nor pedantic, nor locked in an ivory tower. He was involved in public affairs, and took a lifelong interest in public issues, but he was not a philistine and did not judge an academic world by the standards drawn from public life, nor vice versa. He admired practical good sense and administrative ability, and respected all experts and *métiers* as such, and was very suspicious of abstractions and theories in his own subject, which he regarded as essentially applied and not 'pure'. On the other hand, he was not militantly anti-intellectual; he liked any evidence of mental power or elegance; and suffered from neither of those two notorious occupational 'complexes' of dons – a repressed yearning for spectacular worldly success and influence, and a resentful *odium academicum* of those who aspire to it.

His attitude to the great world was balanced and harmonious. He was little worried by official reputations and liked associating

---

[1] *Oxford University Gazette* 83 (1952–3), 85.

with anyone whom he regarded as intelligent, enjoyable or interesting; and of these qualities he was a very good judge. He avoided fools and bores but gave even them little reason for offence. He liked thinking for its own sake and had a streak of imaginative poetry which used to emerge when, in the intimacy of sympathetic company, he would describe old friends or episodes in his Cambridge or London life. His behaviour was always wonderfully normal; there were no antics, no idiosyncrasies, no virtuoso flights, no conscious exercise of charm, no display; yet he felt neither jealousy of such behaviour nor disapproval. He did not resent or dislike cleverness or temperament in others, nor did he resent dimness or pedantry. But he disliked histrionic exhibitions, and every form of hollowness and falsity; he liked the dry and not the wet, the clear and not the obscure, however rich and suggestive. When an occasion presented itself, he took obvious pleasure in torpedoing arguments or schemes which appeared to him foolish or pretentious. He had an acute, ironical humour, was obstinate under attack, and could not be either snubbed or bullied. Ambition he did not seem to me to have, but he had much dignity and a proper sense of his own worth which was never obtruded, but emitted quiet radiations of its own. He did not speak unless he had something to say, and because he often had, talked a great deal, and because he had no fondness for small talk, was also often silent. His mind was just, acute and liberal, free from all personal and social prejudice, distinguished, serious, humane; above all, he was an exceptionally nice man, who remained detached from the normal academic categories, an independent human being on his own; and his premature death was a very great loss to his College and to his University.

J. L. AUSTIN AND THE EARLY BEGINNINGS
OF OXFORD PHILOSOPHY

THE PHILOSOPHICAL trend which afterwards came to be called
'Oxford Philosophy' originated principally in weekly discussions
by a small group of young Oxford philosophers – the oldest was
twenty-seven – which began some time in 1936–7. They were
suggested by J. L. Austin, who remained their leading spirit until
the War brought them to an end. Austin was elected to a
Fellowship at All Souls in the autumn of 1933. He had not then
fully decided on a philosophical career. He was convinced, so he
used to say, that philosophy, as taught in Oxford, was an excellent
training for young men; there was no better way of making them
rational – in those days his highest term of praise – if only because
it generated in them a critical, indeed a sceptical, attitude, the only
antidote, in his view, to what he called 'being chuckle-headed'. He
was to modify his view later: even philosophy as he taught it
proved, in his view, helpless against the traditional pieties and naïve
beliefs of some of his most gifted pupils. He complained that, so far
from undermining their conventional opinions, all his efforts left
the majority of them incurably respectable and dully virtuous. He
knew that he possessed exceptional capacities as a teacher, but he
also had a strong desire to do something more concrete and more
practical, a job of work, something for which, at the end of the day,
there was more to show. He used to tell me that he regretted that
he had spent so much time on the classics instead of learning to be
an engineer, or an architect. However, it was now too late for that:
he was resigned to remaining a theorist. He had a passion for
accurate, factual information, rigorous analysis, testable conclusions, the ability to put things together and to take them to pieces
again, and detested vagueness, obscurity, abstraction, evasion of
issues by escape into metaphor or rhetoric or jargon or metaphysical fantasy. He was from the beginning determined to try to reduce
whatever could be so reduced to plain prose.

Despite his admiration for practical experts, he was, in fact, himself preoccupied by purely philosophical questions, and, when he first came to All Souls, appeared to think about little else. The two living philosophers whom he most admired were Russell and Prichard, the first for his original genius, independence of mind, and powers of exposition; the second because he seemed to him the most rigorous and minute thinker to be found in Oxford at that time. Austin accepted neither Prichard's premises nor his conclusions, but he admired the single-mindedness and tautness of his arguments, and the ferocity and the total lack of respect for great names with which Prichard rejected obscurity and lack of consistency in philosophy, ancient and modern. His own doctrine of the performative function of words seems to me to owe a good deal to Prichard's painful self-questionings, about, for example, the logical character of promises. 'People say that if I say "I agree" to this or that I create rights that were not there before,' Prichard would say. '*Create* rights? What does this mean? Blowed if I know.' Austin did not think this, or Prichard's discussion of the nature of moral obligation, to be either unimportant or ill formulated, and talked about it (to me) a great deal in 1933–5.

Our conversations usually began after breakfast in the smoking room at All Souls. When I had pupils to teach I left him by 11 a.m.; but on other mornings I seem to recollect that we often talked until lunch-time. He had at that time no settled philosophical position, no doctrine to impart. He would simply seize on some current topic of the day, some proposition uttered by a writer or a lecturer, and cut it into smaller and smaller pieces with a degree of skill and intellectual concentration which I met in no one else until I listened to G. E. Moore. The most admired philosopher of the 1930s in Oxford was, I should say, Henry Price, whose lucid, ingenious and beautifully elegant lectures fascinated his audiences, and were largely responsible for putting problems of perception in the centre of Oxford philosophical attention at this time. The counter-influence, so far as the young philosophers were concerned, was the mounting revolt against the entire traditional conception of philosophy as a source of knowledge about the universe. It was led by A. J. Ayer, whose paper on Wittgenstein's *Tractatus*, read, I think, in the spring of 1932, was the opening shot in the great positivist campaign. *Language, Truth and Logic* had not yet been published; nor had Ryle's views yet advanced, publicly at any rate, beyond 'Systematically Misleading Expressions'.[1] Nevertheless the positivist attack, especially in the form of the early articles by John Wisdom at that time appearing in *Mind*, became a source of illumination and excitement to the younger philosophers, and of considerable scandal to their elders. A sweeping anti-metaphysical empiricism was gaining converts rapidly. Price alone, at this time, while in some respects an Oxford realist, showed understanding and sympathy for the new movement, and was regarded by its members as something of an ally in the adversary's camp.

The movement grew apace. It had invaded the pages of *Mind*, and had its own house journal in *Analysis*. This was a source of deep distress and indeed despair to the most influential among the older Oxford philosophers – Prichard, Joseph, Joachim. They reacted very differently. Joachim, who was one of the last and most scrupulous and civilised representatives of moderate Continental Idealism, and lived in a world inhabited by Aristotle, Spinoza, Kant, Hegel and Bradley, ignored this wave as an aberration, a temporary recession to a crude barbarism and irrationality – a view expressed in their different fashions and more passionately by Collingwood and Mure, although Collingwood thought Ayer a much worthier and indeed more dangerous opponent than Joseph, Prichard and their disciples. As for Prichard, he evidently felt contempt for and lack of interest in what appeared to him to be the recurrence of fallacies long exposed, something that belonged to a far cruder order of thought than that of the great sophists who opposed the realist philosophy when he was a young man – Bradley and Bosanquet. But he was so intensely preoccupied by his own continuous effort to 'worry things out', as he called it, and so painfully conscious of his own inability to arrive at adequate formulations of the answers to the questions that tormented him, both epistemological and ethical – the former derived from Cook Wilson, the latter from Kant and the Protestant tradition – that he had no time for dealing with the confusions and errors of his juniors, most of whom he suspected of wasting their time, and in none of whom he was much interested.

The man who suffered most deeply was probably Joseph. He had a very acute sense of the true tradition which he felt it his duty to defend – a tradition which he received at the hands of his deeply

---

[1] *Proceedings of the Aristotelian Society* 32 (1931–2), 139–70; reprinted in Ryle's *Collected Papers* (London, 1971), vol. 2.

admired master Cook Wilson, whose name and fame, despite all his disciples' efforts, are still confined – so far as they survive at all – to Oxford. Plato, Aristotle, to some degree the rationalists, and again Cook Wilson – these Joseph defended to the end of his days. The deadliest enemies of this kind of realist metaphysics were no longer the Idealists, whose day, he agreed with his pupil Prichard, was done, but the empiricists and sceptics headed by the father of fallacies, Hume, followed by Mill, William James, Russell and other intellectually and morally subversive writers whose doctrines he conceived it as his duty to refute and root out. All his life he had been engaged on the great task of weeding the garden of philosophy; and I believe that there were times when he thought that the great task to which he had been called, of restoring the ancient truths, was at last being achieved, at least in the English-speaking world. But as the 1920s wore on, and the '30s began, he saw with horror that rank weeds were springing up again, and not least in Oxford itself, mainly from seeds wafted across from Cambridge – blatant fallacies propagated by Ramsey, Braithwaite, Ayer and their allies, aided and abetted by various pragmatists in the United States. All these ancient heresies were abroad once more, and evidently influenced the young, as if their shallowness and speciousness had not been exposed over and over again by the faithful band of Cook Wilson's disciples. His last lecture, held in New College garden, was a tremendous onslaught on Russell and Co. He died, I suspect, in a state of intellectual despair – the truth was drowning in a sea of falsehoods, a disaster which he was never able to explain to himself.

Austin was himself one of these dangerous empiricists, although he was not a militant controversialist at this stage; nor was his empiricism inhibited by fidelity to any particular tradition. He was not doctrinaire. He did not hold with programmes. He did not wish to destroy one establishment in the interests of another. He treated problems piecemeal as they came, not as part of a systematic reinterpretation. That effort, in so far as it was made (and of course he did try to develop a coherent doctrine of philosophical method), took place much later. I do not think that I ever heard him say anything during this period, that is, before the beginning of the War, which sprang from, or was clearly intended to support, any kind of systematic view. I do not know whether his pupils in Magdalen will bear me out, but it seems to me that he addressed himself to the topics which were part of the then normal curriculum in Oxford with no conscious revolutionary intent. But, of course, he had a very clear, acute and original intellect, and because, when he spoke, there appeared to be nothing between him and the subject of his criticism or exposition – no accumulation of traditional commentary, no spectacles provided by a particular doctrine – he often produced the feeling that the question was being posed clearly for the first time: that what had seemed blurred, or trite, or a play of conventional formulae in the books had suddenly been washed away: the problem stood out in sharp relief, clear, unanswered and important, and the methods used to analyse it had a surgical sharpness, and were used with fascinating assurance and apparently effortless skill.

He always, in those days at any rate, answered one in one's own terminology when he understood what was said to him; he did not pretend that it was not clear until it had been translated into his own language, some special set of terms of his own. In private he used no rhetorical tricks of any kind, and displayed an extraordinary power of distinguishing what was genuine or interesting in what his collocutor said from what was not – from ideological patter, or nervous confusion, or the like. This was not always so in public: opposition made him combative, and in classes or meetings of societies he plainly wished to emerge victorious. But this did not happen, so far as my own experience goes, in private conversation, at any rate not in the presence of those with whom he felt comfortable and unthreatened. I do not mean to say that he was not by temperament dogmatic: he was. But he argued patiently and courteously, and if he failed to convince one, returned to the topic over and over again, with new and highly imaginative examples and first-hand arguments which were intellectually exhilarating whether they produced conviction or not. He still remained throughout this time sceptical about the value of philosophy, except as an educational instrument; but he could not break himself from it: whenever we met during the 1930s he invariably found opportunity of raising some philosophical question, and left one not so much with a set of firm and well-argued positions as with a series of philosophical question-marks strewn along the path, which stopped those who listened to him from resting in the comfortable beds of accepted opinion. I think he was much more authoritarian after the War, and did not, at any rate in public, move his pieces until the entire plan of campaign had been thoroughly thought out, and he felt secure against any possible refutation. One of the criticisms made of him – I think a just one – was that he refused to advance rather than face the smallest possible risk of successful counter-argument. Even so, this did not hold so much in private (I speak only for myself); in the 1930s his pride and his sense of his own position were not so evidently in play, nor did he conceive philosophy as a set of doctrines and a method to which it was his mission to convert the ignorant and the mistaken. It was not until a later period that his philosophical activity became a consciously planned campaign for the dissemination of the truth.

When Ayer's *Language, Truth and Logic* was published in 1936, Austin expressed great admiration for it, and then proceeded to criticise it, during our afternoon walks, page by page and sentence by sentence, without wishing to score points (he did not get far beyond the first chapter, so far as I can remember). Certainly his later polemical ferocity was less in evidence, at any rate so far as the works of his contemporaries – the articles in *Mind* or in *Analysis* on which we fed – were concerned. In 1936, after he had been at Magdalen for about a year he came to my rooms in All Souls one evening and asked me what I had been reading. Had I been reading any Soviet philosophy, and was any of it worth reading? He had visited the Soviet Union as a tourist and had been impressed by his experience. He was attracted by the austerity and sternness and dedication of the grey, impersonal-looking men and women whom he had seen there, had detected the growth of nationalism (of which he did not disapprove) and of admiration (which he shared) for the great men who had worked against gigantic odds, Marx and Lenin for example. His admiration for the founders of Communism was, I think, short-lived. His favourite examples of intellectual virtue in later years were Darwin and Freud, not because he particularly admired their views, but because he believed that once a man had assured himself that his hypothesis was worth pursuing at all, he should pursue it to its logical end, whatever the consequences, and not be deterred by fear of seeming eccentric or fanatical, or by the control of philistine common sense. If the logical consequences were in fact untenable, one would be able to withdraw or modify them in the light of the undeniable evidence; but if one failed to explore a hypothesis to its full logical conclusions, the truth would for ever be defeated by timid respectability. He said that a fearless thinker, pursuing a chosen path unswervingly against mutterings and warnings and criticism, was the proper object of admiration and emulation; fanaticism was preferable to cowardice, and imagination to dreary good sense.

What about Soviet thought? I replied that I had not read anything by any contemporary Communist philosopher which I could genuinely recommend to him – nothing since Ralph Fox, the only English Marxist Austin had read or thought worth reading. But I had, a year or two before, read an interesting book on philosophy called *Mind and the World-Order* by C. I. Lewis, a professor at Harvard of whom I had not previously heard. It says much for the philosophical insulation and self-centredness of Oxford (and other English universities at that time) that so little about American philosophy should have been known to my colleagues and myself. I had come across this book by pure chance on a table in Blackwell's bookshop, had opened it and thought that it looked interesting. I bought it, read it, and thought that its pragmatist transformation of Kantian categories was original and fruitful. I lent it to Austin, who left me almost immediately. He told me that instead of playing his violin – he used to go through unaccompanied Bach partitas evening by evening – he began reading it at once. Three days later he suggested to me that we should hold a class on this book, which had also impressed him.

I may be mistaken about this, but I think that this was the first class or seminar on a contemporary thinker ever held in Oxford. Austin's reputation as a teacher was by this time considerable, and a relatively large number of undergraduates came once a week to our class in All Souls. I had no notion how joint classes were held, and assumed that their holders would begin by a dialogue on points provided by the text, in which they would show each other the almost exaggerated respect which was then common form at philosophical debates among dons. Austin opened by inviting me to expound a thesis. I selected Lewis's doctrine of specific, sensible characteristics – what Lewis called *qualia* – and said what I thought. Austin glared at me sternly and said, 'Would you mind saying that again.' I did so. 'It seems to me', said Austin, speaking slowly, 'that what you have just said is complete nonsense.' I then realised that this was to be no polite shadow-fencing, but war to the death – my death, that is. There is no doubt that Austin's performance at our class had a profound and lasting effect upon some, at any rate, of those who attended it. Some of them later became eminent professional philosophers and have testified to the extraordinary force and fertility of Austin's performance. For a performance it undoubtedly was: as much so as Moore's annual classes held at the joint meetings of the Aristotelian Society and Mind Association. Slow, formidable and relentless, Austin dealt firmly with criticism and opposition of the intelligent and stupid alike, and, in the course of this, left the genuine philosophers in our class not crushed or frustrated, but stimulated and indeed excited by the simplicity and lucidity of the nominalist thesis which he defended against Lewis. 'If there are three vermilion patches on this piece of paper how many vermilions are there?' 'One,' said I. 'I say there are three,' said Austin, and we spent the rest of the term on this issue. Austin conducted the class like a formidable professor at the Harvard Law School. He put questions to the class. If, petrified by terror, everyone remained silent, he would extend a long, thin finger, and after oscillating it slowly to and fro for a minute, like the muzzle of a pistol, would suddenly shoot it forward, pointing at some man, chosen at random, and say in a loud, nervous voice: '*You* answer!' The victim would, at times, be too terrorised to utter. Austin would realise this, answer himself, and return to our normal conditions of discussion. Despite these somewhat terrifying moments, the class remained undiminished in numbers and intensity of interest. We spent the term on nominalism. It was the best class that I have ever attended, and seems to me to mark the true beginning of Austin's career as an independent thinker.

At the end of the summer of 1936 Austin suggested that we hold regular philosophical discussions about topics which interested us and our contemporaries among Oxford philosophers. He wished the group to meet informally, without any thought of publishing our 'results' (if we ever obtained any), or any purpose but that of clearing our minds and pursuing the truth. We agreed to invite Ayer, Macnabb and Woozley, all of whom were at that time teaching philosophy at Oxford; to these Stuart Hampshire, who had been elected to All Souls, and Donald MacKinnon, who had become a Fellow of Keble, were added. The meetings began some time in 1936–7 (I think in the spring of 1937). They took place on Thursdays in my rooms in All Souls after dinner, and continued, with a few intervals, until the summer of 1939. In retrospect they seem to me the most fruitful discussions of philosophy at which I was ever present. The topics were not carefully prepared, nor necessarily announced beforehand, although I think we knew from week to week what we were likely to talk about. The principal topics were four in number: perception – theories of sense data as Price and Broad discussed them; a priori truths, that is, propositions which appeared necessarily true or false, and yet did not appear reducible to rules or definitions and what these entailed; the verification and logical character of counter-factual statements, which I think, in those days, we called unfulfilled hypotheticals or contra-factuals; and the nature and criteria of personal identity, and the related topic of our knowledge of other minds.

When I mentioned perception as one of our subjects, I should have said that what we talked about was principally phenomenalism and the theory of verification with which it was closely bound up, topics on which Ayer held strong, characteristically clear, and well-known opinions. Austin attacked the entire sense-datum terminology, and asked what the criteria of identity of a sense datum were: if one's field of vision contained seven yellow and black stripes like a tiger-skin, did it contain, or consist of, let us say, seven black data and seven yellow ones, or one continuous striped datum? What was the average size of a datum, and what was its average life-span? When could it be said that a single datum changed colour or faded or vanished, or were there as many data as there were hues or saturations of colours or timbres or pitches of sounds? How did one count them? Were there *minima sensibilia* and did they vary from observer to observer? All this apart from the by that time familiar question of how the concept of the observer was itself to be analysed.

Ayer defended positivism and wished to know, if phenomenalism were abandoned, what was to be put in its place. Did Austin suppose that there existed impalpable substrata either in the old, crude Lockean sense, or in the sense in which some modern scientists and philosophers, who were no less confused and much less consistent or honest than Locke, maintained or presupposed the existence of equally unverifiable and metaphysical entities? I cannot remember that Austin ever tried to furnish any positive answers to these questions, or, to begin with at any rate, to formulate any doctrine of his own; he preferred, undoubtedly, to drill holes into solutions provided by others. It was, I think, in the course of one of these sceptical onslaughts, after four or five formulations of the reductionist thesis of pure phenomenalism had been shot down by Austin, that Ayer exclaimed: 'You are like a greyhound who doesn't want to run himself, and bites the other greyhounds, so that they cannot run either.'[1]

There was certainly something of this about Austin. I do not remember that he did altogether, before the War, come out of the wood on phenomenalism; but he did begin saying even then that he could not see that there was all that much wrong with ordinary language as used about the external world. The problems raised by, for example, optical illusions – double images, sticks bent in water, tricks of perspective and the like – were due to the ambiguities of language, mistakenly analysed by philosophers, and not to implausible non-empirical beliefs. Berkeley, whom he admired as against Locke and Hume, was, in his view, right about this. A stick that was 'really' bent was of course something quite different from a stick 'bent in water', and once the laws of the refraction of light were discovered, no confusion need occur: being bent was one thing, and looking bent was another; if a stick were plunged in water and did *not* look bent, then indeed there would be occasion for surprise. The sense-datum language was a sub-language, used for specific purposes to describe the works of impressionist painters, or called for by physicians who asked their patients to describe their symptoms – an artificial usage carved out of ordinary language – language which was sufficient for most everyday purposes and did not itself tend to mislead.

As may be imagined, Ayer, and perhaps others amongst us, stoutly resisted this frontal attack upon the views of Moore and Russell, Broad and Price, and the rejection of the entire apparatus and terminology of the English school of the theory of perception. These discussions led to the emergence of 'Oxford Analysis', not so much as a consequence of Austin's specific theses, as from the appeal to common linguistic usage which was made by us all, without, so far as I recollect, any conscious reference at the time to Wittgenstein's later doctrines, even though the 'Blue Book' was already in circulation in Cambridge, and had, I think, by 1937 or so, arrived in Oxford.

Similar methods were used in discussing counter-factual statements – their extension and their relation to the verification

---

[1] This may have been stimulated by a remark made by Donald Macnabb to the effect that our discussions reminded him of nothing so much as a pack of hounds in full cry (after, presumably, the truth).

principle[1] – as well as the problems of personal identity and its relation to memory. If I remember rightly, the principal example of the latter that we chose was the hero of Kafka's story *Metamorphosis*, a commercial traveller called Gregor Samsa, who wakes one morning to find that he has been transformed into a monstrous cockroach, although he retains clear memories of his life as an ordinary human being. Are we to speak of him as a man with the body of a cockroach, or as a cockroach with the memories and consciousness of a man? 'Neither,' Austin declared. 'In such cases we should not know what to say. This is when we say "Words fail us" and mean this literally. We should need new words. The old ones just would not fit. They aren't meant to cover this kind of case.' From this we wandered to the asymmetry, or apparent asymmetry, between the analysis of propositions made by the speaker about himself and those made by him about others; this was treated from correspondingly differing standpoints by Austin and Ayer, who gradually became the protagonists of two irreconcilable points of view. Austin's particular philosophical position was developed, it seems to me, during those Thursday evenings, in continuous contrast with, and opposition to, the positivism and reductionism of Ayer and his supporters. I do not mean to imply that Austin and Ayer entirely dominated the discussions, and that the rest of us were scarcely more than listeners. We all talked a great deal,[2] although if I asked myself what I myself said or believed, apart from criticising the verification principle, and pure Carnapian logical positivism, I should find it hard to say. All I can recollect is that there was no crystallisation into permanent factions: views changed from week to week, save that Ayer and Austin were seldom, if ever, in agreement about anything.

The discussion of what, for short, I shall call a priori statements

---

[1] As an example, I might say 'If a horse called Sylvia runs in this race it will undoubtedly win.' Suppose no such horse ran or even existed, and I am subsequently asked why I thought that it would win. If I answer that I believed this although – or even because – it was an irrational proposition, that I felt inclined to gamble on its truth because I like gambling, that I had not the slightest desire to know whether there was, or could be, any evidence for the proposition, it seems to follow that the meaning of the counter-factual is detached from 'the means of its verification' in however 'weak' a sense, even if the question of its truth is not.

[2] And interrupted each other unceremoniously; so much so that Austin, with his passion for order, proposed that we acquire 'a buzzer' to introduce discipline. The suggestion was not taken up.

arose out of a paper read by Russell in 1935 to the Cambridge Moral Sciences Club, which Austin and I attended, on 'The Limits of Empiricism'.[1] The thesis was that while such propositions as 'The same object [or surface, or portion of my visual field, or whatever was substituted for this] cannot be red and green at the same time in the same place' appeared to be incontrovertibly true beyond the possibility of falsification, their contradictories did not seem to be self-contradictory. This was so because their truth did not appear to follow from verbal definitions, but from the meaning of colour words, the use of which was learnt or explained by acts of pointing – was fixed by means of what, in those days, used to be called 'ostensive definitions'. The contradictories of such propositions, therefore, seemed better described as absurd or meaningless or unintelligible, and not as contradictions in terms. This stimulated long discussions about verbal and non-verbal definitions, the relation of Carnap's syntactical properties to semantic ones, the difference between the relations of words to words and the relations of words to things, and so on.

The dissimilarity of approach between Austin and Ayer once more showed itself very clearly. Ayer, if he perceived that a given theory entailed consequences which, he was certain, were false or absurd, for example, the existence of impalpable entities or some other gross breach of the verification principle, even in its so-called 'weak' form, felt that the whole argument must be proceeding on fallacious lines, and was prepared to reject the premisses, and try to think of new ones from which these undesirable consequences would not follow. Austin looked at whatever was placed before him, and was ready to follow the argument wherever it led.

It was later maintained by some of his critics (at least in conversation) that this philosophical spontaneity and apparent freedom from preconceived doctrine were not altogether genuine: that in fact they were elaborate Socratic devices which concealed a fully worked-out positive doctrine which he was not yet ready to reveal. I believe this to be false. In 1936–9 he had a philosophically open mind. Indeed, at that time he was full of suspicion of any cut and dried doctrine; if anything, he seemed to take active pleasure in advancing propositions which appeared to him true or at any rate plausible, whatever havoc they might wreak with the systematic

---

[1] The paper was read on 28 November 1935, and published in the *Proceedings of the Aristotelian Society* 36 (1935–6), 131–50.

ideas of writers in, say, *Erkenntnis* or *Analysis*. He was certainly
not free from a certain degree of malicious pleasure in blowing up
carefully constructed philosophical edifices – he did like stopping
the other greyhounds – but his main purpose seemed to me, then
and afterwards, to be the establishing of particular truths with a
view to generalising from them, or eliciting principles at a later
stage. He certainly wished to 'save the appearances', and in this
sense was a follower of Aristotle and not of Plato, of Berkeley and
not of Hume. He disliked clear-cut dichotomies – between, for
instance, universals and particulars (as distinguished in C. I.
Lewis's book), or descriptive and emotive language, or empirical
and logical truths, or verifiable and unverifiable, corrigible and
incorrigible expressions – all such claims to clear and exhaustive
contrasts seeming to him incapable of doing the job they were
expected to do, namely to classify the normal use of words. It
seemed to him then, as it did later, that types and distinctions of
meaning were often reflected in ordinary language. Ordinary
language was not an infallible guide; it was at best a pointer to
distinctions in the subject-matter which language was used to
describe, or express, or to which it was related in some other
fashion; and these important distinctions tended to be obliterated
by the clear-cut dichotomies advanced by the all-or-nothing
philosophies, which in their turn led to unacceptable doctrines
about what there was, and what men meant. Hence when Russell
or others gave examples of propositions asserting irreducible
incompatibilities between Lewis's *qualia* – colours, sounds, tastes
and the like – propositions which did not seem either analytic or
empirical; or when, to take another example, it was maintained that
singular counter-factual statements could be not only understood,
but actually believed, even though it was difficult to see how they
could be verified, even in principle – Austin seized on these
examples and developed them with great force and brilliance,
partly, I suspect, from a desire to discover negative instances which
would blow up general propositions that had been brought to bear
too easily, like distorting moulds, on the complex and recalcitrant
nature of things. He had an immense respect for the natural
sciences, but he believed that the only reliable method of learning
about types of action, knowledge, belief, experience consisted in
the patient accumulation of data about actual usage. Usage was
certainly not regarded by him as sacrosanct, in the sense of
reflecting reality in some infallible fashion, or of being a guaranteed

nostrum against confusions and fallacies. But it was neglected at our peril: Austin did have a Burkean belief that differences of usage did, as a rule, reflect differences of meaning, and conceptual differences too, and thus offered a valuable and relatively neglected path towards establishing distinctions of meaning, of concepts, of possible states of affairs, and in this way did help to clear away muddles and remove obstacles to the discovery of truth. Above all, philosophy was not a set of mechanisms into which untutored expressions had to be fed, and from which they would emerge classified, clarified, straightened out, and cleansed of their delusive properties.

In this sense Austin did not much believe in a specifically philosophical technology – the proliferation of gadgets to deal with difficulties. No doubt his insatiable interest in language and philology as such had something to do with this, and his superb classical scholarship fed his inordinate collector's curiosity, at times at the expense of genuinely philosophical issues. Nevertheless, his implicit rejection of the doctrine of a logically perfect language, which was capable of reflecting the structure of reality, sprang from a philosophical vision not dissimilar to that of Wittgenstein, whose then unpublished but illicitly circulated views he might possibly have looked at, though he did not, I think, pay serious attention to them before the War. Certainly his first published contribution to philosophy – the paper on a priori concepts in which a good deal of his positive doctrine is embodied[1] – owes, so far as I know, nothing to any acquaintance with Wittgenstein's views, unless perhaps, very indirectly, via John Wisdom's articles, which he certainly read.

Occasionally those who met on Thursday evenings talked about moral problems, but this was regarded as an escape, not to be repeated too often, from the sterner demands of the subject. We certainly discussed freedom of the will, in the course of which Austin said to me, *sotto voce*, so as not to provoke Freddie Ayer, who was at that time a convinced determinist, 'They all *talk* about determinism and *say* they believe in it. I've never met a determinist in my life, I mean a man who really did believe in it as you and I believe that men are mortal. Have you?' This endeared him to me

---

[1] 'Are there a priori concepts?', *Proceedings of the Aristotelian Society* supplementary vol. 18 (1939), 83–105; reprinted in Austin's *Philosophical Papers* (Oxford, 1961; 3rd ed., 1979).

greatly. So did his answer to a question that I once put to him during a walk. I asked: 'Supposing a child were to express a wish to meet Napoleon as he was at the battle of Austerlitz, and I said "It cannot be done", and the child said "Why not?", and I said "Because it happened in the past, and you cannot be alive now and also a hundred and thirty years ago and remain at the same age", or something of the kind; and the child went on pressing and said "Why not?", and I said "Because it does not make sense, as we use words, to say that you can be in two places at once or 'go back' into the past", and so on; and this highly sophisticated child said "If it is only a question of words, then can't we simply alter our verbal usage? Would that enable me to see Napoleon at the battle of Austerlitz, and also, of course, stay as I am now, in place and time?" – What [I asked Austin] should one say to the child? Simply that it has confused the material and formal modes, so to speak?' Austin replied: 'Do not speak so. Tell the child to try and go back into the past. Tell it there is no law against it. Let it try. Let it try, and see what happens then.' It seems to me now, as it seemed to me before the last war, that Austin understood the nature of philosophy, even if he was over-pedantic and over-cautious, and insisted on making over-sure of his defences before plunging into the arena – understood, better than most, what philosophy was.

These discussions were fruitful for several reasons: because the number of those who took part in them was small (it never rose above seven and was usually smaller than that); because the participants knew each other well, talked very freely, and were in no sense on show; they were totally spontaneous, and knew that if they went down some false path which led to a precipice or a marsh it did not matter, for they could retrace their steps, whenever they pleased, in the weeks to come. Moreover the intellectual freshness and force, both of Austin and of Ayer, were such that although they were in a state of almost continuous collision – Ayer like an irresistible missile, Austin like an immovable obstacle – the result was not a stalemate, but the most interesting, free and lively discussions of philosophy that I have ever known.

One of the shortcomings of these meetings is something that seems to me to apply to Oxford philosophy in general, at least in those days. We were excessively self-centred. The only persons whom we wished to convince were our own admired colleagues.

There was no pressure upon us to publish. Consequently, when we succeeded in gaining from one of our philosophical peers acceptance or even understanding of some point which we regarded as original and important, whether rightly or, as was more often the case at any rate with me, in a state of happy delusion, this satisfied us completely, too completely. We felt no need to publish our ideas, for the only audience which was worth satisfying was the handful of our contemporaries who lived near us, and whom we met with agreeable regularity. I don't think that, like Moore's disciples at the beginning of the century, of whom Keynes speaks in a memoir on his early ideas,[1] any of us thought that no one before us had discovered the truth about the nature of knowledge or anything else; but, like them, we did think that no one outside the magic circle – in our case Oxford, Cambridge, Vienna – had much to teach us. This was vain and foolish and, I have no doubt, irritating to others. But I suspect that those who have never been under the spell of this kind of illusion, even for a short while, have not known true intellectual happiness.

---

[1] 'My Early Beliefs', in John Maynard Keynes, *Two Memoirs* (London, 1949); reprinted in *The Collected Writings of John Maynard Keynes* (London, 1971–89), vol. 10, *Essays in Biography*.

JOHN PETROV PLAMENATZ

JOHN PLAMENATZ was born in 1912 in Cetinje, the capital of Montenegro. Both his parents belonged to the ruling families of that old, pre-industrial, half-pastoral society, and although his life was lived almost entirely in England, his imagination and his feelings were dominated by his deep attachment to his native land. In 1917, when he was five years old, he was taken by his father to France, and soon after that to England, where he was placed in Clayesmore School, near Winchester, whose headmaster his father knew. There he stayed for the next eleven years, while the school moved from place to place, until he came to Oriel College, Oxford, in 1930. From time to time his parents summoned him to visit them during his school holidays, to Marseilles or Vienna, but for long stretches of time he lived apart from his family, and became used to solitude. He spent four years at Oriel; illness prevented him from completing his papers in PPE and he obtained an *aegrotat*; and, a year later, a First in History. In 1936 he was elected to All Souls, the first Fellow to be elected by thesis since Dearle, early in the century.

He spent the rest of his life in Oxford, and his work and his influence are part of the intellectual history of Britain and of that university. But there is a sense in which he remained in exile all his life. He was never wholly assimilated either to England or to Oxford: when he said 'we' – 'This is the way we think', or 'This is how it is with us' – he usually meant Montenegrins. He once said to me that he had made personal friends among individual English people; that he could feel at home with two or three at a time; but that when more than two or three were gathered in a room, he would become aware of a relationship *between* them, from which he felt excluded. He explained this by saying that he was rooted in a remote culture, that the sudden break in early childhood – the emigration to an alien environment – had forced him to turn, to some degree, in upon himself. Those who knew him can testify to the fact that, like Joseph Conrad (whom in some ways he resembled), all his life he displayed the pride and independence of a noble exile.

'Displayed' is the wrong term: John Plamenatz displayed nothing; he was reserved and reticent; he did not seek to put himself forward or impose his personality in any way on any occasion that I know of. He spoke his mind with candour and precision, and with the great natural courtesy that was an essential attribute of his character; yet, at times, one could not be sure about what was going on inside his mind – there was something remote and unapproachable about him; but when one came to know him well, this melted – he was a warm and affectionate friend. But neither friendship nor its absence ever blinded him to human character and motives; he was acutely perceptive – that somewhat myopic eye saw a very great deal. He was occasionally deceived by persons and situations, but not often. Above all, he was not anxious to judge. At times he commented upon individuals, or on the social scene, with amused irony, but in general he showed the kind of tolerance that only deeply civilised or saintly people can achieve. But, of course, there were qualities he found unbearable: he disliked shoddiness, triviality, ostentation, stridency, vulgarity and opportunism of every sort; he detested rudeness; he was upset by lack of manners, the sources of which he found it difficult to comprehend. He prized privacy and personal relations above all. He was gentle, dignified and wholly uncompetitive; he was interested in the character of others, and sensitive to their feelings, particularly to the feelings of those who, like himself, wished to walk by themselves and found it difficult to fit in with established social patterns. He spoke to such people more easily, and defended them against the criticisms of those who thought them farouche or unattractive. He understood loneliness, unhappiness, vulnerability better, I think, than anyone I have ever known. All Souls, in the years before the War, was full of animated talk by politicians and academics about the burning social and political questions of the day: John Plamenatz avoided such gatherings; his interest in the problems was just as great as that of a good many others, and his understanding of them sometimes more sensitive, but he disliked the noise, the jokes, the rivalry, the repartee, the high spirits – genuine or false – of such exchanges. He seldom attended gaudies.

College meetings were another matter. These he took very

seriously and, though he spoke little, when he did intervene the effect was sometimes decisive: he spoke quietly, with obvious conviction, without the slightest hint of rhetoric. He did not speak unless he had something of central relevance to say or ask: his motives were so completely free from any touch of calculation, his sincerity was so evident, that his apparently simple statements or questions, penetrating as they often did to the heart of some debated issue, tended to have a devastating effect. The word 'integrity' might have been invented for him. His words were listened to with deep respect, and on the rare occasions when he felt genuinely moved, he almost always carried the day. The independence, the scrupulous regard for the truth, the shining impartiality of his judgement were a unique moral asset to every society of which he was a member. It was so at All Souls, and, I am told, it was so at Nuffield also.

It was a singular irony, therefore, that the D.Phil. thesis that he submitted should have been failed by the examiners, on the ground, it was rumoured, of 'lack of judgement'. This was the very thesis on the strength of which he was, a little later, elected to All Souls. When it was published, its quality was plain for all to see. He came to be critical of it himself in later years. Nevertheless, it was, in the opinion of competent critics, probably the best work on political theory produced by anyone in Oxford since the First World War.[1] It was the first in a long line of books that did more than any other single factor to transform the level of the entire discussion of political theory in Oxford. His work served to raise its standards to that of serious philosophical argument. The judgement passed upon it was perhaps the greatest miscarriage of academic justice known to my generation. He was, of course, hurt by it at the time, but in the end ignored it – it left no obvious wound.

His intellectual weapons were derived from that sober, pre-positivist, pre-linguistic, realist tradition in moral philosophy to which his tutor, W. G. Maclagan, belonged, and which was dominant in Oxford in the early 1930s. The purpose of its method was to state the arguments – one's own or those of others, particularly the great thinkers of the past – in the clearest possible fashion – to avoid all vagueness, obscurity, rhetoric, confusion; to expose incoherence; to arrive, by the use of rational methods, at

---

[1] *Consent, Freedom and Political Obligation* (London, 1938).

conclusions acceptable to reasonable and self-critical beings. He believed in this method and defended it, and used it all his life. His purpose was to elucidate and criticise the ideas of those writers who seemed to him to address themselves to problems that were central to men everywhere and at all times. Like Machiavelli, he found a door into a timeless world of the great figures of the past, and questioned them, and sought to understand their basic concepts, their views of man and of society, of what they were and should be. He was never pedantic, and he did not niggle. If the thinkers whom he examined seemed to him dark or confused or even dishonest, he persevered with them if they appeared to him to reveal even glimpses of something important or profound about man's nature, his goals, or his moral or political experience or needs. And while he found clear writers like Machiavelli or Hobbes or the Utilitarians, if not more congenial, at least easier to deal with, he struggled with formidable and difficult theorists in whom he perceived glimmers of genius – Hegel, Marx and his followers – like Jacob wrestling with the Angel of the Lord, who could not let him go until he had received his reward.

His chapters on Hegel and Marx are among the clearest and most valuable expositions of these thinkers in the English language. He worked on these texts with immense tenacity, reading and rereading, writing and rewriting, paying the most scrupulous attention to the criticisms of friends and colleagues, and was more critical of his own work than others were. When argued with, he held on to his own positions with great stubbornness, but nevertheless went back to the texts and to his own commentaries; if the criticisms appeared to him to have any element of justice, he acknowledged them fully and altered his views; the second edition of his book on utilitarianism contains his own review of the first edition, far more severe than anything said by others. His purpose was not to detect inconsistencies in the thought of others, or merely to expose error, or to interpret, but to achieve at least the beginnings of some vision of the complex and elusive truth which thinkers whom he respected seemed to him to approach from this side and from that. His works greatly added to the dignity of the entire subject in England, and indirectly in every English-speaking country.

He was admired by his pupils, and respected by the most distinguished of his opponents, but he occupied no recognisable position and founded no school. Perhaps this was so because he simply said and wrote what seemed to him to be true, in his own unemphatic, careful prose, with all the qualifications that the truth seemed to demand; he did not modify or shape his thought to make it fit into a system, he did not look for a unifying historical or metaphysical structure, he did not exaggerate or over-schematise in order to obtain attention for his ideas – so that those who looked for a system, an entire edifice of thought to attach themselves to, went away dissatisfied. He had no ambition to shine, or to defeat rivals, or to proselytise or found a movement. He only wanted to discover and tell the truth. His methods were essentially English, and indeed local, characteristic of the Oxford of his youth: but they were superimposed on a temperament and outlook very different from the masters who impressed him, Prichard, Ross and the others. His view of human nature and its purposes and its potentialities was taken not only from his reading of the classical philosophers, but equally from his upbringing, from solidarity with, and indeed much nostalgia for, his native land, the customs and outlook of that almost pre-feudal community; and also from his lifelong love of French literature and thought, which he found more sympathetic than its English counterpart. He responded to Donne, Herbert, Wordsworth, but the prose of Montesquieu gave him physical pleasure. The French theatre of the eighteenth century – Marivaux, Jean-Baptiste Rousseau, Beau-marchais – moved him to enthusiasm. His letter to a journal defending Marivaux against charges of shallowness and artificiality, and praising him for true insight and exquisite description of the movements of the shy and innocent human heart, was itself a masterpiece of literary sensibility.

He understood best lonely and unhappy thinkers, who showed the deepest understanding of what men live by, and what frustrates them, of solitude and alienation – he loved best of all Pascal, Jean-Jacques Rousseau – solitary thinkers, given to painful moral and spiritual self-inquisition rather than rational self-examination. He praised Proudhon for knowing what the workers, or the *petit bourgeois*, need, what makes them miserable, because he truly understood them, as the far more gifted Marx, who fitted them into a vast theoretical model, did not bother to do. His acceptance of British empiricism, together with a deeply un-British, romantic vision of the human predicament, imparted to his work a tension that nothing else in English seems to me to have. It was never wholly impersonal: thus, after many pages of sober, Oxford exposition and argument, there would suddenly occur a sharp, original, highly characteristic comment – as when he remarks, 'Passing from German to Russian Marxism, we leave the horses and come to the mules.'[1] In these sudden, often ironical, asides his own authentic voice can be clearly heard. There is something wonderfully fresh, and often devastatingly direct, about these personal passages. Indeed, all his writing was authentic and, as it were, hand-made: it was balanced, unexaggerated, carefully qualified, but nothing in it was mechanical, derived from a model. His books give the impression of being written as if no book on the subject had ever been written before. So, too, with testimonials he wrote for pupils: never over-stated, never conventional, they were illuminated by flashes of acute psychological insight, and carried total conviction. It is this first-hand quality that, added to all its other attributes, lends his work peculiar and irresistible charm.

The War interrupted his work. On Lionel Curtis's advice, he became a member of a somewhat peculiar anti-aircraft battery, which gave full scope for the play of his irony. In time he was transferred to the service of the Yugoslav Embassy, and became a member of the War Cabinet of King Peter. He wrote a pamphlet to answer the detractors of General Mihailovic (it was published in a private, limited edition).[2] After the War he returned to All Souls as a Research Fellow and began to produce a series of essays and books on political thought. In 1951 he was elected to a Fellowship of Nuffield, and in 1967 to the Chair of Social and Political Theory at All Souls.

He told me that a few years later he was visited by some Montenegrin relatives of his, who were engaged in smuggling, I believe, somewhere in the Balkans. They said to him, 'You are a Professor at Oxford – that is a very strange thing for a Montenegrin to be doing.' He added that he thought that they were right. He said he did not feel himself a professor. He found administrative duties a burden; he forced himself to perform them; he attended committees and examined, but without pleasure or satisfaction. He wished to read, to write, to teach. He developed warm personal relations with his pupils; he was an excellent colleague; private life meant far more to him than the busy life of institutions. All Souls suited him better than Nuffield if only

[1] *German Marxism and Russian Communism* (London etc., 1954), p. 191.
[2] *The Case of General Mihailovic* ([London], 1944).

because it made fewer demands on his time. He was grateful to Nuffield, which had come to his aid at a difficult moment; some of his closest friendships were made there. Looking after the college garden gave him genuine pleasure. But what he loved best was privacy. He might have agreed with Pascal that many of the ills of mankind come because men will not stay quietly in a room.

In certain respects he was happier with Americans than he was with the English: like many inward-looking, reticent scholars he was liberated by the openness, the responsiveness, the warmth, the uninhibited natural candour, the unblasé attitude of American students and colleagues, by the deep and genuine desire for the truth with which they sought for answers to intellectual or political problems, by the fact that they took the trouble to understand what he thought and said. He was particularly happy at Columbia University. Yet during the seven long years of his Professorship he longed to be released from it. He was not discontented. Indeed, during his last three or four years, he seemed to me to have grown lighter-hearted, and to have come into something like his own. Friendship, and above all the love and devotion of his wife, were everything to him. He told me that he preferred to live in a village because there relations with neighbours seemed more natural and satisfactory to him – more like the life that human beings have led at all times, everywhere, than artificial existence in an academic enclave.

The heart attack which ultimately proved fatal was the first illness he had had since 1933. He died on 19 February 1975, the very day and month when, fifty-six years before, he had landed at Dover.

His independence, his remoteness from all the least attractive aspects of the life of universities – the idea of trying to involve him in some intrigue was unthinkable – his generous, uncalculating character, his refusal to compromise with whatever seemed to him to distort or ignore or even embellish experience, his distinction as a thinker, his nobility as a human being, were recognised by the academic world here and abroad. He had much pride, but was free from all vanity and snobbery, and treated all men alike: he made no differences between the young and the old, the important and the unimportant, the brilliant and the dull, but behaved towards everyone with the same grave courtesy. He possessed what I can only describe as a quality of moral charm that made all dealings with him delightful. His writings – and this was true of the authors he most admired – were altogether unlike any others. So, in the best and rarest sense, was he.

MAURICE BOWRA

MAURICE BOWRA, scholar, critic and administrator, the greatest English wit of his day, was, above all, a generous and warm-hearted man, whose powerful personality transformed the lives and outlook of many who came under his wide and life-giving influence. According to a contemporary at Cheltenham, he was fully formed by the time he left school for the army in 1916. In firmness of character he resembled his father, of whom he always spoke with deep affection and respect; but unlike him he was rebellious by temperament and, when he came up to New College in 1919, he became the natural leader of a group of intellectually gifted contemporaries, passionately opposed to the conventional wisdom and moral code of those who formed pre-war Oxford opinion. He remained critical of all establishments for ever after.

Bowra loved life in all its manifestations. He loved the sun, the sea, warmth, light, and hated cold and darkness, physical, intellectual, moral, political. All his life he liked freedom, individuality, independence, and detested everything that seemed to him to cramp and constrict the forces of human vitality, no matter what spiritual achievements such self-mortifying asceticism might have to its credit. His passion for the Mediterranean and its cultures was of a piece with this: he loved pleasure, exuberance, the richest fruits of nature and civilisation, the fullest expression of human feeling, uninhibited by a Manichean sense of guilt. Consequently he had little sympathy for those who recoiled from the forces of life – cautious, calculating conformists, or those who seemed to him prigs or prudes who winced at high vitality or passion, and were too easily shocked by vehemence and candour. Hence his impatience with philistine majorities in the academic and official and commercial worlds, and equally with cultural coteries which appeared to him thin, or old-maidish, or disapproving. He believed in fullness of life. Romantic exaggeration, such as he found in the early 1930s in the circle formed round the German poet Stefan George, appealed to him far more than British reticence. With a temperament that resembled men of an older generation – Winston Churchill or Thomas Beecham – he admired genius, splendour, eloquence, the grand style, and had no fear of orchestral colour; the chamber music of Bloomsbury was not for him. He found his ideal vision in the classical world: the Greeks were his first and last love. His first and best book was a study of Homer; this, too, was the topic of his last book, had he lived to complete it.[1] Despite the vast sweep of his literary interests – from the epic songs of Central Africa to the youngest poets of his own day – it is Pindar, Sophocles, the Greek lyric poets who engaged his deepest feelings. Murray and Wilamowitz meant more to him than scholars and critics of other literatures.

Endowed with a sharp, quick brain, a masterful personality, an impulsive heart, great gaiety, a brilliant, ironical wit, contempt for all that was solemn, pompous and craven, he soon came to dominate his circle of friends and acquaintances. Yet he suffered all his life from a certain lack of confidence: he needed constant reassurance. His disciplined habits, his belief in, and capacity for, hard, methodical work, in which much of his day was spent, his respect for professionalism and distaste for dilettantism, all these seemed, in some measure, defensive weapons against ultimate self-distrust. So, indeed, was his Byronic irony about the very romantic values that were closest to his heart. The treatment of him at New College by that stern trainer of philosophers, H. W. B. Joseph, undermined his faith in his own intellectual capacity, which his other tutor in philosophy, Alick Smith, who did much for him, and became a lifelong friend, could not wholly restore.

Bowra saw life as a series of hurdles, a succession of fences to take: there were books, articles, reviews to write; pupils to teach, lectures to deliver; committees, even social occasions, were so many challenges to be met, no less so than the real ordeals – attacks by hostile critics, or vicissitudes of personal relationships, or the hazards of health. In the company of a few familiar friends, on whose loyalty he could rely, he relaxed and often was easy, gentle and at peace. But the outer world was full of obstacles to be taken

---

[1] Nine out of ten chapters were found after his death, and the book (*Homer*) was published in London in 1972. His first book was *Tradition and Design in the Iliad* (Oxford, 1930).

at a run; at times he stumbled, and was wounded: he took such reverses with a stiff upper lip; and then, at once, energetically moved forward to the next task. Hence, it may be, his need and craving for recognition, and the corresponding pleasure he took in the many honours he received. The flat, pedestrian, lucid, well-ordered but, at times, conventional style and content of his published writings may also be due to this peculiar lack of faith in his own true and splendid gifts. His private letters, his private verse, and above all his conversation, were a very different matter. Those who know him solely through his published works can have no inkling of his genius.

As a talker he could be incomparable. His wit was verbal and cumulative: the words came in short, sharp bursts of precisely aimed, concentrated fire, as image, pun, metaphor, parody seemed spontaneously to generate one another in a succession of marvellously imaginative patterns, sometimes rising to high, wildly comical fantasy. His unique accent, idiom, voice, the structure of his sentences became a magnetic model which affected the style of speech, writing, and perhaps feeling, of many who came under its spell. It had a marked effect on some among the best-known Oxford-bred writers of our time. But his influence went deeper than this: he dared to say things which others thought or felt, but were prevented from uttering by rules or convention or personal inhibitions. Maurice Bowra broke through some of these social and psychological barriers, and the young men who gathered round him in the 1920s and '30s, stimulated by his unrestrained talk, let themselves go in their turn.

Bowra was a major liberating force: the free range of his talk about art, personalities, poetry, civilisations, private life, his disregard of accepted rules, his passionate praise of friends and unbridled denunciation of enemies, produced an intoxicating effect. Some eyebrows were raised, especially among the older dons, at the dangers of such licence. They were wholly mistaken. The result, no matter how frivolous the content, was deeply and permanently emancipating. It blew up much that was false, pretentious, absurd; the effect was cathartic; it made for truth, human feeling, as well as great mental exhilaration. The host (and he was always host, whether in his own rooms or those of others) was a positive personality; his character was cast in a major key: there was nothing corrosive or decadent or embittered in all this talk, no matter how irreverent or indiscreet or extravagant or unconcerned with justice it was.

As a scholar, and especially as a critic, Bowra had his limitations. His most valuable quality was his deep and unquenchable love of literature, in particular of poetry, of all periods and peoples. His travels in Russia before the Revolution, when as a schoolboy he crossed that country on his way to his family's home in China, gave him a lifelong interest in Russian poetry. He learnt Russian as a literary language, and virtually alone in England happily (and successfully) parsed the obscurest lines of modern Russian poets as he did the verse of Pindar or Alcaeus. He read French, German, Italian and Spanish, and had a sense of world literature as a single firmament, studded with works of genius, the quality of which he laboured to communicate. He was one of the very few Englishmen equally well known to, and valued by, Pasternak and Quasimodo, Neruda and Seferis, and took proper pride in this. It was all, for him, part of the war against embattled philistinism, pedantic learning, parochialism. Yet he was, with all this, a stout-hearted patriot, as anyone could testify who heard him in Boston, for example, when England was even mildly criticised. Consequently, the fact that no post in the public service was offered him in the Second World War distressed him. He was disappointed, too, when he was not appointed to the Chair of Greek at Oxford (he was offered chairs by Harvard and other distinguished universities). But later he came to look on this as a blessing in disguise; for his election as Warden of Wadham eventually made up and more than made up for it all.

Loyalty was the quality which, perhaps, he most admired, and one with which he was himself richly endowed. His devotion to Oxford, and in particular to Wadham, sustained him during the second, less worldly, portion of his life. He did a very great deal for his college, and it did much for him. He was intensely and, indeed, fiercely proud of Wadham, and of all its inhabitants, senior and junior; he seemed to be on excellent terms with every undergraduate in its rapidly expanding population; he guided them and helped them, and performed many acts of kindness by stealth. In his last decades he was happiest in his Common Room, or when entertaining colleagues or undergraduates; happiest of all when surrounded by friends, old or young, on whose love and loyalty he could depend.

After Wadham his greatest love was for the University: he served it faithfully as Proctor, member of the Hebdomadal Council, and of many other committees, as Delegate of the Press, finally as Vice-Chancellor. Suspected in his younger days of being a cynical epicure (no less cynical man ever breathed), he came to be respected as one of the most devoted, effective and progressive of academic statesmen. He had a very strong institutional sense: his presidency of the British Academy was a very happy period of his life. Under his enlightened leadership the Academy prospered. But it was Oxford that claimed his deeper allegiance: the progress of the University filled him with intense and lasting pride. Oxford and Wadham were his home and his life; his soul was bound up with both. Of the many honours which he received, the honorary doctorate of his own University gave him the deepest satisfaction: the opinion of his colleagues was all in all to him. When the time for retirement came, he was deeply grateful to his college for making it possible for him to continue to live within its walls. His successor was an old personal friend: he felt sure of affection and attention.

Increasing ill health and deafness cut him off from many pleasures, chief among them committees and the day-to-day business of administration, which he missed as much as the now less accessible pleasures of social life. Yet his courage, his gaiety, his determination to make the most of what opportunities remained did not desert him. His sense of the ridiculous was still acute; his sense of fantasy remained a mainstay. New faces continued to feed his appetite for life. Most of all he now enjoyed his contact with the young, whose minds and hearts he understood, and whose desire to resist authority and the imposition of frustrating rules he instinctively shared and boldly supported to the end. They felt this and responded to him, and this made him happy.

He was not politically minded. But by temperament he was a radical and a nonconformist. He genuinely loathed reactionary views and had neither liking nor respect for the solid pillars of any establishment. He sympathised with the unions in the General Strike of 1926; he spoke with passion at an Oxford meeting against the suppression of socialists in Vienna by Dollfuss in 1934; he detested oppression and repression, whether by the right or by the left, and in particular all dictators. His friendship with Hugh Gaitskell was a source of pleasure to him. If political sentiments which seemed to him retrograde or disreputable were uttered in his presence, he was not silent and showed his anger. He did not enjoy the altercations to which this tended to lead, but would have felt it shameful to run away from them; he possessed a high degree of civil courage. He supported all libertarian causes, particularly minorities seeking freedom or independence, the more unpopular the better. Amongst his chief pleasures in the late 1950s and '60s were the Hellenic cruises in which he took part every year. But when the military regime in Greece took over, he gave them up.

His attitude to religion was more complicated and obscure: he had a feeling for religious experience; he had no sympathy for positivist or materialist creeds. But to try to summarise his spiritual outlook in a phrase would be absurd as well as arrogant. As Warden he is said scarcely ever to have missed Chapel.

The last evening of his life was spent at a convivial party with colleagues and undergraduates. This may have hastened the heart attack of which he died; if so, it was as he would have wished it to be: he wanted to end swiftly and tidily, as he had lived, before life had become a painful burden.

He was, in his prime, the most discussed Oxford personality since Jowett, and in every way no less remarkable and no less memorable.

DAVID CECIL

Lord David Cecil was born the second son of the fourth Marquess of Salisbury, and spent his boyhood and much of his youth at the family house at Hatfield. His earliest memories, as a boy, were of a house full of talk – sharp, articulate, amusing. He spoke of the atmosphere of total freedom and spontaneity in which everything was discussed at his parents' hospitable table, in particular, as was very often the case, when his uncles Robert and Hugh – the political sons of the great Victorian Prime Minister – and the future Bishop of Exeter, William, were present. Politics, history, religion, stories about the behaviour of British cabinets, episodes in Parliament (serious and comical), elaborate analyses of the personal relations of public personalities – all this was part of the daily pabulum of this famous and dominant clan.

When their cousin the Prime Minister, Arthur Balfour, came to stay, as he often did, the talk became particularly lively and vehement and indiscreet and intimate – but interspersed with discussions of moral and religious principles and issues – with the result that David Cecil's naturally keen and eager mind and wit developed early, and he acquired opinions, the capacity for clear and articulate expression, and a tendency to relate abstract ideas to the vicissitudes of public, social and personal lives, and the interplay of individual characters and doctrines to their public environment and their place in history – all this as a naturally uninhibited process.

Books were everywhere, prose and poetry; he read them at odd moments, at various times, in no particular order, and so became familiar with Clarendon, Dickens, Spenser, Shakespeare, Jane Austen, Carlyle, Lamb, Byron, Shelley, Macaulay, Disraeli; he had absorbed volumes or chapters or fragments of these writings by the time he went to Eton. He had, as a schoolboy, from all evidence, unusual charm and ease of manner, intellectual gaiety and delight in human gifts and foibles. But he was a bookish boy, and this did not stand him in particularly good stead at Eton. He did not like his years there. His contemporary, Edward Sackville-West, later a well-known musical critic, said that Cecil truly blossomed only when he left Eton and came to Oxford, and entered Christ Church. The strongest cultural influence on him at Eton was probably Aldous Huxley, who was a temporary master there during the First World War, and opened his eyes to realms of poetry which were new to him; his love of English poetry, particularly Christian poetry, stayed with him for the rest of his life.

At Oxford Cecil became deeply interested in English history, particularly the Stuarts and the rise of the Tory Party, with which his family's fortunes were so deeply bound up – this was strongly encouraged by his learned and sensitive history tutor, Keith Feiling, who thought him one of the cleverest as well as one of the most attractive undergraduates he had ever known. And indeed Cecil's reputation for natural charm, combined with a very sharp and nimble intelligence, both clear- and hard-headed, critical both of what he read and of what he wrote, and an unflagging interest in people (more than ideas) and imagination (more than intellect), characterised him at all times.

He was always conscious of his origins and his social position in the hierarchical structure of British society. He once said that it was difficult for English aristocrats to be original artists or writers because, unless their circumstances were very unusual, they tended to be brought up to be all things to all men, and this, he thought, was an obstacle to the withdrawal and concentration needed for original artistic creation – Tolstoy and Byron and perhaps Shelley were exceptions. Those brought up as he was, he thought, were tempted to take too much interest in the lives, both personal and social, by which they were surrounded to dedicate themselves to hard, life-absorbing tasks. He was, all his life, too deeply fascinated by too great a variety of individual experiences, as well as books, above all novels and poetry, stories and literary essays, to be able to do more than describe them and the worlds they expressed, give his own impressions, convey what they seemed to him to say and be; and this left no room for the self-disciplined, preoccupying creative labour after which, at times, he hankered.

After his First in History at Oxford he attempted All Souls, but was not taken, and was elected to a Fellowship at Wadham

College, where he remained from 1924 until 1930. He taught
English literature (and sometimes history) there – it was then that
he began to exercise his extraordinary capacity for understanding
casts of mind and for eliciting from pupils and making them aware
of the precise content of what they thought and felt and groped
for, their roots and their goals, and, conversely, conveying his own
vividly imaginative and concrete sense of what he himself thought
and understood and knew about the writers and works which were
being discussed. This gift for seeing in stunted-seeming seeds the
particular kinds of blooms that might be encouraged to grow made
him (especially after he became a tutor at New College, and then,
from 1939 to 1970, Professor) a remarkable influence on his pupils,
an unusually large number of whom became distinguished teachers
of English literature themselves, at Oxford and other universities,
and held him in affection and admiration for ever after. At least five
among the most distinguished literary luminaries at Oxford alone
acknowledged a deep intellectual and personal debt to him as a
wonderfully sympathetic and inspiring teacher. Until fashions
changed, his lectures were vastly attended.

His interest did not lie in scholarship, but he did not look down
on the minutiae of learning, on the most scrupulous textual or
philological investigations, let alone creative reconstruction of the
past: he respected this deeply, and looked on as masters and
personal friends some of the best-known literary scholars in
Oxford at this time – C. S. Lewis, J. R. R. Tolkien, Helen Gardner,
F. P. Wilson, Helen Darbyshire, L. P. Wilkinson, Nevill Coghill –
who, in turn, liked him greatly and respected his judgement. But
his heart was not in learning. He had a very definite doctrine of the
proper aim of the study of literature, at least as he conceived of it,
though he did not exclude other possibilities. He was not
favourable to historical, biographical, sociological, sociolinguistic
approaches to a writer, and the interpretation of his work in the
light of them. His approach was aesthetic. Like T. S. Eliot, he
thought that works of art shone by their own radiance, and that
knowledge of the artist's life added little. Like Proust, he was
against Sainte-Beuve's methods. He did not care for Edmund
Wilson or the semantics of I. A. Richards, or the cultural moralism
of F. R. Leavis (who duly attacked him). This was not what he
wished to do, even when he admitted that it was, in its own way,
well done. He thought that the task of a critic, and of a teacher of
literature, was to make clear to himself and convey to others the

creative process of the writer, the process of the particular imaginative act of composition, whether it obeyed rules or departed from them, or derived from examples, or was directed against other modes of expression, or created its own. He thought that this task resembled that of a teacher of composition in a musical *conservatoire* who describes the process of evolution of successive drafts of a Beethoven sonata, or Wagner's development of the organisation of orchestral forces and the relationship of this to his mythological invention. This entailed a degree of imaginative insight, as well as accurate knowledge where it was available, which alone could bring out the inwardness, and, in particular, convey the specific quality, of a piece of writing, its inner pulse, its poetic imagery and changing forms, which were part and parcel of its meaning, of the artist's way of achieving artistic effects. It was this wish to see nothing between him and the object of attention, and a consequent distaste for theories of literature, systems of aesthetics – sociological, psychological, philosophical, methodo-logical approaches – that gave Cecil's teaching and his writing their particular character. It was this, too, that often enabled him to encourage a particular approach, and suggest further steps along the grain of a pupil's mind or imagination. He made no attempt to indoctrinate or impose correct methods, as some of his less formidable colleagues seemed, in the 1930s and late '40s, keen to do.

Cecil's books, which reflect his deepest interests, both in literature and life, show that what he loved best was what was most English in English life and letters, and everything outside England which seemed closest to its, to him, most valuable qualities – a sense of lives as they are lived, the inwardness, the awareness of the poetry of quiet existence in the country, the often complex self-absorption of solitary lives, as well as their part in and interplay with the facets of various kinds of English social life, particularly when the observation is authentic, and concerned with the personal and private, and the effects of distortion or destruction by disasters or false values. His first important work, *The Stricken Deer* (1929), is a beautifully written, deeply sympathetic study of a melancholy, introspective, semi-solitary, lyrical Christian poet living out his life in the country. Cecil had a natural affinity with uneasy, cloistered, fantasy-filled, inwardly rich lives, and the deep, unquenchable lyrical impulse which they fed – Cowper, Gray, Lamb, the Brontës (as in his *Early Victorian Novelists* of 1934), Dorothy Osborne in an earlier century (*Two Quiet Lives*, 1948) – and this is conveyed by the best pages of *Poets and Story-Tellers* (1949), by his essay on Walter de la Mare, and especially by his excellent, original and deeply-felt lectures on Thomas Hardy, perhaps the best of all his books.

But he was not confined to this genre: he gave an interesting account of Scott's early grasp of the collision of social classes, of conflicts of individuals in societies in flux, which owed nothing to Lukács. His lecture on Walter Pater in 1955 is something else again – an exquisite appreciation of the aesthetic approach to life, which meant a very great deal to him, and which he defended in an unfavourable climate, as emerged in his Inaugural Lecture. Against the current streams of the time, in 1949 and again in 1957, he declared that the central purpose of art was to give delight, not to instruct, nor to disturb, nor to explain, nor to praise or condemn a movement, an idea, a regime, nor to help build a better world in the service of a Church, a party, a nation, a class, but to irradiate the soul with a light which God had granted the artist the power to shed, and the reader or listener to absorb, understand, delight in, and thereby be drawn nearer its divine creator.

The true love of his life was, of course, Jane Austen. He wrote about her during his freelance life in London in 1935, and after he retired from Oxford in 1978: the *Portrait of Jane Austen* was his most finished study of her. Everything in her appealed to him: the dry light upon, and profound understanding of, the human heart; the unswerving pursuit of what she perceived to be the real nature of human beings and the world they lived in; the calm good sense and unalterably just appraisals; the steady gaze; the light but calculated weight; the perfection of marksmanship of every word; the pervasive irony, the deceptively quiet tone; the capacity to convey the nuances of every tremor of feeling and passion and painful thought in these well-mannered, genteel, provincial heads and hearts. He laughed at the strictures of social, especially Marxist, critics – what, no mention of the French or the Industrial Revolutions? Nothing about the condition of the poor? Or Napoleon? Or class warfare? Or the technological transformation which altered everything in the society about which she purported to write? Nothing but individual experience, personal relationships, children, adolescents, marriage, a thousand indescribable feelings, intimations? As if this were not enough, not the essence of life and of art.

She wrote of an England he knew and understood, and he responded to those who described it with genius. He felt this in a smaller degree about Mrs Gaskell and, in his own time, Jean Rhys. George Eliot was a genius, he knew, but for him too unaesthetic and too ideological. For this he was reproached by members of the Bloomsbury coterie, but he was defiantly unrepentant.

He was, of course, well acquainted with Bloomsbury; he had married the daughter of Desmond MacCarthy, who was brought up at the heart of it, and he went to Bloomsbury parties. He delighted in the wit and irreverence of its members. Lytton Strachey did have a strong and lasting influence upon him – he believed that Strachey was the creator of biography as a conscious art form alongside the novel, and as a biographer he confessed himself to be his disciple. *The Young Melbourne* and its successor, *Lord M.*, probably his most widely read works, owe a great deal to Strachey; the sure touch with which the brilliant world of the Whig aristocracy is brought to life has surely some foundation in Cecil's familiarity with his own social world before the War, and is perhaps a trifle anachronistic, as Tolstoy's society in *War and Peace* is, for much the same reason. Both volumes are most enjoyable reading – Strachey would have been much more ironical, mischievous, cruel, would have played with the facts to the point of caricature, but the genre is similar: Cecil is at once more high-spirited, kinder and more conventional. He liked the Partridges, thought E. M. Forster very clever, amusing, skilful, but recoiled from their moral values – they conflicted obviously with his own religious and perhaps more worldly ones. He compared Forster unfavourably with Turgenev, who seemed to him equally gifted, indeed, more so, equally clever, amusing, perceptive and humane, but with a lyrical imagination denied, in his view, to Forster.

He looked on Bloomsbury with some irony, as a kind of sect, a self-contained, unreal little society which had its own orthodoxies and its own experts on everything, rather like the Roman Catholic or Marxist or Freudian establishments. But the person in Bloomsbury he most deeply admired, and, indeed, looked up to almost uncritically, was, of course, Virginia Woolf. He thought her novels works of undeniable genius, but what meant most to him was *The Common Reader*, her critical essays. These formed his ideal model – the revelation of the varieties of the actual processes of creation, the literary analogue to the teaching of musical composition – in which he so deeply believed, and which he tried to write, all his life. He shared his sense of Woolf's dazzling genius with his lifelong friend, Elizabeth Bowen, whose novels spoke to him directly. He thought Elizabeth Bowen, as well as his intimate friend the novelist L. P. Hartley, to be endowed beyond others with a sensibility to the texture of life as it is lived, a gift which, for him, Chekhov possessed to a supreme degree. He loved Tolstoy – he preferred his sunlit world – 'Tolstoy was surely the cleverest man who ever lived', he said of him – to the crushing misanthropy of Flaubert or the unceasing discords and infernal regions of Dostoevsky. The most valuable quality for him in people was, I think, a capacity for self-understanding – for knowing what one could and could not be and do. Genius as she was, Virginia Woolf did not completely possess that – and Vita Sackville-West, for example, and indeed, the rest of Bloomsbury, then a dominant literary influence, not at all. He was too hard-headed and undeceivable not to look on this literary mandarinate with amused detachment, and mocked at the snobbishness, both social and artistic, of most of its members (acute even in his heroes, Strachey and Woolf) as being a genuine defect.

Towards the end of his life he did many other things. He wrote an excellent life of Max Beerbohm (*Max*), which Max, on his deathbed, had asked his widow to propose to him. He wrote about his own family and their house, first in the early 1950s, then again in his later years, in 1973. He wrote about his father-in-law, Desmond MacCarthy; and he edited anthologies, of Christian verse in 1940, and of his own choice (*Library Looking-Glass*) in 1935. He wrote *Visionary & Dreamer*, about the painters Samuel Palmer and Burne-Jones (1969), on whom he had lectured in the United States. He took no interest in 'the modern movement' – T. S. Eliot, James Joyce, Wyndham Lewis, Ezra Pound and their successors. The new schools – deconstruction and its successors, formalism, neo-Freudianism, neo-Marxism and the rest – seemed to him arid, academic exercises, or else dark mysteries conjured up by foreign mystagogues, which he was only too happy not to seek to penetrate.

All in all he was one of the most intelligent, irresistibly attractive, gifted, life-enhancing, shrewd and brilliant literary personalities of his time. He confined himself to what he liked, admired and enjoyed, and described it and his reasons for it with great talent. He saw through pretence and sham quickly and infallibly. Some

declared that he wrote with undeniable charm, style and distinction, but with a lack of originality, that his opinions were often
familiar enough though 'ne'er so well expressed'. This is not just.
His pen had a very sharp edge, and often cut deeper than cruder, if
stronger, weapons. However this may be, he was certainly the
most delightful human being that anyone could ever hope to meet.

MEMORIES OF VIRGINIA WOOLF

I REMEMBER that in 1933 Virginia Woolf was invited to stay the night by her first cousin H. A. L. Fisher, Warden of New College.

Mrs Fisher told me that she did not care for her much, as she thought her somewhat arrogant, but Herbert Fisher had a high regard for her, apart from his close relationship. The dinner party was given in the Warden's Lodgings, and there were present, apart from the guest of honour and the host and Mrs Fisher, John Sparrow, then a Fellow of All Souls (as, indeed, was I), Richard Crossman, whom Mrs Fisher greatly liked, C. S. Lewis, who could not bear feminine company and disapproved of women writers particularly, and a classical tutor from Brasenose College called Alan Kerr, who was, I think, a friend of the Fisher family. Virginia Woolf, who was certainly the most beautiful woman I had ever seen, then or perhaps even later, looked exceedingly nervous and unseeing – she did not exactly stumble against the furniture, but she made her way to the table very uncertainly. I sat at Fisher's left, she on his right. Mrs Fisher, flanked by Crossman and Lewis, was at the other end of the table. Mary Fisher (now Mrs Bennett), Fisher's daughter, who fell totally under her cousin's spell, and her friend Rachel Walker were also present.

Mrs Woolf twitched nervously, and when her neighbour, the don from Brasenose, asked whether Mr Woolf would be coming also, did not reply. The explanation apparently was that Leonard Woolf was convinced that Fisher had been responsible, at any rate in part, for inventing the Black and Tans to quell the Irish rebellion in 1921, and refused to be in the same room with so wicked a member of Lloyd George's Cabinet.

Mrs Woolf was silent, so was the host. Then, to break the silence, he said, 'Do you do much reading, Virginia? Have you been reading novelists at all – Scott, for example?' To which she replied, 'No, not Scott, I think it's all terrible rubbish. I know that

David Cecil has just published a lecture about him, God knows what he finds in him, I didn't like the lecture either.' After that, another silence.

'Do you go for walks at all, Virginia?' asked Fisher a little desperately. 'Yes, I do. Not much in London. Mostly in the country.'

'What do you notice most on your walks?'

'I think mostly goats on hillsides, they look so ecclesiastical.'

Meanwhile, at the other end of the table, in loud voices, the company was saying how much they liked Uppingham (I do not vouch for my recollection of the actual words spoken).

'I like hearty schools,' said Crossman, 'none of your arty-tarty people there – there were some at Winchester when I was there, but not all that many. Eton, of course, is much worse.' Mrs Fisher, I think, agreed.

Lewis said he found it difficult to teach introverts at Magdalen – 'Arty-tarty, that's very good: Betjeman, Pryce-Jones, I found they had no genuine grasp of either prose or poetry, either modern or old – I was greatly relieved when they left.'

Mrs Woolf winced at the tone, the loudness, the sentiments, and Fisher quickly tried to intervene. They talked about people they had known, about travel in Italy and the like – I have no recollection of what either of the young women said. Then we went to the drawing room, where no fewer than forty or fifty graduates and undergraduates of New College who were thought suitable had been gathered to see and hear the great writer.

She stood in front of them, silent, nervous, her gaze fixed on some distant point, unable to utter – it was a little like an execution, or perhaps like a very shy bishop about to confirm a class of schoolboys or undergraduates. Finally she spoke.

'Has anyone here ever read *Jane Eyre*?' she said, looking at the ceiling, then at the windows, trying not to look at anyone's face.

One young man raised his hand. 'Can you tell me the plot?' said Mrs Woolf.

The young man did his best, he took ten minutes or so over it.

'Has anyone here read *Wuthering Heights*?'

The same process followed.

'What about *The Moonstone*?' Someone had read that too.

'Do you like reading detective stories?' There were mixed answers about that. Then, looking really at her wits' end, she said,

'I cannot go on talking like this, I am so sorry. Let us mingle like human beings.' And we did so.

It was by now near 10 o'clock, and Mrs Fisher announced that she was going to bed, but that those who wished to stay could do so. Fisher asked Mrs Woolf whether she liked Handel, Mozart, Haydn, Beethoven. She said she liked them all – 'What a very catholic taste you have,' he said. After that we broke up into little groups and she talked most amiably in a corner with two or three young women, perhaps her cousin Mary among them, and we all went to bed.

Much later, I think in 1938, Mrs Woolf asked me to dinner in her house in Tavistock Square. On her postcard she wrote: 'If you knock on my little grey door I shall open it.'

Apart from myself the only persons present were Leonard, Ben Nicolson and Sally Graves, niece of Robert Graves, by then married as Mrs Chilver, who later became Principal of Lady Margaret Hall in Oxford – Mrs Woolf obviously had a passion for her and had been cross-examining her (so Mrs Chilver told me) about whether there was much free love going on among young people: was lesbianism known at all? And so on. I rather think she must have cross-examined her nieces about that kind of thing too – she had a feeling that she knew too little about the contemporary world in England.

She began describing a visit which one of the Royal Princesses, I think Princess Beatrice, had paid to Duncan Grant's studio, and how delightful this was. Leonard, who, with a trembling hand, was fumbling to light the gas fire, said, 'I don't know why you think that – royalty are exactly like everybody else, there's no difference between them and ordinary people.' 'You are quite wrong, Leonard,' she said, 'they are quite different. Quite wonderful. Quite marvellous. Not at all like ordinary people. I was very excited on that occasion and I'm not ashamed of it.' Then she turned to Ben Nicolson – there was always someone she evidently liked to tease – and said, 'Ben, do tell us [he was the Assistant Keeper of the King's pictures], do you have to wear knee-breeches when you go to Buckingham Palace or Windsor? Do you bow very low? Do you go down on one knee? Do you ever speak before you are spoken to? Do you ever ask any questions? When you leave the King's presence do you walk backwards?' And so on.

Ben answered as best he could, without smiling, quite solemnly as was his way, and did finally burst out, 'You always tease me,

Virginia. I'll never forget when you asked poor Hugh Walpole whether his car was lined with gold.'

She then turned to me. 'What is that book that you came in with? I saw it.'

I said it was Henry James's book on Hawthorne.

'I expect there are no bats in your belfry, Mr Berlin,' she said, 'I can see that – you don't look to me like someone interested in dreams or fancies – or are you?'

I cannot remember what I answered. I expect I faltered out of pure terror at her presence. She did convey the presence of genius, and her conversation, which I cannot hope to reproduce, was full of wonderful images and analogies, and was more fascinating to listen to than that of I think anyone I have ever met – Pasternak was the only person who came close to it.

'Henry James,' she said, 'well everybody reads him now, of course, but by the time I met him he was nothing but a frozen-up old monster. I don't read many modern novels, not even those that we publish, Leonard and I. Stephen Spender told us how marvellous he thought *In a Province* by Laurens van der Post was – we published it, you know. Quite decent, I thought, but wonderful? No. Have you read *Murder in the Cathedral*, or seen it? I rather liked it.'

'I walked out of it in the middle, I couldn't bear it,' said Leonard, 'Tom Eliot is too obscurantist for me. All that religious nonsense.'

I can remember no more, but I spent three of the most wonderful hours of my life in the presence of that not entirely sympathetic and certainly not very kind, but wonderfully gifted writer, a writer of genius, as I still regard her – more and more so as I reread the works of her middle period.

EDMUND WILSON AT OXFORD

I MET Edmund Wilson, I think, sometime in the early spring of 1946, after I had come back from Moscow to finish the job I was doing at the British Embassy in Washington. I had been in Washington during the war years, and my friend the Russian composer Nicolas Nabokov, who, like his cousin Vladimir, was a friend of Wilson's, thought that he might like to meet me (I had expressed my intense admiration for *Axel's Castle* and *The Triple Thinkers*) and talk about Russian literature and other topics. Wilson refused. He was convinced that any British official could want to meet him only in order to rope him into the British propaganda machine. He was acutely isolationist: his Anglophobia, which in any case had been fairly acute, was increased by the reflection that England had once again managed to drag America into a dreadful and totally unnecessary war, and he had no wish to meet any representative of that country. However, once the War was over he evidently decided that he was no longer in any danger of being inveigled into pro-British activities, and asked me to lunch at the Princeton Club in New York.

I was, I own, rather taken aback by his appearance. I do not know what I had imagined a distinguished literary critic to look like, but there stood before me a thickset, red-faced, pot-bellied figure, not unlike President Hoover in appearance; but once he began to talk, almost before we had sat down, I forgot everything save his conversation. He spoke in a curiously strangled voice, with gaps between his sentences, as if ideas jostled and thrashed about inside him, getting in each other's way as they struggled to emerge, which made for short bursts, emitted staccato, interspersed with gentle, low-voiced, legato passages. He spoke in a moving and imaginative fashion about the American writers of his generation, about Dante, and about what the Russian poet Pushkin had meant to him. He described his visit to the Soviet Union in 1935 and the appalling effect which this had had upon him, for, like many other members of the American intelligentsia, he had once tended to idealise the Communist regime.

The climax of his visit was a meeting with Prince D. S. Mirsky. Mirsky was a brilliant, highly original émigré writer in English on Russian literature who had become a convert to Marxism in England; he then returned to Russia and soon after this published a book denouncing British writers and intellectuals, some of whom had befriended him. Wilson found him in Moscow in a very low and wretched state (two years later he was arrested and sent to a camp, where he died). Mirsky's downfall and pathetic condition had made an indelible impression on Wilson, and he spoke long and bitterly about the passing of his own political infatuation. He then talked about Russian literature in general, and particularly about Chekhov and Gogol, as well as I have ever heard anyone talk on any literary topic. I was completely fascinated; I felt honoured to have met this greatly gifted and morally impressive man. We became friends. I did not return to the United States until 1949, when I went to teach at Harvard, and stayed a night with Wilson at Wellfleet, where he was living with his wife Elena. I went to see them both on subsequent visits in the 1950s.

In 1954 he came to England and telephoned virtually from the airport to tell me that he wished to come to Oxford and stay with me for a day or two. I welcomed this. Since I was not married then, I was living in All Souls College. Wilson did stay two nights with me in a not very attractive college room (which he describes with characteristic acerbity in his diary).[1] He was in a splendidly Anglophobic mood. On the first morning, before lunch, we went for a walk to look at the colleges. When we passed Christ Church, he looked at the decaying building of the Library (not then yet refaced, as it would be later, with the assistance of the Rockefeller Foundation) and said, 'Oh, most of these buildings look in very poor shape – I think they're actually falling down', and looked delighted. 'I think that's the case with a lot of England,' he went on, 'I think your country deserves a bit of this.'

He then launched into a sweeping attack on academic life and academics in general as murderers of all that was living and real in literature and art – classical, medieval, modern. I asked him

---

[1] Edmund Wilson, *The Fifties*, ed. Leon Edel (New York, 1986), p. 135 (entry for 20–21 January 1954).

whether there were no academics he liked or admired. He said that there were indeed a few: one was Christian Gauss, his teacher at Princeton, whose lectures he had greatly admired and whom he had liked and deeply respected as a man; another was Norman Kemp Smith, who had been a professor of philosophy at Princeton in his day and was now living in retirement in Scotland. (Wilson had gone to see him during a visit to England in 1945, the visit on which the pages about England in *Europe Without Baedeker* were founded.) Apart from these he could for the moment think of no one.

The diatribe continued (I had no idea of whether this was a passing mood, induced by Oxford, or a permanent attitude): he could wish for no worse fate for anyone than to hold a job at a university, particularly if it were connected with literary studies; he had heard that Archibald MacLeish contemplated becoming, or had become, a professor somewhere, was it Harvard? It was a fate that that ass deserved (I had read Wilson's devastating parody, 'The Omelet of A. MacLeish', and had realised that this poet was not one of his favourites). Then there had been the ridiculous Ted Spencer at Harvard, who tried to seek him out but had died before any relationship could be attempted; and there was also Spencer's protégé, Harry Levin – a clever man, and widely read, with interesting things to say, who had had it in him to become something if only he had not chosen to make a career at Harvard, which had turned him into a pedantic schoolmaster, buried in trivial detail, a Dryasdust, who turned everything into dust, a kind of coloured dust. 'Oh, but I can't explain it,' he said, 'I talked to him about Howells – he doesn't think Howells is any good at all.' He went on to say that Harry Levin was, in spite of all this, not a bad fellow; he could be highly perceptive and interesting, but he was ridiculous about Howells. I was under the impression that they were friends (as I feel sure in fact they were), and was taken aback by these remarks about Levin, whom I admired and whose essay on Stendhal I thought a remarkable piece of work. But he would not relent. His next target was Perry Miller; then C. S. Lewis; he went on and on in a ferocious fashion. Perhaps Tennyson talked about Churton Collins in this way when he called him a louse in the locks of literature. I saw no reason to doubt that he spoke of me in similar fashion; it was obviously part of him; I loved him as he was.

He asked me whether it was to be his fate to meet more

academics at lunch or dinner. I relieved his fears about lunch by saying the guests would be Stephen Spender and another man of letters (I cannot remember who); in the evening, however, if he wished to dine in All Souls as he had suggested, he might well meet some academics. Would he prefer to dine in a restaurant? No, he said, he wished to plumb the depths of old, decayed, conservative English academic life in its death-throes. I remember his words: 'It can't be long now,' he said ominously, 'I think we're in at the kill.' I did not ask him to develop this theme, but tried to divert him on to other subjects. No good. He said that in England – London – writers and the like formed little cliques, jealous coteries engaged in keeping each other out; there was no real literary world; Evelyn Waugh could not be in a room with Peter Quennell, a perfectly decent man of letters; both had spoken ill of Cyril Connolly; Auden was ostracised; nobody had a kind word to say about MacNeice or Angus Wilson; and so on and so on. Most of this seemed absurdly misconceived to me. To get him off this topic I asked him – unwisely, as it turned out – what his last visit to England had been like. But by then it was time for lunch. He seemed to enjoy the company, denounced the writers of the *Partisan Review*, said that Philip Rahv was able enough but, like the rest of them, used literature to make political points, and praised V. S. Pritchett as one of the few critics whose thought was free and who had something to say.

After lunch he reminded me of my earlier question and told me what had occurred during his previous London visit. He had arrived as a kind of war correspondent, and the wartime British Ministry of Information had detached the well-known publisher Hamish Hamilton, who was then a member of that ministry and was half American, to look after him. Hamilton had organised a party of eminent members of the British literary establishment. According to Wilson, he saw at the party, among others, T. S. Eliot, one or two Sitwells, Cyril Connolly, Siegfried Sassoon, Harold Nicolson, Peter Quennell and, I think, Rosamond Lehmann. He wished to talk to none of these. 'T. S. Eliot', he said, 'is a gifted poet, but somewhere inside him there is a scoundrel. When I see him, which is not often, I just cannot take him. I do not wish to meet him, although I think some of his poetry is wonderful – it repels me, but it is poetry.' The Sitwells he dismissed as being of no interest. The only person there that he was able to speak to was Compton Mackenzie – they swapped stories about life before and during the First World War, and he found the appearance, manner and conversation of the old buccaneer quite entrancing.

I gradually realised that there is a sense in which Wilson belonged to an earlier generation than the literary intelligentsia of England at that time; that the kind of people he preferred were the Edwardians – full-blooded, masculine men of letters, with sometimes coarse (and even to some degree philistine) but vital personalities – and that this was the world to which Compton Mackenzie truly belonged. Desmond MacCarthy had once described to David Cecil and myself a typical dinner he had attended some years before the First World War in a London club – the Reform, or it may have been the Travellers'. Present were Rudyard Kipling, H. G. Wells, Max Beerbohm, Hilaire Belloc, G. K. Chesterton, Arnold Bennett and Bernard Shaw, as well as Henry James and the young Hugh Walpole. There was no talk about literature or the arts, or friendship or nature or morality or personal relations or the ends of life – the kinds of things that were discussed in Bloomsbury. There was not a touch of anything faintly aesthetic – the talk was hearty, concerned with royalties, publishers, love-affairs, absurd adventures, society scandals, and anecdotes about famous persons, accompanied by gusts of laughter, puns, limericks, a great deal of mutual banter, jokes about money, women and foreigners, and a great deal of drink. The atmosphere was that of a male dining-club of vigorous, amusing, sometimes rather vulgar friends. These were the best-known authors of the time, the 'blind leaders of the blind' so much disliked and disapproved of by Bloomsbury. It seemed to me that Edmund Wilson, for all his unerring sense of quality and his moral preoccupations, had an affinity with these masters. I do not think that he would have greatly enjoyed tea with Virginia Woolf or an evening with Lytton Strachey.

Hence the literary party in London did not suit him at all, and, after a few perfunctory words with E. M. Forster about Jane Austen, he told Hamish Hamilton that he wanted to get away from it as soon as possible. After the conversation with Compton Mackenzie he swiftly withdrew, to the disappointment, so Hamilton told me, of some of those invited. All he wished to do was to go to Scotland and see his mentor, Kemp Smith. Hamish Hamilton, who had probably never heard of this Kantian scholar, did his best to arrange for the journey to Scotland. Wilson did manage to see him – he told me that he had had a good time with him, that they had talked about the old times with great pleasure and had discussed the decline in the standards of European scholarship. Then he came back to London to be met at the station by the courteous and indefatigable Hamilton, who tried to persuade him to get into a taxi to go to his hotel. It was evening; Wilson had become convinced (so he told me) that what Hamilton was mainly anxious to do was to prevent him from seeing the prostitutes who then walked the streets of London in exceptional numbers (so he had been told). He did his best to evade Hamilton, for whom he had by then conceived one of his violent, irrational dislikes (by this time reciprocated by Hamilton, who told me on a later occasion that Wilson was one of the most unpleasant and difficult people he had ever encountered). Wilson did get into a taxi, but, by God, he got out of it after five minutes, and he *did* walk the streets, particularly Park Lane, and he *did* see prostitutes, and he felt that he had scored off the officials who had been sent to escort him, almost, he thought, in the manner of the Russian secret police.

I tried to persuade him that all that Hamish Hamilton had attempted to do was to extend the kind of courtesies which cultural institutions thought to be his due. Wilson would have none of that: he was certain that an attempt was being made to bear-lead him in London, to prevent him from meeting unsuitable people whom in fact he might have liked to meet. This conviction – that there was a general conspiracy in England, of a Soviet type, not to let him meet unsuitable people – obsessed him, and was to surface later in Oxford. I asked him if he had disliked every literary person he had met in London. He said, 'No, I like Evelyn Waugh and Cyril Connolly best.' Why? 'Because I thought they were so nasty.' Perhaps this referred to later meetings, because I do not know if Evelyn Waugh was in London during the War, in which he served as a soldier. He had also taken to Angus Wilson because he reminded him of the heartfelt human feelings of the kind of Americans with whom he felt at home. It was the aestheticism, the prissiness, the superciliousness, the cliquishness, the thin, piping voices, the bloodlessness, the preoccupation with one's own emotions both in life and in literature – all of which he (no less than D. H. Lawrence) attributed to Bloomsbury – that irritated him. He thought the whole of English literary life was infected by this. I don't know what he would have said about J. B. Priestley – I think that he was, perhaps, below his angle of vision. He could not bear the thought of the Huxleys, Aldous or Julian.

Evening fell, and it was time for dinner in the Common Room of All Souls College. He had me on one side and the senior Fellow dining, the historian A. L. Rowse, on the other. He hardly spoke to Rowse, although Rowse tried to speak to him. He turned to me brusquely and engaged in conversation about mutual friends in America – Justice Felix Frankfurter and his wife, Nicolas Nabokov and his wives, the playwright Sam Behrman, Mary McCarthy (to whom Wilson had been married), Conrad Aiken, Arthur Schlesinger, Judge Learned Hand and others. Reluctantly he turned to his other side and allowed himself to be addressed by Rowse. He answered in monosyllables. After coffee, when we came back to my rooms, he complained that a flood of British nationalist propaganda had been poured over him by Rowse at dinner, that he had not come to Oxford to be made a victim of cultural chauvinists. I think that on a later occasion, when Rowse went to see him in the United States, they may have got on a little better – but on this occasion he was in a grumpy mood and would not let up.

He said that he realised why the All Souls college servants removed the plates so rapidly, hardly letting him finish a single dish – he spoke of a Barmecide feast – it was because they were acutely class-conscious, hated their masters, wanted to serve them as gracelessly as possible and get away from their hated presence as quickly as they could. He had noticed, he said, that class-consciousness was clearly rampant in this ancient establishment. I did not argue with him – he was, I think, past convincing on this and most other points. What he said was characteristic wonderful nonsense, of course. The majority of scouts (servants) in Oxford were certainly then, and perhaps are still, among the most conservative of its inhabitants; they were conscious carriers of ancient college traditions, old retainers if ever there were such, who for the most part – certainly at that time – refused to be unionised, on the ground that this was an insult to what they conceived to be their status and very special function. The servants at All Souls exemplified this type almost to the point of caricature.

It was plain that Wilson on that day – as on many others – lived in a world of angry fantasy, particularly in the case of anything British, and although I was devoted to him, felt deep admiration and respect for him to his dying day, and remain intensely proud of the friendship that bound us, I knew that it was useless to argue with him once he got the bit between his teeth. This was certainly the case during his stay with me in Oxford. After dinner I had invited my colleague David Cecil, the novelist Iris Murdoch and her husband the critic John Bayley, and the philosopher Stuart Hampshire to meet him. It was not a happy evening. He took against everyone in the room. He mistook Bayley for the critic Humphry House (with whom he might well have got on) and virtually ignored him and everyone else. He became listless, answered in monosyllables, gurgled, drank a great deal of whisky, and looked with hateful eyes at everyone. Although Iris, who is the soul of courtesy and kindness, tried to make things go, and John Bayley, a beguiling talker, did his best, the old bear remained in his lair, glaring balefully from time to time and trying to drown his boredom in drink. The evening came to an early end. At the end of it he burst out about these feeble creatures – aristocrats who dabbled in literature were useless; the dons were all bloodless monks, cut off from all that mattered. Why could I not have invited one of the few academics with guts, like A. J. P. Taylor, whom he wanted to meet because he liked his radical polemics? I said that I knew and liked Taylor, despite a slight *froideur* caused by a somewhat disparaging review he had written of a small book I had just published, but that I would gladly arrange a meeting between them – and did so on the following day.

Taylor was most amiable to us both. Wilson said that he had quite enjoyed his visit to Taylor's rooms in Magdalen College. But then Taylor had taken him to a lecture by Steven Runciman on a Byzantine subject, which bored him stiff; once again he heard the over-refined and, to him, deeply depressing accents of Blooms-bury, those high, thin voices which he could not bear. (I do not know how many of these voices he had ever actually heard.) I also arranged for him to see the Jewish historian Cecil Roth, because at this time he took an increasing interest in Jewish history and was learning Hebrew – it was not long before the publication of his book on the Dead Sea Scrolls. That visit also went well, particularly as I had warned him that Roth was something of a bore, though a worthy and learned antiquary; those mildly disparaging words were enough to make Wilson like him. He muttered something about being kept from people he admired by persons (myself) who for some reason decided to 'blackball' them – more fantasy, more mild paranoia.

Once he had formed a sociological and psychological hypothesis, he held on to it grimly with a kind of pleased deliberate
perversity, against all evidence. He told me that the only persons he
had truly enjoyed meeting in England, apart from his old friend
Sylvester Gates, whom he had known at Harvard many years
before, were Connolly (again because what he said was so
malicious), Taylor, Roth and Angus Wilson. The rest seemed to
him repellent. 'And Compton Mackenzie? And Kemp Smith?' Yes,
indeed, these too, but that was all. The most hateful figure to him
in England, he said, was Winston Churchill, who was nothing but
a typical low-grade American journalist. If it were not for Sylvester
Gates and myself he would not have come to England. Did Oxford
still contain a ridiculous puffed-up fellow called Maurice Bowra,
whom he had met with Gates and who, for all his knowledge of
languages, had no understanding whatever of literature? He loved
literature – that was evident – a pity that he had nothing of interest
to say about it; he gathered that he was a friend of mine: how could
this be? His conversation was banal and empty to a degree, just a
lot of shouting. He could not understand how such writers as
Cyril Connolly and Evelyn Waugh could be said to owe so much
to this inflated philistine – they were at least gifted, he was a
caricature John Bull. The diatribes went on. By this time he had
drunk a great deal and his eyes were almost closed. I managed to
get him to his bedroom, not without some difficulty.

Next day he was serene and gentle. We talked about Russian
writers, about his life in Talcottville, which he pressed me to visit
with him, about Hebrew tenses and the structure of the Hungarian
language (which he contemplated acquiring), about his intense
admiration for the poetry of W. H. Auden, about the interesting
position of the New Yorker in American cultural life, about the
monstrously patronising attitude of Europeans, not only the
despicable English but the French and even the Italians, towards
American culture, towards such great poets as Walt Whitman and
such prose writers as Herman Melville and Henry James – they
were recognised, but the fact that they were Americans had always,
it seemed to him, to be explained away or apologised for. But
America would show them. There was a wonderful generation of
young technologists and engineers coming up in America, confident, gifted, clear-headed, uncluttered men in thin drill suits (I
remember this odd description), inventors of excellent new
gadgets; these men were building a new, fresh, highly practical

civilisation that would respond to new human needs and would
open prospects of wonderful new comforts of life, and this
would supersede the decay and self-conceit and squalor of a fast-
declining, petty-minded European culture. Nevertheless, these
boutades of his were less violent than on the day before, and rarer.
Wilson was in a calmer and happier mood, quite relaxed. He
explained that his life was, and always had been, literature and
writers, that music[1] and even painting meant less, even though they
did mean a great deal: Malraux was marvellous on sculpture.
Nothing had contributed so much to his ideas about life and art –
to what seemed to him to matter, politics and all – as the great
Russian masters. Pushkin had begun to move him more than
Shakespeare, but not more than Dante; what terrible nonsense
Orwell had written about Tolstoy and *Lear*. He said that his
distaste for the English had been increased by the knock-kneed
creatures he met in London and Oxford. Did I know his friend
Jason Epstein? He was, he thought, himself misanthropic enough,
but Epstein outdid him – his dislike of mankind was phenomenal.
He liked Epstein, and liked that in him.

After which he left. It could not be regarded as a successful visit.
In spite of this, he did come back to Oxford with his wife Elena to
stay for a couple of days with me and my wife – by that time we
were living in a house of our own – and I took care not to invite
Oxford academics to meet him, however great their eagerness and
admiration. I preferred to meet him in Boston, London and New
York.

He was, in my eyes, a great critic, and a noble and moving
human being, whom I loved and respected and wanted to have a
good opinion of me; I was deeply touched when, not long before
he died, he made me inscribe a line from the Bible with a diamond
upon the window-pane of his house in Wellfleet, a privilege
reserved for friends. The line was a verse from Isaiah, with whom,
he insisted, I had obviously identified myself – another ineradicable
fantasy, like his obstinate insistence that I had written as I did
about Tolstoy only because I, too, was a fox, longing to be, indeed
believing myself to be, a hedgehog. Nothing said to deny this
absurdity made the faintest impression on him. He knew that 'like

---

[1] I once asked him, I cannot think why, whether he liked Wagner. He said, I
think, 'Yes, yes, I did, yes, when I was much younger, but it is not the kind of
stuff I can listen to now.'

all Jews' I sought unity and a metaphysically integrated organic world; in fact, I believe the exact opposite. The constructions of his inner world withstood all external evidence. He was prey to wild fantasies, to absurd conjectures, to irrational hatreds and loves. The fact that my prejudices largely coincided with his own was, of course, an immense source of sympathy and endearment. It was perhaps this more than anything else that brought us together.

His judgements were often erratic, and he was prey to delusions, but his humanity and integrity were total. When he went off on a tangent it might end anywhere. His review in the *New Yorker* of Pasternak's *Doctor Zhivago* was the best and most understanding, I think, in any language; but his speculation in a later article on the meaning of various names and symbols in the novel was crazy to a degree.[1] He managed to combine profound insight and extraordinary vision into cultures not his own with turbulent prejudices, hatreds and a great deal of pure nonsense; he sometimes misfired totally and missed the target by miles; yet most of his denunciations were deserved. He was the last major critic in the tradition of Johnson, Sainte-Beuve, Belinsky and Matthew Arnold; his aim and practice were to consider works of literature within a larger social and cultural frame – one which included an absorbed, acutely penetrating, direct, wonderfully illuminating view of the author's personality, goals and social and personal origins, the surrounding moral, intellectual and political worlds, and the nature of the author's vision – and to present the writer, the work and its complex setting as interrelated, integrated wholes. He told me during his visit that the modern tendency towards purely literary scholarship, towards an often deliberate ignoring of the texture of the writer's life and society, for him lacked all genuine content. I agreed with him, fervently. Art shone for him, but not by its own light alone. He is gone, and has not left his peer.

---

[1] The two articles are 'Doctor Life and his Guardian Angel', *New Yorker*, 15 November 1958, 201–26, and (with Barbara Deming and Evgenia Lehovich) 'Legend and Symbol in "Doctor Zhivago" ', *Nation* 188 No 16 (18 April 1959), 363–73, and *Encounter* 12 No 6 (June 1959), 5–16; both were reprinted in Wilson's *The Bit Between My Teeth: A Literary Chronicle of 1950–1965* (London, [1966]).

AUBERON HERBERT

In the early spring of 1946, when I was still a government official, I had occasion to go to Paris for a few days, and was staying as a guest in the British Embassy, then presided over by the infinitely hospitable Duff and Diana Cooper. At dinner on my last night in Paris I found myself sitting opposite an officer in uniform, proclaimed by the metal strip on his shoulder to be a member of the Polish Army. He was tall, generously built, with a fine Roman bust and head, looking like (as someone once described him) a kindly Nero. For a Pole, which I took him to be, he seemed to me to speak English with remarkable purity and a rich and imaginative vocabulary; some question on my part about where he had served stimulated him to a magnificent outpouring of words reminiscent in style of an older and more stately world. Although I am far from taciturn myself, I was, for once, perfectly content to listen. The stream of vivid, somewhat formal, eloquence flowed on like a mountain torrent, carrying all before it; at moments it was diverted this way and that by questions or interruptions by the other guests, but not for long: it always returned to its original course, sweeping away, or twisting round, every obstacle in its path, until a full account had been given of the picaresque adventures of his wartime experience.

He continued to talk to me, to my great pleasure, after dinner. Held, like the wedding guest, by this strange and plainly gifted Pole, who plied me with drink after drink long after the hosts had gone to bed, I finally made my excuses and made my way to my bedroom for a few hours' sleep, until the car that was to take me to Boulogne arrived at five in the morning. This was not to be. My new friend followed, settled himself on the edge of my bed and continued to talk. Some might have found this excessive. I did not; I thought it a strange but delightful experience.

By this time I had discovered that he was Auberon Herbert; that his father had died before he could know him, that he was devoted to his mother and his sisters; that he had joined the Polish forces because he had been rejected on medical grounds by those of his own country. I learnt, too, that he had, not very long before, nearly lost his life in a fracas with some Canadian soldiers, which he described in horrifying detail, mitigated by his rolling Victorian periods. His gift for languages was remarkable: he spoke Polish, Ukrainian, Dutch, as well as French and German, a little Russian (enough to indicate his extreme disapproval of the regime of that country), some Czech, and, of course, Italian, since he had spent many months in his family's house in Portofino. (He could manage some Genoese and Provençal too.) We turned out to have a good many acquaintances in common, of each of whom he was prepared to provide pungent vignettes; and he judged them by the ancient criteria of the traditional ruling classes of many lands: whether they had courage, moral or intellectual distinction, nobility of character, generosity, personal beauty, charm, breeding, and – most important of all – correct political and religious beliefs. These standards were applied in a confident, direct, unswerving fashion, with fine extravagance of speech and expression. I found that on a good many of our common friends and acquaintances his judgements at times diverged sharply from my own. He listened to my qualifications courteously, but without much attention: everyone he knew had his and her place in the coherent and vividly coloured world constructed by his fervid imagination, which now and again seemed to me to exist at a certain distance from the world of what most of us regard as reality.

This chance meeting resulted in an acquaintance which ripened into friendship. We met occasionally in London and Oxford; from time to time he would invite me (I was then single) to Pixton, but something always intervened. Ten years passed since our first meeting in Paris. In 1956 I married, and that September my wife and I, with some friends, came to stay in Portofino. There we saw a good deal of Mary Herbert and Auberon, who was most hospitable to us all; we greatly delighted in their company. In Portofino even more than in England, Auberon's quixotic qualities became overwhelmingly evident. He was high-souled and morally fastidious, fearless in his devotion to noble, knightly virtues, and the order in which alone they could flourish, deeply repelled as he was by the modern world, from which he sought refuge in an imaginary older world, to which his social, moral and religious code could be made to apply. Like Don Quixote, he was, above and beyond everything – to use that obsolescent concept – a gentleman. He was totally free from anything in the least small-minded, ignoble, petty, opportunist – anything that in Bloomsbury used to be called 'squalid'. His passion for the causes of the oppressed, which he supported in his own exceedingly individual-istic manner, seemed to me to stem mainly from his religious convictions, with which his chivalrous instinct was closely inter-woven. Don Quixote may not have achieved worldly success, but his life was nothing if not a triumphant affirmation of the Christian soul in a workaday society. Neither Don Quixote nor Auberon were realists. But then, when men say 'I am afraid I am rather a realist', what they often mean is that they are about to tell a lie or do something shabby. From this Auberon was immeasurably remote. Everything that was eccentric and, at times, comical about him sprang from his inability to compromise with the exception-ally 'realistic' values of some of the times and places in which he spent his not altogether happy life.

This was very evident in Portofino. The inhabitants of that portion of the Ligurian coast are not given to exaggerated idealism. They are dry-eyed, tough-minded, not liable to excessive compas-sion, and concerned with their immediate interests, beyond, perhaps, those of other Italian provinces. Auberon was, in a sense, well aware of this – he talked about it often and amusingly, but his penchant for living in an idealised universe led him to magnify the minor intrigues of the inhabitants of this resort, as well as his own relationships with neighbouring landowners and peasants, into dramatic feuds or wonderful alliances, conducted in a world drawn from the pages of Scott or Manzoni or Mary Renault, or at times even from the fantasies of J. R. R. Tolkien, to whose works he was deeply addicted; and this enabled him to live his life at a level at which he could breathe without too much moral discomfort. His vision of life was filled with plots and counter-plots, sinister political conspiracies, secret alliances and mysterious operations of men engaged sometimes in local purposes in Portofino or Genoa or Rome, around the papal throne, or in far-flung world-wide political or financial schemes into which ruthless and wicked men lured innocents to their destruction – schemes which, at any rate at the local Ligurian level, he believed himself able to penetrate and even to foil and turn to his own or other good people's advantage.

All this was done with immense gaiety, fancy, and sometimes

obsessive saga-spinning (which not everyone was always prepared to hear out to the end), but also with a certain unexpected half-awareness of its incomplete reality: moments of fancy (which stimulated some of his 'business' activities) were, it seemed to me, succeeded by periods of clear-eyed vision in which he knew that the world, as he described it to himself and others, was not perhaps wholly what he insisted on its being. Heroes and martyrs who had died for his faith populated his world; so, of course, did the oppressed peoples whose causes he took up zealously: Poles, Ukrainians, Belorussians. What the members of these movements in fact thought of him I do not know, but they were fortunate to find someone who was prepared to work for them so passionately, so disinterestedly, and to involve so many of his bemused friends, bemused but loyal to him, and therefore prepared, against all motives of prudence, to be wafted by him into all kinds of unlikely predicaments, on public platforms and stranger places, in pursuit of some usually Utopian goal.

Auberon was not only pure-hearted, generous, honourable, and a generator of marvellous Chestertonian fantasies, but warm-hearted, morally perceptive, and always responsive to the states of mind and fortune, the feelings, the moods, the joys and the miseries of his friends. Passionate and unswerving as his political convictions were – no one who approved of the Yalta agreement could be spoken to, at any rate with comfort; as for those who were tolerant of the totalitarian regimes east of the Iron Curtain, they were either fools or knaves and to be treated accordingly – the claims of friendship transcended even these barriers. Although he saw the world politically in terms of black and white, this nevertheless did not blind him to the true character of the human beings he met and came to know. More often than not he recognised honesty, goodness, purity of heart when he met them, however deplorable the political or religious opinions of those who possessed these properties; but sometimes he was deceived, and found his trust betrayed, especially by those he helped, who, at least on one occasion, exploited him shamelessly and used him ill. He bore no grudges and harboured no resentment. He was entirely free from malice and from ill will. But if my words tend to suggest the character of a remote dreamer, self-absorbed, detached from common concerns, living in a feudal Middle Age of his own, I have failed to convey a true image of Auberon. He was the very opposite of a prig or prude, noble but humourless, not of this world. Unlike Don Quixote, he possessed an acute sense of the incongruous, and, indeed, of the ridiculous, even in his own knight-errantry. He knew that his efforts to be elected to Parliament were not likely to bear fruit, and gave highly entertaining, self-deprecating accounts of his political ambitions and activities. There was a sense in which he knew that he could do relatively little for the Polish or Ukrainian groups which he supported, that a good many of the persons who clustered round him were less worthy than he told himself and others that they must surely be; and that the entire undertaking, however great its moral worth, had rickety foundations in the world of serious social and political action.

It is, perhaps, a property of the romantic temperament to be at once dedicated to pursuing unattainable goals, demanding of the world what it can never give – to develop a kind of spiritual maximalism – and also to remain ironically aware that such claims bear little relation to what can be achieved on earth. It is this that enabled Auberon not to be shocked or offended when he perceived that others, among them persons he liked and respected, stopped their ears to his propaganda, or looked on him as politically inept, whether or not they were personally fond of him, or were touched by his stout-hearted integrity. He was at once prepared to make light of his own endeavours and yet persist with them. The universe of his imagination, the semi-feudal, nostalgic, historical romance which he lived out so movingly, so gallantly and painfully, had become second nature to him, and perhaps, despite moments of penetrating self-awareness – the bitter moments when reality broke through the fantasy – had become one with his basic character and nature.

He was talented, civilised, very well bred, and hated moderation in all things. He was fiercely anti-utilitarian, pursued ends for their own sakes, to extremes, and despised those who did not. He disliked philistines, policemen, cowards and hypocrites more than liars, barbarians or cunning adventurers. More than almost anything he liked style, dash, lunatic courage. He was highly cultivated in an eighteenth-century sort of way. Apart from his gift for languages, he explored byways of philology, preferably of languages and dialects spoken by semi-submerged local populations – Basques or Genoese or Maltese or Lusatian Sorbs, or Dalmatians, or Greek enclaves in Magna Graecia – and had accumulated an extraordinary store of out-of-the-way historical knowledge which fed his past-directed imagination and his acute aesthetic sense. His taste, expressed in the delightful disorder of his life and the charm and distinction of the houses he inhabited in England and in Italy, remained impeccable; so were his manners, whether he was tipsy or sober. He made excellent jokes. Nothing he said could ever make one wince. He was sometimes monotonous and glazed, never embarrassing. He was a loyal and affectionate friend and behaved beautifully to those who worked for him.

His life at Pixton, the management of the broad but not on the whole rich lands which he owned, his country concerns, his hunting and the open-handed hospitality dispensed by his mother – to whom he remained utterly and deeply, perhaps too deeply, devoted – and which continued after her death, not long before his own, were as much as he could do to keep the traditions of an older world going, a world in which he breathed more freely and suffered less acutely. He was visited by a sense of frustration, desolation and, still more, acute loneliness. His faith (if someone as remote from it as I am may speak of it), which was deep, childlike, beset by no genuine doubts, and the supreme value which guided his entire being, preserved him and kept him from ultimate despair. He was, above all, an extraordinarily good man. This shone through everything he did and said. I was not among his intimates, but I knew him, loved and admired him, and mourn his passing, and the world of fantasy which vanished with him.

ALDOUS HUXLEY

THE CLASSICAL and History Middle and Upper Eighth forms at St Paul's School were, in the middle and late 1920s, an unusually sophisticated establishment. This was not directly induced by the masters, who were (with one exception – an obscure, eccentric, devoted contemporary and follower of Lytton Strachey) solid, sentimental and unimaginative. While the most civilised among them recommended Shaw, Wells, Chesterton, Gilbert Murray, Flecker, Edward Thomas, Sassoon and the *London Mercury*, we read Joyce, Firbank, Edward Carpenter, Wyndham Lewis, Schiller's Logic,[1] Havelock Ellis, Eliot, the *Criterion* and, under the impulse of Arthur Calder-Marshall, whose elder brother was then in America and favoured them, the works of H. L. Mencken, Carl Sandburg, Sherwood Anderson; we also took an interest in Cocteau, *transition*, the early surrealists. We looked down on *Life and Letters*, edited by Desmond MacCarthy, as tame and conventional. Among our major intellectual emancipators were J. B. S. Haldane, Ezra Pound, Aldous Huxley.

I cannot myself claim to have been liberated by anyone; if I was in chains then, I must be bound by them still. But, as men of letters – led by Voltaire, the head of the profession – rescued many oppressed human beings in the eighteenth century; as Byron or George Sand, Ibsen and Baudelaire, Nietzsche, Wilde and Gide and perhaps even Wells or Russell have done since; so members of my generation were assisted to find themselves by novelists, poets and critics concerned with the central problems of their day. Social and moral courage can, on occasion, exercise a more decisive influence than sensibility or original gifts. One of my own contemporaries, a man of exceptional honesty, intellectual power

[1] F. C. S. Schiller, *Formal Logic: A Scientific and Social Problem* (London, 1912).

and moral responsiveness, inhibited and twisted by an uncertain social position and bitter puritanism on the part of his father, was morally freed (as others have been by psychoanalysis, or Anatole France, or living among Arabs) by reading Aldous Huxley: in particular *Point Counter Point*, and one or two short stories. Light had been thrown for him on dark places, the forbidden was articulated, intimate physical experience, the faintest reference to which used to upset him profoundly and affect him with a feeling of violent guilt, had been minutely and fully described. From that moment my friend advanced intellectually, and became one of the most admired and productive men of learning of our day. It is not this therapeutic effect, however, that appealed to the young men of my generation so much as the fact that Huxley was among the few writers who, with all his constantly commented upon inability to create character, played with ideas so freely, so gaily, with such virtuosity, that the responsive reader, who had learnt to see through Shaw or Chesterton, was dazzled and excited. The performance took place against a background of relatively few simple moral convictions; they were disguised by the brilliance of the technical accomplishment, but they were there, they were easily intelligible, and, like a monotonous, insistent, continuous ground bass slowly pounding away through the elaborate intellectual display, they imposed themselves on the minds of the boys of seventeen and eighteen – still, for the most part, eager and morally impressionable, no matter how complex or decadent they may in their *naïveté* have conceived themselves to be.

I suspect that the impact diminished as the ground bass – the simple repetitive pattern of Huxley's moral and spiritual philosophy – became increasingly obsessive in his later novels, and destroyed the exhilarating, delightfully daring, 'modern', neo-classical upper lines of the music, in combination with which alone his novels seemed such masterpieces. The grave, noble, humane, tolerant figure of the 1940s and '50s inspired universal respect and admiration. But the transforming power – the impact – was that of the earlier, 'cynical', God-denying Huxley, the object of fear and disapproval to parents and schoolmasters, the wicked nihilist whose sincere and sweetly sentimental passages – especially about music – were swallowed whole, and with delight, by those young readers who supposed themselves to be indulging in one of the most dangerous and exotic vices of those iconoclastic post-war times. He was one of the great culture heroes of our youth.

When I met him in 1935 or 1936, in the house of a mutual friend, Lord Rothschild, in Cambridge, I expected to be overawed and perhaps sharply snubbed. But he was very courteous and very kind to everyone present. The company played intellectual games, so it seemed to me, after nearly every meal; it took pleasure in displaying its wit and knowledge; Huxley plainly adored such exercises, but remained uncompetitive, benevolent and remote. When the games were over at last, he talked, without altering his low, monotonous tone, about persons and ideas, describing them as if viewed from a great distance, as queer but interesting specimens, odd, but no odder than many others in the world on which he seemed to look as a kind of museum or encyclopaedia. He spoke with serenity and disarming sincerity, very simply. There was no malice and very little conscious irony in his conversation, only the mildest and gentlest mockery of the most innocent kind. He enjoyed describing prophets and mystagogues, but even such figures as Count Keyserling, Ouspensky and Gurdjieff, whom he did not much like, were given their due and indeed more than their due; even Middleton Murry was treated more mercifully and seriously than in the portrait in *Point Counter Point*. Huxley talked very well: he needed an attentive audience and silence, but he was not self-absorbed or domineering, and presently everyone in the room would fall under his peaceful spell; brightness and glitter went out of the air, everyone became calm, serious, interested and contented. The picture I have attempted to draw may convey the notion that Huxley, for all his noble qualities, may (like some very good men and gifted writers) have been something of a bore or a preacher. But this was not so at all, on the only occasions on which I met him. He had great moral charm and integrity, and it was these rare qualities (as with the otherwise very dissimilar G. E. Moore), and not brilliance or originality, that compensated and more than compensated for any lack-lustre quality, and for a certain thinness in the even, steady flow of words to which we all listened so willingly and respectfully.

The social world about which Huxley wrote was all but destroyed by the Second World War, and the centre of his interests appeared to shift from the external world to the inner life of men. His approach to all this remained scrupulously empirical, directly related to the facts of the experience of individuals of which there is record in speech or in writing. It was speculative and imaginative only in the sense that in his view the range of valuable human experience had often been too narrowly conceived; that the hypotheses and ideas which he favoured about men in their relations to each other and to nature illuminated the phenomena commonly described as paranormal or supernormal better than much conventional physiology or psychology, tied to inappropriate models as they seemed to him to be. He had a cause and he served it. The cause was to awaken his readers, scientists and laymen alike, to the connections, hitherto inadequately investigated and described, between regions artificially divided: physical and mental, sensuous and spiritual, inner and outer. Most of his later writings – novels, essays, lectures, articles – revolved round this theme. He was a humanist in the most literal and honourable sense of that fearfully abused word; he was interested in human beings as objects in nature in the sense in which the *philosophes* of the eighteenth century had been, and he cared about them as they had. His hopes for men rested on the advance of self-knowledge: he feared that humanity would destroy itself by over-population or by violence; from this only greater self-understanding would save them – above all, understanding of the intimate interplay of mental and physical forces, of man's place and function in nature, on which so much alternate light and darkness seemed to him to have been cast both by science and by religion.

He was sceptical of all those who have tried to systematise the broken glimpses of the truth that had been granted to mystics and visionaries, whom he thought of as uncommonly sensitive or gifted or fortunate men whose power of vision could be cultivated and extended by devoted, assiduous practice. He recognised no supernatural grace; he was not a theist, still less an orthodox Christian believer. In all his writings, whether inspired by Malthusian terrors, or by hatred of coercion and violence, or by opposition to what he called idolatry – the blind worship of some single value or institution to the exclusion of others, as something beyond rational criticism or discussion – or by Hindu and Buddhist classics, or by Western mystics and writers gifted with capacity for spiritual or psychological insight – Maine de Biran, Kafka, Broch (Huxley was a remarkable discoverer of original talent) – or by composers, sculptors, painters, or by poets in all the many languages that he read well – whatever his purpose or his mood, he always returned to the single theme that dominated his later years: the condition of men in the twentieth century. Over and over again he contrasted on the one hand their new powers to create works of unheard-of power and beauty and live wonderful lives – a future far wider and more brilliant than had ever stretched before mankind – with, on the other hand, the prospect of mutual destruction and total annihilation, due to ignorance and consequent enslavement by irrational idols and destructive passions – forces that all men could in principle control and direct, as some individuals had indeed already done. Perhaps no one since Spinoza has believed so passionately or coherently or fully in the principle that knowledge alone liberates, not merely knowledge of physics or history or physiology, or psychology, but an altogether wider panorama of possible knowledge which embraced forces, open and occult, which this infinitely retentive and omnivorous reader was constantly discovering with alternate horror and hope.

His later works, novels and tracts – the frontiers were at times not clear – were everywhere respectfully received; respectfully, but without marked enthusiasm. Those who saw him as a latter-day Lucian or Peacock complained that the wit, the virtuosity, the play of facts and ideas, the satirical eye had disappeared; that the sad, wise, good man who lived in California was but the noble ghost of the author who had earned himself an assured place in the history of English letters. In short, it was alleged that he had turned into a lay preacher, who, like other poets and prophets, had been abandoned by the spirit, so that, like Newton and Robert Owen, Wordsworth and Swinburne, he had ended with little to say, and went on saying it earnestly, honourably, tediously, to an ever-dwindling audience. Such critics were mistaken in at least one fundamental respect: if he was a prophet, he was so in a literal sense. Just as Diderot's *Le Rêve de d'Alembert* and the *Supplément au voyage de Bougainville* (particularly the former) anticipated biological and physiological discoveries of the nineteenth and twentieth centuries, and expressed in the form of audacious speculation some of the major advances in the natural sciences, so Aldous Huxley, with that special sensibility to the contours of the future which impersonal artists sometimes possess, stood on the edge of, and peered beyond, the present frontiers of our self-knowledge. He was the herald of what will surely be one of the great advances in this and following centuries – the creation of new psychophysical sciences, of discoveries in the realm of what at present, for want of a better term, we call the relations between body and mind; a field in which modern studies of myth and ritual, the psychological roots of social and individual behaviour, the relations of the physiological and the logical foundations of linguistics, as well as the phenomena of paranormal psychology, psychical therapy and the like, are but the earliest and most rudimentary beginnings.

Huxley was well aware of this. There is a sense in which he knew that he stood on the frontier between the old astrology that was passing and the new astronomy that was beginning in the sciences of man; and he therefore bore the frequent accusations of betraying his original rationalism in favour of a confused mysticism, of a sad collapse into irrationalism as a means of escape from his own private miseries and the bleakness of his particular world, of a weak abandonment of his old belief in the clear, the precise, the tangible, for the comforting obscurity of hazy, facile, pseudo-religious speculation – he bore these charges with great sweetness and patience. He was perfectly aware of what was being said: no one could have composed a better caricature of precisely these attitudes if he had wished. He persisted not because of some softening of a once gem-like intellect, but because he was convinced that his chosen field was the region in which the greatest and most transforming advance would be made by mankind.

On the last occasion on which I met him, he would – at least in public – speak of nothing but the need for the re-integration of what both science and life had divided too sharply: the restoration of human contact with non-human nature, the need for antidotes to the lopsided development of human beings in the direction of observation, criticism, theory, and away from the harmonious development of the senses, of the 'vegetative soul', of that which man has in common with animals and plants. Others have spoken of this. The great modern protest against alienation springs as much from a sense of isolation from natural processes as from lack of social harmony and common purpose. But Huxley did not, it is evident, believe in the possibility of repairing the texture through institutional change, whether gradualist or revolutionary; nor solely through psychological therapy, though he attached great importance to it. He believed that there were regions in the world, among primitive peoples and in non-European cultures, where forms of life persisted, or had at any rate not been wholly lost, the rediscovery of which would offer a shorter and surer path, based as it was on tradition and experience, than Acts of Parliament or social revolutions or mechanical inventions, or even educational innovations in which he deeply believed. Much of what he said may one day seem vague or unreal in the light of the future experiences of men. Much of it, too, may prove delusive, or fantastic, as often happens with pioneers and those who have an intuitive sense of what is to come. But I must own that I think him wholly right to have directed his excellent mind towards the problems of psychophysical relationships and the control of mental – or what he would have preferred to call spiritual – factors, in which he thought that the Indians, ancient and modern, had advanced beyond the West.

His warnings, whether in *Brave New World*, which is certainly the most influential modern expression of disillusionment with purely technological progress, or in his other novels and essays, and his premonitions, even at their flattest and least artistic, have enough genius to have created a new genre, the pessimistic, frightening Utopia – a vision of unintended consequences of what a good many uncritical liberals and Marxists still conceive, in E. H. Carr's complacent words, as 'old-fashioned belief in progress'. These novels create a genuine uneasiness by getting near the bone (the rotting bone, he would have said) of the contemporary experience of the West. He was a victim of a deep and universal malaise, against which he rightly perceived that too many contemporary antidotes were and are useless because they are too practical and therefore too short-sighted, or operate with concepts which are too shallow, too crude and ephemeral, too vulgar and insulting to the nature of man, particularly to those – to him all-important – still concealed and neglected powers in it about which he wrote. He was conscious of this fatal inadequacy in much contemporary politics, sociology and ethics. There is no coherent body of doctrine, no systematic exposition in his works. But that he had a sense of what men stood and stand in need of, and a premonition of the direction in which, if mankind survives at all, it will be moving – of that I feel convinced. If I am right, justice will one day be done to those very pages over which even his admirers at present shake their heads, some sadly, others patronisingly.

I was delighted to meet him in India in 1961, when he and I found ourselves as delegates at the same congress in New Delhi. He spoke on his usual theme, the poet as *vates* – a man with powers of discerning what other eyes could not see – the poet's claims to prophetic powers in a literal sense. He was received, of course, with immense respect in a country with which his beliefs gave him special ties. We – Huxley, the American delegate Louis

Untermeyer and I – went to a reception at which six or seven hundred students came to do him homage and collect his autograph. There was dead silence as he stood, distinguished and embarrassed, looking beyond their heads. An ironical young man broke the silence with some such words as these: 'After the late Mr Gandhi the Taj Mahal is certainly the most precious possession of the Indian people. Why then did you, Mr Huxley, in your book *Jesting Pilate*, speak in so disparaging a fashion of it? May I enquire, Sir, if you continue to adhere to this unfavourable view?' Huxley was amused and faintly put out. He said that perhaps he had spoken a little too harshly about the Taj Mahal, that he had not intended to wound anyone's feelings, that aesthetics was an uncertain field, that tastes were incommensurable, and then he gradually slid from this perilous ground to his central Tolstoyan theme – the unnatural lives that men lead today. But he wondered afterwards whether perhaps he had been unjust, and so we decided to revisit Agra. We travelled separately: he and his wife with the well-known Indian novelist Mulk Raj Anand; my wife and I in a separate car. We met in Agra and went together to Fatehpur Sikri, Akbar's dead city. Huxley adored it. He moved with the slow, sure-footed, slightly gliding steps of a somnambulist: his grave and urbane charm was moving and very delightful.

On the way to Fatehpur Sikri, he described his earlier visit to India in the 1920s, when he had stayed with one of his Oxford contemporaries, now a member of the Upper House in India, a distinguished man who had welcomed him on this occasion too. He described Jawaharlal Nehru's father, Motilal, who, he said, was a man of exquisite appearance and manners, and sent his shirts to be washed in Paris; he had belonged to the rich and power-loving aristocracy that had sought to use Gandhi for its purposes; but they found that he had outwitted them, that the attempt to harness this great force, or at any rate the flood of popular emotion which Gandhi had brought into being, proved fruitless, that Gandhi ended by controlling them and not, as they had hoped, the other way about. Huxley described the relations of these distinguished and autocratic Brahmins to Gandhi with a kind of benevolent irony, even-toned, slow, deliberate and exceedingly entertaining. He went on to an elaborate enumeration of the wiles and stratagems that he used, whether in California or in India, to escape the bores by whom his life was menaced. He was very simple, very serene, very easy to talk with. The fact that, a few weeks before, his house and all his books had been destroyed by fire seemed hardly to trouble him at all, nor did he by the slightest allusion reveal the fact that he knew that he was suffering from a mortal disease; he complained of his eyesight – his old, familiar infirmity – but said nothing about the cancer that was ultimately to end his life.

When he finally saw the Taj Mahal again, he relented; and decided that it was not as unsightly as he had supposed, but on the contrary, except for the minarets – 'chimney pots' which he still thought a mistake – it was a creditable building after all. We spent the evening together; I think that Jean Guéhenno, the French writer, was also there part of the time. Guéhenno, a melancholy, interesting and idealistic man, was not likely – nor did he intend – to raise anyone's spirits; and the lights in the hotel were very low owing to some permanent power failure. One might have thought that the whole occasion would be one of extreme, if dignified, gloom and depression. But it was not. Huxley was simple, natural and unselfconscious, what he said was unusual and absolutely authentic. Everything about him was so sincere and so interesting that the occasion was wholly enjoyable, and inspired, at any rate in me, a lasting affection and a degree of respect bordering on veneration.

Huxley had spent a great deal of his time collecting facts; he much preferred to be told facts rather than opinions – opinions he could form for himself. But despite this he did not, contrary to common belief, talk like an encyclopaedia. Nor were the hatred of the flesh, the puritanical streak, the ascetic's obsession with scatological detail which his writings sometimes betray, ever in evidence; nor was his conversation strewn with oddly assorted bric-à-brac of abstract knowledge; nor did he ever behave like a writer conscious of his status as a great man. He was courteous, serious and charming, and his movements and his words possessed a dignity and humanity wholly unrelated to the popular image of him in the 1920s. He seemed to be more interesting, and his thought, despite his deliberate manner, seemed to be more direct, spontaneous and moving, more personal and authentic than his writings, which even at their best have something mechanical and derivative. But the recollection that will remain in my mind for the rest of my life is that of a wholly civilised, good and scrupulous man, and one of the greatest imaginable distinction.

MEETINGS WITH RUSSIAN WRITERS
IN 1945 AND 1956

> Every attempt to produce coherent memories amounts
> to falsification. No human memory is so arranged as
> to recollect everything in continuous sequence. Letters
> and diaries often turn out to be bad assistants.

Anna Akhmatova[1]

I

IN THE SUMMER of 1945, while I was working as a temporary
official in the British Embassy in Washington, I was informed that
I was to be seconded to our Moscow Embassy for a few months;
the reason given was that it was short-handed, and since I knew
Russian, and had, at the San Francisco Conference (and long before
it), learnt something of official and unofficial American attitudes to
the Soviet Union, I might be of some use in filling a gap until the

I wish to acknowledge my gratitude to Miss Amanda Haight, Dr George
Katkov, Dr Aileen Kelly, Dr Robin Milner-Gulland, Professor Dimitri Obolensky, Mr Peter Oppenheimer, Mrs Josephine Pasternak, Mrs Lydia Pasternak-
Slater, Mr John Simmons and Mrs Patricia Utechin, all of whom were kind
enough to read the first draft of this account. I have greatly profited by their
suggestions, nearly all of which I have followed. For all the faults that remain, I
am, of course, solely responsible. I have never kept a diary, and this account is
based on what I now remember, or recollect that I remembered and sometimes
described to my friends during the last thirty or more years. I know only too well
that memory, at any rate my memory, is not always a reliable witness of facts or
events, particularly of conversations which, at times, I have quoted. I can only say
that I have recorded the facts as accurately as I can recall them. If there is
documentary or other evidence in the light of which this account should be
amplified or corrected, I shall be glad to learn of it. I.B. 1980.

[1] Quoted from L. A. Mandrykina, 'Nenapisannaya kniga: "Listki iz dnevnika"
A. A. Akhmatovoi' ('An Unwritten Book: Anna Akhmatova's "Pages from a
Diary" '), in *Knigi, Arkhivy, Avtografy* (Moscow, 1973), pp. 57–76; the quotation
appears on p. 75. Mandrykina's article is based on material in the archive of A. A.
Akhmatova in the V. I. Lenin State Library in Moscow (archive 1073, Nos 47–69);
the quotation appears in No 47, sheet 2.

New Year, when someone less amateur would be free to come. The War was over. The Potsdam Conference had led to no overt rift among the victorious allies. Despite gloomy forebodings in some quarters in the West, the general mood in official circles in Washington and London was cautiously optimistic; among the general public and in the Press it was much more hopeful and even enthusiastic: the outstanding bravery and appalling sacrifices of Soviet men and women in the war against Hitler created a vast wave of sympathy for their country which, during the second half of 1945, silenced many of the critics of the Soviet system and its methods; mutual understanding and co-operation at every level. were very widely and ardently desired. It was during this season of good feeling, which, one was told, reigned equally in the Soviet Union and in Britain, that I left for Moscow.

I had not been in Russia since my family left in 1920 (when I was eleven years old) and I had never seen Moscow. I arrived in the early autumn, was given a table in the Chancery, and did such odd jobs as were assigned to me. Although I reported for work at the Embassy every morning, the task (the only one I was ever asked to do) of reading, summarising and commenting on the content of the Soviet Press was not exactly arduous: the contents of periodicals were, by comparison with the West, monochrome, predictable and repetitive, and the facts and propaganda virtually identical in them all. Consequently I had plenty of spare time on my hands. I used it to visit museums, historic places and buildings, theatres, bookshops, to walk idly about the streets, and so on; but unlike many foreigners, at any rate non-Communist visitors from the West, I had the extraordinary good fortune to meet a number of Russian writers, at least two among them persons of outstanding genius. Before I describe my meetings with them, I should say something about the background of the literary and artistic situation in Moscow and Leningrad as it appeared to me during the fifteen weeks that I spent in the Soviet Union.

The magnificent flowering of Russian poetry which had begun in the 1890s – the bold, creative, numerous, vastly influential experiments in the arts at the beginning of the twentieth century, the main currents within the new movements, the symbolist, post-impressionist, cubist, abstract, expressionist, futurist, suprematist and constructivist movements in painting and sculpture; their various tributaries and confluences in literature, as well as Acmeism, ego- and cubo-futurism, imagism, 'trans-sense' (the *zaumnye*) in poetry; realism and anti-realism in the theatre and the ballet – this vast amalgam, so far from being arrested by war and revolution, continued to derive vitality and inspiration from a vision of a new world. Despite the conservative artistic tastes of the majority of the Bolshevik leaders, anything that could be represented as a 'slap in the face' to bourgeois taste was in principle approved and encouraged: and this opened the way to a great outpouring of exciting manifestos and audacious, controversial, often highly gifted experiments in all the arts and in criticism, which, in due course, were to make a powerful impact on the West. The names of the most original among the poets whose work survived the Revolution, Alexander Blok, Vyacheslav Ivanov, Andrey Bely, Valery Bryusov and, in the next generation, Mayakovsky, Pasternak, Velemir Khlebnikov, Osip Mandel'shtam, Anna Akhmatova; of the painters, Benois, Roerich, Somov, Bakst, Larionov, Goncharova, Kandinsky, Chagall, Soutine, Klyun, Malevich, Tatlin, Lissitzky; of the sculptors, Arkhipenko, Gabo, Pevsner, Lipchitz, Zadkine; of the producers,[1] Meyerhold, Vakhtangov, Tairov, Eisenstein, Pudovkin; of the novelists, Aleksey Tolstoy, Babel', Pil'nyak – all these became widely known in the West. They were not isolated peaks, but were surrounded by foothills. There was a genuine renaissance, different in kind from the artistic scene in other countries, in Russia during the 1920s. Much cross-fertilisation between novelists, poets, artists, critics, historians, scientists took place, and this created a culture of unusual vitality and achievement, an extraordinary upward curve in European civilisation.

Plainly all this was too good to last. The political consequences of the devastation of war and civil war, of the famine, the systematic destruction of lives and institutions by the dictatorship, ended the conditions in which poets and artists could create freely. After a relatively relaxed period during the years of the New Economic Policy, Marxist orthodoxy grew strong enough to challenge and, in the late 1920s, crush all this unorganised revolutionary activity. A collectivist proletarian art was called for; the critic Averbakh led a faction of Marxist zealots against what was described as unbridled individualistic literary licence – or as formalism, decadent aestheticism, kowtowing to the West, opposition to socialist collectivism.

[1] Today called 'directors'.

Persecution and purges began; but since it was not always possible to predict which side would win, this alone, for a time, gave a certain grim excitement to literary life. In the end, in the early 1930s, Stalin decided to put an end to all these politico-literary squabbles, which he plainly regarded as a sheer waste of time and energy. The leftist zealots were liquidated; no more was heard of proletarian culture or collective creation and criticism, nor yet of the non-conformist opposition to it. In 1934 the Party (through the newly created Union of Writers) was put in direct charge of literary activity. A dead level of State-controlled orthodoxy followed: no more argument; no more disturbance of men's minds; the goals were economic, technological, educational – to catch up with the material achievements of the enemy – the capitalist world – and overtake it. If the dark mass of illiterate peasants and workers was to be welded into a militarily and technically invincible modern society, there was no time to be lost; the new revolutionary order was surrounded by a hostile world bent on its destruction; vigilance on the political front left no time for high culture and controversy, or concern for civil liberties and basic human rights. The tune must be called by constituted authority; writers and artists, the importance of whose influence was never denied or ignored, must dance to it.

Some conformed, some did not, to a lesser or greater degree; some felt state tutelage to be oppressive, others accepted and even welcomed it, since they told themselves, and one another, that it conferred upon them a status denied them by the philistine and indifferent West. In 1932 there were some symptoms of a coming relaxation; it did not come. Then came the final horror: the Great Purge, heralded by the repression which followed the assassination of Kirov in 1934 and the notorious political show trials, and culminating in the Ezhov Terror of 1937–8, the wild and indiscriminate mowing down of individuals and groups, later of whole peoples. While Gorky, with his immense prestige in the Party and the nation, was alive, his mere existence may have exercised some moderating influence. The poet Mayakovsky, whose fame and reputation as a voice of the Revolution were almost equal to Gorky's, had committed suicide in 1930 – Gorky died six years later. Soon after that Meyerhold, Mandel'shtam, Babel', Pil'nyak, Klyuev, the critic D. S. Mirsky, the Georgian poets Yashvili and Tabidze – to mention only the most widely known – were arrested and done to death. A few years later, in 1941, the poetess Marina Tsvetaeva, who had not long before returned from Paris, committed suicide. The activities of informers and false witnesses exceeded all previously known bounds; self-prostration, false and wildly implausible confessions, bending before, or active co-operation with, authority, usually failed to save those marked for destruction. For the rest it left painful and humiliating memories from which some of the survivors of the Terror were never completely to recover.

The most authentic and harrowing accounts of the life of the intelligentsia during that murderous period, neither the first nor, probably, the last in the history of Russia, are to be found in Nadezhda Mandel'shtam's and Lydia Chukovskaya's memoirs; and, in a different medium, in Akhmatova's poem *Requiem*. The number of writers and artists exiled and destroyed was such that in 1939 Russian literature, art and thought emerged like an area that had been subjected to a terrible bombardment, with some splendid buildings still relatively intact, but standing bare and solitary in a landscape of ruined and deserted streets. Finally Stalin called a halt to the proscriptions: a breathing space followed; nineteenth-century classics were again treated with respect, old street-names replaced revolutionary nomenclature. The period of convalescence was virtually blank so far as the creative and critical arts were concerned.

Then came the German invasion, and the picture changed again. Such authors of distinction as had survived the Great Purge and had managed to retain their human semblance responded passionately to the great wave of patriotic feeling. Some degree of truth returned to literature: war poems, not only those by Pasternak and Akhmatova, sprang from profound feeling. In the days when all Russians were caught up in the high tide of national unity, and the nightmare of the purges was succeeded by the tragic but inspiring and liberating sense of patriotic resistance and heroic martyrdom, writers, old and young, who expressed it, particularly those who had a vein of genuine poetry in them, were idolised as never before. An astonishing phenomenon took place: poets whose writing had been regarded with disfavour by the authorities, and who had consequently been published rarely and in very limited editions, began to receive letters from soldiers at the fronts, as often as not quoting their least political and most personal lines. I was told that

the poetry of Blok, Bryusov, Sologub, Esenin, Tsvetaeva, Mayakovsky was widely read, learnt by heart and quoted by soldiers
and officers and even political commissars. Akhmatova and
Pasternak, who had for a long time lived in a kind of internal exile,
received an amazingly large number of letters from the front,
quoting from both published and unpublished poems, for the most
part circulated privately in manuscript copies; there were requests
for autographs, for confirmation of the authenticity of texts, for
expressions of the author's attitude to this or that problem. In the
end this did not fail to impress itself on some of the Party leaders:
the value of such writers as patriotic voices of which the State
might one day be proud came to be realised by the bureaucrats of
literature. The status and personal security of the poets were
improved in consequence.

During the immediate post-war years, and, indeed, until the end
of their lives, the most distinguished among the older writers found
themselves in an odd condition of being objects of simultaneous
worship on the part of their readers and of a half-respectful, half-
suspicious toleration by the authorities: a small, diminishing
Parnassus, sustained by the love and admiration of the young.
Public readings by poets, as well as the reciting from memory of
poetry at private gatherings and parties of all kinds, had been
common in pre-revolutionary Russia; what was novel was a fact
described to me by both Pasternak and Akhmatova, that when
they read their poems before the vast audiences who packed
assembly halls to hear them, and occasionally halted for a word,
there were always scores of listeners present who prompted them
at once – with passages from works both published and unpublished (and in any case not publicly available). No writer could
help being moved or could fail to draw strength from this most
genuine form of homage; they knew that their status was unique,
that this absorbed attention was something that poets in the West
might well envy; and yet, despite this sense of contrast, which most
Russians feel between what they regard as the open, passionate,
spontaneous, 'broad' Russian nature and the dry, calculating,
civilised, inhibited, sophisticated approach usually attributed to the
West (enormously exaggerated by Slavophils and populists), a
good many among them still believed in the existence of an
unexhausted Western culture, full of variety and free creative
individuality, unlike the grey on grey of daily life in the Soviet
Union, broken only by sudden acts of repression; nothing I could

say – I speak of more than thirty years ago[1] – could shake this passionate conviction.

However this may be, famous poets were, at this time, heroic figures in the Soviet Union. It may well be so still. What is certain is that the vast increase in literacy, together with the wide circulation of the best-known Russian and foreign literary classics, particularly of translations into the various national languages of the USSR, created a public the responsiveness of which was, and probably still is, unique in the world. There is plenty of evidence that the majority of the avid readers of foreign masterpieces tended at that time to think that life in England and France was similar to that described by Dickens or Balzac; but the intensity of their vision of the worlds of these novelists, their emotional and moral involvement, their often childlike fascination with the lives of characters in these novels, seemed to me to be more direct, fresh, un-used-up, far more imaginative, than the corresponding response of the average readers of fiction in, say, England or France or the United States. The Russian cult of the writer as hero – which began early in the nineteenth century – is bound up with this. I do not know how it is today: perhaps it is all quite different – I can testify only that in the autumn of 1945 the crowded bookshops, with their understocked shelves, the eager literary interest – indeed, enthusiasm – of the government employees who ran them, the fact that even *Pravda* and *Izvestiya* sold out within a few minutes of their appearance in the kiosks, argued a degree of intellectual hunger unlike that found elsewhere. The rigid censorship which, with so much else, suppressed pornography, trash and low-grade thrillers such as fill railway bookstalls in the West, served to make the response of Soviet readers and theatre audiences purer, more direct and naïve than ours; I noticed that at performances of Shakespeare or Sheridan or Griboedov members of the audience, some of them obviously country folk, were apt to react to the action on the stage or to lines spoken by the actors – rhyming couplets in Griboedov's *Woe from Wit*, for example – with loud expressions of approval or disapproval; the excitement generated was, at times, very strong and, to a visitor from the West, both unusual and touching. These audiences were, perhaps, not far removed from those for which Euripides or Shakespeare wrote; my neighbours in the theatre,

---

[1] This essay, written in 1980, contains several references to the then present which have mostly not been altered in the light of more recent events. Ed. 1997.

when they talked to me, often seemed to look on the dramatic action with the sharp and unspoilt eyes of intelligent adolescents – the ideal public of the classical dramatists, novelists and poets. It may be that it is the absence of this kind of popular response that has made some avant-garde art in the West at times seem mannered, contrived and obscure – in the light of this the condemnation of much modern literature and art by Tolstoy, however sweeping, dogmatic and wrong-headed, becomes more intelligible. The contrast between the extraordinary receptivity and interest, critical and uncritical, of the Soviet public in anything that seemed authentic, new, or even true, and the inferiority of the pabulum provided by government-controlled purveyors, astonished me. I had expected a far greater degree of colourless, depressing conformity at all levels. At the official level, which included critics and reviewers, this was indeed so; but not among those to whom I spoke in theatres and cinemas, at lectures, football matches, in trains and trams and bookshops.

When, before my journey to Moscow, I was given advice by British diplomats who had served there, I was warned that meetings with Soviet citizens were difficult to achieve. I was told that a certain number of carefully selected high bureaucrats were to be met at official diplomatic receptions, and that these tended by and large to repeat the Party line and avoid all real contact with foreigners, at any rate those from the West; that ballet-dancers and actors were occasionally permitted to attend such receptions because they were thought to be the simplest-minded and least intellectual among artists, and consequently least likely either to be infected by unorthodox thoughts or to give anything away. In short, the impression I received was that, apart from linguistic obstacles, the general fear of association with foreigners, in particular those coming from capitalist countries, together with specific instructions to members of the Communist Party not to engage in such activities, left all Western missions culturally insulated; that their members (and most journalists and other foreigners) lived in a kind of zoo, with intercommunicating cages, but cut off by a high fence from the outside world. I found that this was to a large extent true, but not as much as I had been led to expect. I did, during my brief stay, meet not only the same well-regimented group of ballet-dancers and literary bureaucrats who were to be seen at all receptions, but also a number of genuinely gifted writers, musicians and producers, among them two poets of genius. One of these was the man I most of all wished to meet, Boris Leonidovich Pasternak, whose poetry and prose I deeply admired. I could not bring myself to seek his acquaintance without some excuse, however transparent. Fortunately I had met his sisters, who were living in Oxford, and one of them had asked me to take a pair of boots for her brother the poet. This was the pretext I needed, and I was most grateful for it.

I arrived in Moscow just in time to attend a dinner arranged by the British Embassy to celebrate an anniversary of its Russian-language publication, *The British Ally*, to which Soviet writers had been invited. The guest of honour was J. B. Priestley, who was then regarded as a firm friend by the authorities of the Soviet Union; his books were much translated, and two of his plays were, I seem to recollect, then being performed in Moscow. That evening Priestley seemed out of humour: he was, I think, exhausted by being taken to too many collective farms and factories – he told me that although he had been well received, he had found the majority of these official visits inconceivably tedious; in addition to this, his royalties had been blocked, conversation through interpreters was horribly stilted, in short he was not enjoying himself, was very tired and longed to go to bed. So, at any rate, his interpreter and guide from the British Embassy whispered to me; he proposed to accompany the guest of honour back to his hotel, and asked me if I would try to do something to fill the awkward gap left by Mr Priestley's early departure. I readily agreed and found myself sitting between the famous director Tairov and the equally distinguished literary historian, critic, translator and inspired writer of children's verse, Korney Chukovsky. Opposite me was the best known of all Soviet film directors, Sergey Eisenstein. He looked somewhat depressed: the reason for this, as I learned later, was not far to seek.[1] I asked him to what years of his life he looked back

[1] A short while before he had been severely reprimanded by Stalin, who had been shown the second part of his film *Ivan the Terrible*, and had expressed his displeasure, mainly, I was told, because Tsar Ivan (with whom Stalin may, to some degree, have identified himself) had been represented as a deeply disturbed young ruler, violently shaken by his discovery of treason and sedition among his boyars, tormented by the need to apply savage measures if he was to save the State and his own life, and transformed by this experience into a lonely, gloomy despot, suspicious to the point of neurosis, even while he was raising his country to a pinnacle of greatness.

with the greatest pleasure. He replied that the early post-revolutionary period was far and away the best in his own life as a creative artist, and in the lives of many others. It was a time, he said wistfully, when wild and marvellous things could be done with impunity. He remembered with particular delight an occasion at the beginning of the 1920s when pigs covered with grease were let loose among the audience of a Moscow theatre, who leapt on to their seats, terrified; people shrieked, the pigs squealed. 'This was just what was required by our surrealist spectacle. Most of us who were active in those days were happy to be living and working then; we were young and defiant and full of ideas; it did not matter whether we were Marxists or formalists or futurists – painters, writers or musicians – we all met and quarrelled, sometimes very bitterly, and stimulated each other; we really did enjoy ourselves, and produced something, too.'

Tairov said much the same. He, too, spoke wistfully about the experimental theatre of the 1920s, about the genius of both Vakhtangov and Meyerhold; about the boldness and vitality of the short-lived Russian modern movement, which, in his view, was far more interesting than anything achieved on the stage by Piscator or Brecht or Gordon Craig. I asked him what had brought the movement to an end: 'Things change,' he said, 'but it was a wonderful time; not to the taste of Stanislavsky or Nemirovich, but absolutely wonderful.' The actors of the Moscow Art Theatre were not now educated enough, he said, to understand what Chekhov's characters were really like: their social status, their attitudes, manners, accents, their entire culture, outlook, habits were a closed book to the rising actors and actresses of the present; no one had been more aware of this than Chekhov's widow, Olga Knipper, and, of course, Stanislavsky himself; the greatest actor who survived from those days was the peerless, but rapidly ageing, Kachalov; he would soon retire and then, with modernism gone and naturalism in decay, would something new spring up? He doubted it: 'A few minutes ago I said to you "Things change." But they also do not change. This is even worse.' And he fell into gloomy silence.

Tairov proved right on both scores. Certainly Kachalov was the best actor I have seen in my life. When he was on the stage as Gaev in Chekhov's *Cherry Orchard* (he played the part of the student in the original performance) he literally fascinated the audience, nor did the other actors take their eyes off him: the beauty of his voice and the charm and expressiveness of his movements were such that one wished to go on looking at him and listening to him for ever; this may have distorted the balance of the play, but Kachalov's performance that night, like Ulanova's dancing in Prokofiev's *Cinderella*, which I saw a month later (and Chaliapin in *Boris Godunov* many years before), remains in my memory as an unsurpassed summit in terms of which to judge all later performances. So far as power of expression on the stage is concerned, these Russians still seem to me to have no equals in the twentieth century.

The neighbour on my right, the critic Korney Chukovsky, talked with rare wit and charm about writers, both Russian and English. He said that his brisk dismissal by the guest of honour reminded him of the visit to Russia of the American journalist Dorothy Thompson. She came with her husband, Sinclair Lewis, whose fame in Russia in the 1930s was very great: 'Several of us called on him in his hotel room – we wished to tell him how much his wonderful novels had meant to us. He sat with his back to us, typing away on his machine, and did not once turn his head to look at us; he did not utter a sound. This had a certain sublimity.' I did my best to assure him that his own works were read and greatly admired by Russian scholars in English-speaking countries; by Maurice Bowra, for example (who, in his memoirs, gives an account of meeting him during the First World War), and by Oliver Elton – the only English writers interested in Russian literature whom at that time I knew personally. Chukovsky told me of his two visits to England, the first at the beginning of the century when he was very poor and earned a few shillings by casual work – he had learned English by reading Carlyle's *Past and Present* and *Sartor Resartus*, the second of which he had bought for one penny, and which he extracted for me there and then out of his waistcoat pocket. He was a frequenter in those days, he told me, of the Poetry Bookshop, whose celebrated owner, the poet Harold Monro, befriended him and introduced him to various British men of letters including Robert Ross, Oscar Wilde's friend, of whom he retained an agreeable memory. He felt, he said, at ease in the Poetry Bookshop, but nowhere else in England; like Herzen, he admired and was amused by the social structure and the manners of the English, but like him had made no friends among them. He loved Trollope: 'What wonderful parsons [*popy*], charming, eccentric –

nothing like that here, in old Russia; here they were sunk in sloth and stupidity and greed. They were a miserable crew. The present ones, who have had a difficult time since the Revolution, are a much better lot: at least they can read and write; some are decent and honourable men. But you will never meet our priests – why should you want to? I am sure that English clergymen are still the most delightful people in the world.' He then told me about his second visit, during the First World War, when he came with a party of Russian journalists to report on the British war effort; they were entertained by Lord Derby, with whom he had found little common ground, at a weekend at Knowsley, of which he also gave an exceedingly entertaining and not very respectful account.

Chukovsky was a writer of high distinction who had made his name before the Revolution. He was a man of the left, and welcomed the Revolution; like all intellectuals of any independence of mind, he had had his share of harassment by the Soviet authorities. There are more ways than one of preserving one's sanity under a despotism: he achieved his own by a kind of ironical detachment, careful behaviour and considerable stoicism of character; the decision to confine himself to the relatively calm waters of nineteenth-century literature in Russian and in English, of children's verse, of translation, may have saved himself and his family, if only just, from the dreadful fate of some of their closest friends. He informed me that he had one overmastering wish; if I could satisfy it he would do almost anything for me in return: he longed to read Trollope's autobiography. His friend Ivy Litvinov, the wife of Maxim Litvinov, the former Foreign Minister and Ambassador to the United States, who was living in Moscow, could not find her own copy and thought it unsafe to order one from England in view of the extreme suspicion in which all relations with foreign countries were held; could I supply it? I did so a few months later, and he was delighted by it. I said that what I in my turn wished for most of all was to meet Boris Pasternak, who was living in the writers' village of Peredelkino, where Chukovsky, too, had a cottage. Chukovsky said that he admired Pasternak's poetry deeply; personally, although he loved him, he had had his ups and downs with him – his interest in Nekrasov's civic poetry and in populist writers of the late nineteenth century had always irritated Pasternak, who was a pure poet out of tune with the Soviet regime, with a particular distaste for committed – *engagé* – literature of any kind; nevertheless, he was at the moment on good terms with him, would arrange a meeting, and warmly invited me to visit him too, on the same day.

This was, as I was soon to discover, a courageous, not to say foolhardy, act: contact with foreigners – especially members of Western embassies, all of whom were regarded by the Soviet authorities, and particularly by Stalin himself, as spies – was, to say the least, strongly discouraged. Realisation of this fact led me later, in some cases too late, to exercise caution in meeting Soviet citizens informally – it placed them in a degree of danger which not all those who wished to see me seemed fully to realise; some did so, and knew that in meeting me they were taking a risk, but took it because their desire to be in contact with life in the West was overwhelming. Others were less reckless, and I respected their well-grounded fears and met fewer Soviet citizens, especially those not protected to some extent by their fame abroad, than I could have wished, for fear of compromising them. Even so, I probably did inadvertent harm to innocent people whom I met accidentally, or because they assured me, in some cases, as it turned out, mistakenly, that it involved no risk for them. Whenever I hear of the subsequent fate of some of these, I feel qualms of conscience, and blame myself for not having resisted the temptation of meeting some of the most unspoilt, delightful, responsive, moving human beings I have ever come across, with a quality of intellectual gaiety astonishing in their circumstances, consumed, for the most part, with an enormous curiosity about life beyond the frontiers of their country, anxious to establish a purely human relationship with a visitor from that outer world who spoke their language and, it seemed to them, understood them and was understood by them. I do not know of any case of imprisonment or worse, but I do know of cases of harassment and persecution to which meetings with me may have contributed. It is difficult to tell, for the victims often never knew why they were punished. One can only hope that survivors do not feel too bitterly towards the foreign visitors for the harm of which, unwittingly and perhaps too unthinkingly, we may have been a cause.

The visit to Peredelkino was arranged for a week after the dinner at which I met Korney Chukovsky. In the meanwhile, at another festivity in honour of Priestley (for whose presence I am still grateful, since it helped to open doors to me), I met Mme

Afinogenova, a Hungarian-American dancer, the widow of a playwright 'honourably' killed – in an air-raid on Moscow in 1941 – who was evidently authorised, and perhaps instructed, to organise a salon for foreign visitors with cultural interests. At any rate, she invited me to it, and there I met a number of writers. The best known among them was the poet Ilya Sel'vinsky ('Sel'vinsky had his hour, but it is, thank God, long past,' said Pasternak to me later), who had had the temerity to suggest that if socialist realism was the correct genre of imaginative writing, it might perhaps be equally compatible with Communist ideology to develop a literature of socialist romanticism – a freer use of the imagination, equally impregnated with total loyalty to the Soviet system. He had recently been harshly reproved for this, and when I met him was in an obviously nervous state. He asked me whether I agreed that the five greatest English writers were Shakespeare, Byron, Dickens, Wilde and Shaw; with perhaps Milton and Burns as runners-up. I said that I had no doubt about Shakespeare and Dickens, but before I could continue he went on to say that it was our new writers that they were interested in – what about Greenwood and Aldridge? What could I say about them? I realised that these were names of contemporary writers, but confessed that I had never heard of them – this was, perhaps, because I had been abroad during the greater part of the War – what had they written?

This was clearly not believed. I discovered later that Aldridge was an Australian Communist novelist and that Greenwood had written a popular novel called *Love on the Dole*; their works had been translated into Russian and published in large editions. Ordinary Soviet readers had little idea of what scales of values obtained in other societies, or sections of them; an official literary committee, directed by the cultural department of the Party's Central Committee, decided what was to be translated and how widely it was to be distributed, and modern British writing at that moment was in effect represented principally by A. J. Cronin's *Hatter's Castle*, two or three plays by Somerset Maugham and Priestley, and – so it seemed – the novels of Greenwood and Aldridge (the age of Graham Greene, C. P. Snow, Iris Murdoch and the 'angry young man' – who have since been extensively translated – had not yet dawned).

It was my impression that my hosts thought that I was less than honest when I said that I knew nothing of the two authors whom they mentioned, because I was an agent of a capitalist power, and therefore obliged to ignore the merits of left-wing writers, much as they themselves were committed to real or pretended ignorance of most émigré Russian writers and composers. 'I know,' said Sel'vinsky, speaking loudly, with great rhetorical force, as if he were addressing a much wider audience, 'I know that we are called conformists in the West. We are. We conform because we find that whenever we deviate from the Party's directives it always turns out that the Party was right and that we were wrong. It has always been so. It is not only that they say that they know better: they do; they see further: their eyes are sharper, their horizons are wider, than ours.' The rest of the company looked uncomfortable: these words were plainly intended for the concealed microphones without which we could scarcely have met as we did. Under dictatorships public and private expressions of opinion may differ; but Sel'vinsky's outburst was, perhaps because of the insecurity of his own position, too clumsy and overdone: hence the embarrassed silence which followed. I realised none of this at the time, and argued that free discussion, even of political issues, was no danger to democratic institutions: 'We are a scientifically governed society,' said a handsome lady who had once been one of Lenin's secretaries and was married to a famous Soviet writer, 'and if there is no room for free thinking in physics – a man who questions the laws of motion is obviously ignorant or mad – why should we, Marxists, who have discovered the laws of history and society, permit free thinking in the social sphere? Freedom to be wrong is not freedom; you seem to think that we lack freedom of political discussion; I simply do not understand what you mean. Truth liberates: we are freer than you in the West.' Lenin was quoted, so was Lunacharsky. When I said that I remembered propositions of this sort in the works of Auguste Comte, that this was the thesis of French positivists in the nineteenth century, whose views were surely not accepted by Marx or Engels, a chill fell upon the room, and we passed on to harmless literary gossip. I had learnt my lesson. To argue about ideas while Stalin was in power was to invite predictable answers from some, and to put those who remained silent in some jeopardy. I never saw Mme Afinogenova or any of her guests again. I had obviously behaved with conspicuous absence of tact, and their reaction was perfectly comprehensible.

II

A few days later, accompanied by Lina Ivanovna Prokofiev, the composer's estranged wife, I took the train to Peredelkino. Gorky, I was told, had organised this colony to provide recognised writers with an environment in which they could work in peace. Given the temperament of creative artists, this well-intentioned plan did not always lead to harmonious coexistence: some of the personal and political tensions could be sensed even by an ignorant stranger like myself. I walked down the tree-lined road which led to the houses inhabited by the writers. On the way there we were stopped by a man who was digging a ditch; he climbed out of it, said his name was Yazvitsky, asked after our names, and spoke at some length about an excellent novel that he had written called *The Fires of the Inquisition*; he warmly recommended it to us and told us that we should read an even better novel he was in the course of writing about Ivan III and medieval Russia. He wished us Godspeed and returned to his ditch. My companion thought it all somewhat uncalled-for, but I was charmed by this unexpected, direct, open-hearted and utterly disarming monologue; the simplicity and immediacy, even when it was naïve, the absence of formalities and small talk which seemed to hold everywhere outside official circles, was, and is, wonderfully attractive.

It was a warm, sunlit afternoon in early autumn. Pasternak, his wife and his son Leonid were seated round a rough wooden table in the tiny garden at the back of the dacha. The poet greeted us warmly. He was once described by his friend the poetess Marina Tsvetaeva as looking like an Arab and his horse: he had a dark, melancholy, expressive, very *racé* face, now familiar from many photographs and his father's paintings; he spoke slowly, in a low tenor monotone, with a continuous, even sound, something between a humming and a drone, which those who met him almost always remarked; each vowel was elongated as if in some plaintive, lyrical aria in an opera by Tchaikovsky, but with more concentrated force and tension.

With an awkward gesture I offered him the parcel that I was holding in my hands, and explained that I had brought him a pair of boots sent him by his sister Lydia. 'No, no, what is all this?' he said, visibly embarrassed, as if I were offering him a charitable gift: 'It must be a mistake, this must be for my brother.' I, too, became acutely embarrassed. His wife, Zinaida Nikolaevna, tried to put me at my ease and asked me whether England was recovering from the effects of the War. Before I could answer, Pasternak broke in: 'I was in London in the '30s – in 1935 – on my way back from the Anti-Fascist Congress in Paris. Let me tell you what happened. It was summer, I was in the country, when two officials, probably from the NKVD – not, I think, the Writers' Union – called – we were not quite so afraid of such visits then, I suppose – and one of them said "Boris Leonidovich, an Anti-Fascist Congress is taking place in Paris. You have been invited to it. We should like you to go tomorrow. You will go via Berlin: you can stay there for a few hours and see anyone you wish: you will arrive in Paris on the next day and will address the Congress in the evening." I said that I had no suitable clothes for such a visit. They said that they would see to that. They offered me a formal morning coat and striped trousers, a white shirt with stiff cuffs and a wing collar, a magnificent pair of black patent leather boots which, I found, fitted perfectly. But I somehow managed to go in my everyday clothes. I was later told that pressure had been brought to bear at the last minute by André Malraux, one of the chief organisers of the Congress, to get me invited. He had explained to the Soviet authorities that not to send me and Babel' might cause unnecessary speculation, since we were very well known in the West, and there were, at that time, not many Soviet writers to whom European and American liberals would be so ready to listen. So, although I was not on the original list of Soviet delegates – how could I possibly be? – they agreed.'

He went via Berlin, as arranged, where he met his sister Josephine and her husband, and said that when he arrived at the Congress many important and famous people – Dreiser, Gide, Malraux, Forster, Aragon, Auden, Spender, Rosamond Lehmann and other celebrities – were there. 'I spoke. I said "I understand that this is a meeting of writers to organise resistance to Fascism. I have only one thing to say to you about that. Do not organise. Organisation is the death of art. Only personal independence matters. In 1789, 1848, 1917 writers were not organised for or against anything; do not, I implore you, do not organise." I think they were very surprised. But what else could I say? I thought I would get into trouble at home after that, but no one ever said a word to me about it, then or now.[1] I went on from Paris to

---

[1] I asked André Malraux about this many years later. He said that he did not remember this speech.

London, where I saw my friend Lomonosov, a most fascinating man, like his namesake, a kind of scientist – an engineer. Then I travelled back to Leningrad in one of our boats, and shared a cabin with Shcherbakov, then the Secretary of the Writers' Union, who was tremendously influential.[1] I talked without ceasing, day and night. He begged me to stop and let him sleep. But I went on and on. Paris and London had awoken me, I could not stop. He begged for mercy, but I was relentless. He must have thought me quite deranged; it may be that I owe a good deal to his diagnosis of my condition.' Pasternak did not explicitly say that what he meant was that to have been thought a little mad, or at least very eccentric, might have helped to save him during the Great Purge; but the others present told me that they understood this all too well, and explained it to me later.

Pasternak asked me whether I had read his prose – in particular *The Childhood of Lüvers*, which I greatly admired. I said that I had. 'I can see by your expression', he said, quite unjustly, 'that you think that these writings are contrived, tortured, self-conscious, horribly modernist – no, no, don't deny it, you do think this and you are absolutely right. I am ashamed of them – not of my poetry, but of my prose – it was influenced by what was weakest and most muddled in the symbolist movement, which was fashionable in those years, full of mystical chaos – of course Andrey Bely was a genius – *Petersburg, Kotik Letaev* are full of wonderful things – I know that, you need not tell me – but his influence was fatal – Joyce is another matter – all I wrote then was obsessed, forced, broken, artificial, no good [*negodno*]; but now I am writing something entirely different: something new, quite new, luminous, elegant, harmonious, well-proportioned [*stroinoe*], classically pure and simple – what Winckelmann wanted, yes, and Goethe; and this will be my last word, and most important word, to the world. It is, yes, it is, what I wish to be remembered by; I shall devote the rest of my life to it.'

I cannot vouch for the accuracy of all these words, but this is how I remember them and his manner of speaking. This projected work later became *Doctor Zhivago*. He had in 1945 completed a draft of a few early chapters, which he asked me to read and take to his sisters in Oxford; I did so, but was not to know about the plan

---

[1] Shcherbakov later became a powerful member of Stalin's Politburo, and died in 1945.

for the entire novel until much later. After that, he was silent for a while; none of us spoke. He then told us how much he liked Georgia, Georgian writers, Yashvili, Tabidze, and Georgian wine, how well received he always was there. He then politely asked me about what was going on in the West; did I know Herbert Read and his doctrine of personalism? Here he explained that the doctrine of personalism basically derived from the moral philosophy – in particular the idea of individual freedom – of Kant, and of his interpreter Hermann Cohen, whom he had known well and greatly admired when he was his student in Marburg before the First World War. Kantian individualism – Blok had misinterpreted him completely, had made him a mystic in his poem *Kant* – did I know it? Did I know Stefan Schimansky, a personalist who had edited some of his, Pasternak's, work in translation? There was nothing here in Russia about which he could tell me. I must realise that the clock had stopped in Russia (I noticed that neither he nor any of the other writers I met ever used the words 'Soviet Union') in 1928 or so, when relations with the outer world were in effect cut off; the description of him and his work in, for instance, the Soviet Encyclopaedia, made no reference to his later life or work.

He was interrupted by Lydia Seifullina, an elderly, well-known writer who came in while he was in mid-course: 'My fate is exactly the same,' she said: 'the last lines of the Encyclopaedia article about me say "Seifullina is at present in a state of psychological and artistic crisis" – this has not been changed in the last twenty years. So far as the Soviet reader is concerned, I am still in a state of crisis, of suspended animation. We are like people in Pompeii, you and I, Boris Leonidovich, buried by ashes in mid-sentence. And we know so little: Maeterlinck and Kipling, I know, are dead; but Wells, Sinclair Lewis, Joyce, Bunin, Khodasevich – are they alive?' Pasternak looked embarrassed and changed the subject to French writers generally. He had been reading Proust – French Communist friends had sent him the entire masterpiece – he knew it, he said, and had reread it lately. He had not then heard of Sartre or Camus,[1] and thought little of Hemingway ('Why Anna Andreevna [Akhmatova] thinks anything of him I cannot imagine,' he said). He pressed me warmly to visit him in his Moscow apartment – he would be there from October.

[1] By 1956 he had read one or two of Sartre's plays, but nothing by Camus, who had been condemned as reactionary and pro-Fascist.

He spoke in magnificent, slow-moving periods, with occasional intense rushes of words; his talk often overflowed the banks of grammatical structure – lucid passages were succeeded by wild but always marvellously vivid and concrete images – and these might be followed by dark words when it was difficult to follow him – and then he would suddenly come into the clear again; his speech was at all times that of a poet, as were his writings. Someone once said that there are poets who are poets when they write poetry and prose-writers when they write prose; others are poets in everything that they write. Pasternak was a poet of genius in all that he did and was; his ordinary conversation displayed it as his writings do. I cannot begin to describe its quality. The only other person who seems to me to have talked as he talked was Virginia Woolf, who, to judge from the few occasions on which I met her, made one's mind race as he did, and obliterated one's normal vision of reality in the same exhilarating and, at times, terrifying way.

I use the word 'genius' advisedly. I am sometimes asked what I mean by this highly evocative but imprecise term. In answer, I can only say this: the dancer Nijinsky was once asked how he managed to leap so high. He is reported to have answered that he saw no great problem in this. Most people when they leapt in the air came down at once. 'Why should you come down immediately? Stay in the air a little before you return, why not?' he is reported to have said. One of the criteria of genius seems to me to be the power to do something perfectly simple and visible which ordinary people cannot, and know that they cannot, do – nor do they know how it is done, or why they cannot begin to do it. Pasternak at times spoke in great leaps; his use of words was the most imaginative I have ever known; it was wild and very moving. There are, no doubt, many varieties of literary genius: Eliot, Joyce, Yeats, Auden, Russell did not (in my experience) talk like this.

I did not wish to overstay my welcome: I left the poet, excited, and indeed overwhelmed, by his words and by his personality. I went on to Chukovsky's neighbouring dacha, and although he was charming, friendly, interesting, remarkably penetrating and, indeed, brilliantly amusing as a talker, I could think only about the poet with whom I had been an hour before. At Chukovsky's house I met Samuil Marshak, translator of Burns and also a writer of children's verse, who, by standing aside from the main stream of ideology and political storms, and, perhaps, because he enjoyed the protection of Maxim Gorky, managed to survive intact during the darkest days. He was one of the few writers permitted to meet foreigners. During my weeks in Moscow he showed me much kindness, and was, indeed, one of the nicest and most warm-hearted members of the Moscow intelligentsia whom it was my good fortune to meet; he talked freely and painfully about the horrors of the past, showed little faith in the future, and preferred to discuss English and Scottish literature, which he loved and understood, but about which he seemed to me to have little of interest to say. There were others there, among them a writer whose name, if it was mentioned, I had not taken in. I asked him about the Soviet literary scene: who were the most notable authors? He mentioned various writers, among them Lev Kassil'. I said, 'The author of *Shvambraniya* [a fantasy for adolescents]?' 'Yes,' he said, 'the author of *Shvambraniya*.' 'But that is a poor novel,' I said: 'I read it some years ago – I thought it had no imagination and was both dull and naïve – do you like it?' 'Yes,' he said, 'I do rather – it seems to me sincere and not badly written.' I disagreed. Some hours later, when darkness fell and I said that I was very bad at finding my way anywhere, he volunteered to accompany me to the railway station. As we were parting I said to him 'You have been wonderfully kind to me all day – I am so sorry that I never took in your name.' 'Lev Kassil',' he said. I stood rooted to the ground in shame and remorse, crushed by my gaffe. 'But', I said, 'why didn't you tell me? *Shvambraniya* . . .'. 'I respect you for saying what you really thought – the truth is not easy for us writers to come by.' I went on apologising until the train arrived. No one in my experience has ever behaved so admirably; I have never before or since met an author so free from vanity or *amour propre* of any kind.

While I was waiting for the train it began to rain. There were only two other persons on the platform, a young-looking couple, and we all huddled for cover under the only protection we could find – some planks jutting over an old, dilapidated fence. We exchanged a few words – they turned out to be young students – the young man said he was a chemist, the girl was a student of nineteenth-century Russian history, in particular of revolutionary movements. We were in complete darkness – the station had no light – and we could scarcely see each other's faces; consequently they felt reasonably secure with a total stranger and talked freely. The girl said that they were taught that in the last century the Russian Empire was a huge prison with no liberty of thought or expression: but although they thought this generally true, radicals did seem to have got away with quite a lot, and dissidence without actual terrorism did not then, as a rule, mean torture and death; and even terrorists escaped. 'Why', I said, I admit not altogether innocently, 'can people not speak their minds now on social issues?' 'If anyone tries,' said the young man, 'he is swept away as with a broom, and we do not know what happens to him; no one ever sees him or hears from him again.' We changed the subject and they told me that what young Russians at this time read most avidly were nineteenth-century novels and stories: not Chekhov, it turned out, nor Turgenev, who seemed to them antiquated and preoccupied with problems of little interest to them; nor Tolstoy – perhaps because (so they said) they were fed on *War and Peace* as the great national patriotic epic too insistently during the War. They read, when they could get them, Dostoevsky, Leskov, Garshin, and the more accessible foreign masters – Stendhal, Flaubert (not Balzac or Dickens), Hemingway and, somewhat unexpectedly, O. Henry. 'And Soviet writers? What about Sholokhov, Fedin, Fadeev, Gladkov, Furmanov?' I said, reeling off the first names of contemporary Soviet authors that came into my head. 'Do *you* like them?' the girl asked. 'Gorky is sometimes good,' said the young man, 'and I used to like Romain Rolland. I suppose you have great and marvellous writers in your country?' I said 'No, not marvellous', but they seemed incredulous, and may have thought that I was peculiarly jaundiced about British writers, or else was a Communist who did not care for bourgeois artists of any kind. The train arrived and we entered different carriages – the conversation could not have continued before others.

Like these students, many Russians (at least at that time) seemed convinced that in the West – England, France, Italy – there was a magnificent flowering of art and literature, inaccessible to them. When I threw doubts on this I was never really believed: at best, it was attributed to politeness or world-weary capitalist ennui. Even Pasternak and his friends were firmly convinced that there was a golden West where writers and critics of genius had created, and were creating, masterpieces concealed from them. This belief was very widespread. Most of the writers whom I met in 1945 and 1956, Zoshchenko, Marshak, Seifullina, Chukovsky, Vera Inber, Sel'vinsky, Kassil' and a dozen others, and not only writers but musicians like Prokofiev, Neuhaus, Samosud, producers like Eisenstein and Tairov, painters and critics whom I met in public places, at official receptions given by VOKS (the Society for Promoting Cultural Relations with Foreigners) and very occasionally in their own homes, philosophers whom I met at a session of the Academy of Sciences which I was invited to address on the initiative of none other than Lazar' Kaganovich, just before his fall from grace and power – all these persons were not only immensely curious about – indeed, hungry for news of – progress in arts and letters in Europe (rather less in America), but were firmly convinced that marvellous works of art and literature and thought were ceaselessly being born there, hidden from their eyes by the rigid Soviet censors. *Omne ignotum pro magnifico*. I had no wish to denigrate Western achievements, but I tried to indicate that our cultural development was less irresistibly triumphant than they generously supposed. It may be that some of those who emigrated to the West are still looking for this rich cultural life, or else feel disillusioned. The campaign against 'rootless cosmopolitans' was clearly directed in part against this extraordinary pro-Western enthusiasm, aroused in the first place, perhaps, by rumours of life in the West stemming from returned Soviet soldiers, both ex-prisoners and the conquering battalions themselves, as well as being the inevitable reaction to the steady and very crude campaign of vilification of Western culture in the Soviet press and on the radio. Russian nationalism used as an antidote against such unhealthy interest on the part of, at any rate, the educated section of the population, and fed, as so often, by ferocious anti-Semitic propaganda, in its turn produced strong pro-Jewish and pro-Western feeling which seemed to me to have taken deep root among the intelligentsia. By 1956 there was rather less ignorance about the West, and perhaps correspondingly less enthusiasm, but still a great deal more than the reality justified.

After Pasternak returned to Moscow, I visited him almost weekly and came to know him well. He always spoke with his peculiar brand of vitality, and flights of imaginative genius which no one has been able to convey; nor can I hope to describe the transforming effect of his presence, his voice and gestures. He talked about books and writers; I wish I had made notes at the time. At this distance of years I can remember only that of modern Western writers he loved Proust most of all, and was steeped in his novel and in *Ulysses* (he had not read Joyce's later work). When, some years later, I brought to Moscow with me two or three volumes of Kafka in English, he took no interest in them, and later, so he told me, gave them to Akhmatova, who admired them intensely. He spoke about French symbolists and about Verhaeren and Rilke, both of whom he had met and the second of whom he greatly admired as both a man and a writer. He was steeped in Shakespeare. He was dissatisfied with his own renderings, particularly of *Hamlet* and *Romeo and Juliet*: 'I have tried to make Shakespeare work for me,' he said early in the conversation, 'but it has not been a success.' And he then quoted examples of what he regarded as his own failures in translation, which, unfortunately, I have forgotten. One evening during the War, he told me, he was listening to the BBC and heard poetry being read aloud – he understood spoken English with difficulty but this seemed to him wonderful. He asked himself 'Who is this by?' – it seemed familiar. 'Why, it is by me,' he said to himself; but it turned out to be a passage from Shelley's *Prometheus Unbound*.

He grew up, he said, in the shadow of Tolstoy, whom his father knew well – to him an incomparable genius, greater than Dickens or Dostoevsky, a writer who stood with Shakespeare and Goethe and Pushkin. His father, the painter, had taken him to see Tolstoy on his deathbed, in 1910, at Astapovo. He found it impossible to be critical towards him: Russia and Tolstoy were one. As for Russian poets, Blok was of course the dominant genius of his time, but he did not find his quality of feeling sympathetic. He would not enlarge on this. Bely was closer to him, a man of strange, unheard-of insights, magical and a holy fool in the tradition of Russian Orthodoxy. Bryusov he considered a self-constructed, ingenious, mechanical musical-box, a clever, calculating operator, not a poet at all. He did not mention Mandel'shtam. He felt most tenderly towards Marina Tsvetaeva, to whom he had been bound by many years of friendship.

His feelings towards Mayakovsky were more ambivalent: he had known him well, they had been close friends, and he had learnt from him; he was, of course, a titanic destroyer of old forms but, he added, unlike other Communists, he was at all times a human being – but no, he was not a major poet, not an immortal god like Tyutchev or Blok, not even a demi-god like Fet or Bely; time had diminished him; he was needed, he was indispensable in his day, what those times had called for – there are poets, he said, who have their hour, Aseev, poor Klyuev – liquidated – Sel'vinsky – even Esenin – they fulfil an urgent need of the day, their gifts are of crucial importance to the development of poetry in their country, and then they are no more; Mayakovsky was far and away the greatest of these – *The Cloud in Trousers* had a central historical importance, but the shouting was unbearable: he inflated his talent and tortured it until it burst: the sad rags of the multicoloured balloon still lay in one's path if one was a Russian – he was gifted, important, but coarse and not grown up, and ended as a poster-artist; Mayakovsky's love-affairs had been disastrous for him as a man and a poet; he had loved Mayakovsky as a man – his suicide was one of the blackest days in his own life.

Pasternak was a Russian patriot – his sense of his own historical connection with his country was very deep. He told me again and again how glad he was to spend his summers in the writers' village, Peredelkino, for it had once been part of the estate of that great Slavophil, Yury Samarin: the true lines of tradition led from the legendary Sadko to the Stroganovs and the Kochubeys, to Derzhavin, Zhukovsky, Tyutchev, Pushkin, Baratynsky, Lermon-tov, to the Aksakovs, Tolstoy, Fet, Bunin, Annensky – to the Slavophils in particular – not to the liberal intelligentsia, which, as Tolstoy maintained, did not know what men lived by. This passionate, almost obsessive, desire to be thought a Russian writer with roots deep in Russian soil was particularly evident in his negative feelings towards his Jewish origins. He was unwilling to discuss the subject – he was not embarrassed by it, but he disliked it: he wished the Jews to assimilate, to disappear as a people. Apart from his immediate family, he had no interest in relatives, past or present. He spoke to me as a believing, if idiosyncratic, Christian. Among consciously Jewish writers he admired Heine, Hermann Cohen (his neo-Kantian philosophical mentor in Marburg), whose ideas – in particular, his philosophy of history – he evidently thought profound and convincing. If I mentioned Jews or Palestine, this, I observed, caused him visible distress; in this respect he differed from his father, the painter. I once asked Akhmatova whether others of her intimate Jewish friends – Mandel'shtam or Zhirmunsky or Emma Gerstein – were sensitive on this subject: she said that they had little liking for the conventional Jewish bourgeoisie from which they sprang, but did not deliberately avoid the subject as Pasternak was apt to do.

His artistic taste had been formed in his youth and he remained faithful to the masters of that period. The memory of Scriabin – he had at one time thought of becoming a composer himself – was sacred to him; I shall not easily forget the paean of praise offered by Pasternak and Neuhaus (the celebrated musician and former husband of Pasternak's wife Zinaida) to Scriabin, by whose music they had both been influenced, and to the symbolist painter Vrubel', whom, with Nicholas Roerich, they prized above all contemporary painters. Picasso and Matisse, Braque and Bonnard, Klee and Mondrian seemed to mean as little to them as Kandinsky or Malevich.

There is a sense in which Akhmatova and Gumilev and Marina Tsvetaeva are the last great voices of the nineteenth century (with Pasternak and, in his very different fashion, Mandel'shtam in some interspace between the centuries), and remain the last representatives of what can only be called the second Russian renaissance, for all that the Acmeists wished to relegate symbolism to the nineteenth century, and declared themselves poets of their own time. They seemed basically untouched by the modern movement – their contemporaries, Picasso, Stravinsky, Eliot, Joyce – even when they admired them, a movement which, like many others, was aborted in Russia by political events.

Pasternak loved everything Russian, and was prepared to forgive his country all her shortcomings, all save the barbarism of Stalin's reign; but even that, in 1945, he regarded as the darkness before a dawn which he was straining his eyes to detect, the hope expressed in the last chapters of *Doctor Zhivago*. He believed himself to be in communion with the inner life of the Russian people, to share its hopes and fears and dreams, to be its voice as, in their different fashions, Tyutchev, Tolstoy, Dostoevsky, Chekhov and Blok had been (by the time I knew him he conceded nothing to Nekrasov). In conversation with me during my Moscow visits, when we were always alone, before a polished desk on which not a book or a scrap of paper was to be seen, he repeated his conviction that he lived close to the heart of his country, and sternly and repeatedly denied this role to Gorky and Mayakovsky, especially to the former, and felt that he had something to say to the rulers of Russia, something of immense importance which only he could say, although what this was – he spoke of it often – seemed dark and incoherent to me. This may well have been due to lack of understanding on my part – although Anna Akhmatova told me that when he spoke in this prophetic strain, she, too, failed to understand him.

It was when he was in one of these ecstatic moods that he told me of his telephone conversation with Stalin about Mandel'shtam's arrest, the famous conversation of which many differing versions circulated and still circulate. I can only reproduce the story as I remember that he told it me in 1945. According to his account he was in his Moscow flat with his wife and son and no one else, when the telephone rang and a voice told him that it was the Kremlin speaking, and that comrade Stalin wished to speak to him. He assumed that this was an idiotic practical joke and put down the receiver. The telephone rang again and the voice somehow convinced him that the call was authentic. Stalin then asked him whether he was speaking to Boris Leonidovich Pasternak; Pasternak said that it was indeed he. Stalin asked whether he was present when a lampoon about himself, Stalin, was recited by Mandel'shtam:[1] Pasternak answered that it seemed to him of no importance whether he was or was not present, but that he was enormously happy that Stalin was speaking to him; that he had always known that this would happen, that they must meet and speak about matters of supreme importance. Stalin then asked whether Mandel'shtam was a master: Pasternak replied that as poets they were very different; that he admired Mandel'shtam's poetry but felt no affinity with it; but that in any case this was not the point at all.

Here, in recounting the episode to me, Pasternak again embarked on one of his great metaphysical flights about cosmic turning-points in the world's history, which he wished to discuss with Stalin – it was of supreme importance that he should do so – I can easily imagine that he spoke in this vein to Stalin too. At any rate, Stalin asked him again whether he was or was not present when Mandel'shtam read the lampoon. Pasternak answered again that what mattered most was his indispensable meeting with Stalin, that it must happen soon, that everything depended on it, that they must speak about ultimate issues, about life and death. 'If I were Mandel'shtam's friend I should have known better how to defend him,' said Stalin, and put down the receiver. Pasternak tried to ring back but, not surprisingly, failed to get through to the leader. The episode evidently preyed deeply upon him: he repeated to me the version I have just recounted on at least two later occasions, and told the story to other visitors, although, apparently, in somewhat different forms. His efforts to rescue Mandel'shtam, in particular

[1] See Nadezhda Mandelstam, *Hope Against Hope*, trans. Max Hayward (London, 1971), p. 13 and chapter 32.

his appeal to Bukharin, probably helped to preserve him at least for a time – Mandel'shtam was finally destroyed some years later – but Pasternak clearly felt, perhaps without good reason, but as anyone not blinded by self-satisfaction or stupidity might feel, that perhaps another response might have done more for the condemned poet.[1]

He followed this story with accounts of other victims: Pil'nyak, who anxiously waited ('was constantly looking out of the window') for an emissary to ask him to sign a denunciation of one of the men accused of treason in 1936, and because none came, realised that he too was doomed. He spoke of the circumstances of Tsvetaeva's suicide in 1941, which he thought might have been prevented if the literary bureaucrats had not behaved with such appalling heartlessness to her. He told the story of a man who asked him to sign an open letter condemning Marshal Tukhachevsky; when Pasternak refused and explained the reasons for his refusal, the man burst into tears, said that the poet was the noblest and most saintly human being that he had ever met, embraced him fervently, and then went straight to the secret police and denounced him.

Pasternak then said that despite the positive role which the Communist Party had played during the War, and not in Russia alone, he found the idea of any kind of relationship with it increasingly repellent: Russia was a galley, a slave-ship, and these were the overseers who whipped the rowers. Why, he wished to know, did a diplomat from a remote British 'territory', then in Moscow, whom I surely knew, a man who knew some Russian and claimed to be a poet, and visited him occasionally, why did this person insist, on every possible and impossible occasion, that he, Pasternak, should get closer to the Party? He did not need gentlemen who came from the other side of the world to tell him what to do – could I tell this man that his visits were unwelcome? I promised that I would, but did not do so, partly for fear of rendering Pasternak's none too secure position still more precarious. The Commonwealth diplomat in question shortly afterwards left the Soviet Union, and, I was told by his friends, later changed his views.

Pasternak reproached me too; not, indeed, for seeking to impose my political or any other opinions on him, but for something that

---

[1] Akhmatova and Nadezhda Mandel'shtam (according to Lydia Chukovskaya) decided that he deserved four out of five for his conduct in this situation.

to him seemed almost as bad: here we both were, in Russia, and wherever one looked everything was disgusting, appalling, an abominable pigsty, yet I seemed to be positively exhilarated by it, I wandered about and looked at everything (he declared) with bemused eyes – I was no better than other foreign visitors who saw nothing and suffered from absurd delusions, maddening to the poor miserable natives.

Pasternak was acutely sensitive to the charge of accommodating himself to the demands of the Party or the State – he seemed afraid that his mere survival might be attributed to some unworthy effort to placate the authorities, some squalid compromise of his integrity to escape persecution. He kept returning to this point, and went to absurd lengths to deny that he was capable of conduct of which no one who knew him could begin to conceive him to be guilty. One day he asked me whether I had read his wartime volume of poems *On Early Trains*; had I heard anyone speak of it as a gesture of conformity with the prevailing orthodoxy? I said truthfully that I had never heard this, that it seemed to me a ludicrous suggestion.

Anna Akhmatova, who was bound to him by the deepest friendship and admiration, told me that when she was returning to Leningrad from Tashkent, where in 1941 she had been evacuated from Leningrad, she stopped in Moscow and visited Peredelkino. Within a few hours of arriving she received a message from Pasternak that he could not see her – he had a fever – he was in bed – it was impossible. On the next day the message was repeated. On the third day he appeared before her looking unusually well, with no trace of any ailment. The first thing he did was to ask her whether she had read his latest book of poems: he put the question with so painful an expression on his face that she tactfully said that she had not read them yet; at which his face cleared, he looked vastly relieved and they talked happily. He evidently felt needlessly ashamed of these poems, which, in fact, were not well received by the official critics. It evidently seemed to him a kind of half-hearted effort to write civic poetry – there was nothing he disliked more intensely than this genre.

Yet, in 1945, he still had hopes of a great renewal of Russian life as a result of the cleansing storm that the War had seemed to him to be – as transforming in its own terrible fashion as the Revolution itself – a vast cataclysm beyond our puny moral categories. Such vast mutations cannot, he held, be judged; one must think and think about them and seek to understand as much of them as one can, all one's life; they are beyond good and evil, acceptance or rejection, doubt or assent; they must be accepted as elemental changes, earthquakes, tidal waves, transforming events which are beyond all moral and historical categories. So, too, the dark nightmare of betrayals, purges, massacres of the innocent, followed by an appalling war, seemed to him a necessary prelude to some inevitable, unheard-of victory of the spirit.

I did not see him again for eleven years. By 1956 his estrangement from his country's political order was complete. He could not speak of it, or its representatives, without a shudder. By that time his friend Olga Ivinskaya had been arrested, interrogated, maltreated, sent to a labour camp for five years. 'Your Boris,' the Minister of State Security, Abakumov, had said to her, 'your Boris detests us, doesn't he?' 'They were right,' Pasternak said to me: 'she could not and did not deny it.' I had travelled to Peredelkino with Neuhaus and one of his sons by his first wife, Zinaida Nikolaevna, who was now married to Pasternak. Neuhaus repeated over and over again that Pasternak was a saint: that he was too unworldly – his hope that the Soviet authorities would permit the publication of *Doctor Zhivago* was plainly absurd – martyrdom of the author was far more likely. Pasternak was the greatest writer produced by Russia for decades, and he would be destroyed, as so many had been destroyed, by the State; this was an inheritance from the tsarist regime – whatever the difference between Russia old and new, suspicion and persecution of writers were common to both. His former wife had told him that Pasternak was determined to get his novel published somewhere; he had tried to dissuade him, in vain. If Pasternak mentioned the matter to me, would I – it was important – more than important – perhaps a matter of life and death, who could tell, even in these days? – would I try to persuade him to hold his hand? Neuhaus seemed to me to be right: Pasternak probably did need to be physically saved from himself.

By this time we had arrived at Pasternak's house. He was waiting for me by the gate and let Neuhaus go in, embraced me warmly and said that after eleven years during which we had not met, much had happened, most of it very evil. He stopped and said 'Surely there is something you want to say to me?' I said, with monumental tactlessness (not to say unforgivable stupidity), 'Boris Leonidovich, I am happy to see you looking so well: but the main thing is that you have survived – it seemed almost miraculous to some of us' (I was thinking of the anti-Jewish persecution of

Stalin's last years). His face darkened and he looked at me with real anger: 'I know what you are thinking,' he said. 'What, Boris Leonidovich?' 'I know, I know it, I know exactly what is in your mind,' he replied in a breaking voice – it was very frightening – 'do not prevaricate, I can see more clearly into your mind than I can into my own.' 'What am I thinking?' I asked again, more and more disturbed by his words. 'You think – I know that you think – that I have done something for *them*.' 'I assure you, Boris Leonidovich, that I never conceived of this – I have never heard this suggested by anyone, even as an idiotic joke.' In the end he believed me. But he was visibly upset. Only after I had assured him that admiration for him, not only as a writer, but as a free and independent human being, was, among civilised people, world-wide, did he begin to return to his normal state. 'At least', he said, 'I can say, like Heine, "I may not deserve to be remembered as a poet, but surely as a soldier in the battle for human freedom." '[1]

He took me to his study. There he thrust a thick envelope into my hands: 'My book,' he said, 'it is all there. It is my last word. Please read it.' I began to read *Doctor Zhivago* immediately on leaving him, and finished it on the following day. Unlike some of its readers in both the Soviet Union and the West, I thought it was a work of genius. It seemed – and seems – to me to convey an entire range of human experience, to create a world, even if it contains only one genuine inhabitant, in language of unexampled imaginative power. When, two or three days later, I saw him again I found it difficult to say this to him, and only asked what he intended to do with his novel. He told me that he had given it to an Italian Communist, who worked in the Italian Section of the Soviet radio and at the same time acted as an agent for the Communist Milanese publisher Feltrinelli; he had assigned world rights to Feltrinelli – he wished his novel, his testament, the most authentic, most complete of all his writings – his poetry was nothing by comparison (although the poems in the novel were, he thought, perhaps the best he had written) – he wished his work to travel over the entire world, to 'lay waste with fire' (he quoted from Pushkin's famous poem *The Prophet*) 'the hearts of men'.[2]

[1] Cf. *Heinrich Heines Sämtliche Werke*, ed. Oskar Walzel (Leipzig, 1911–20), vol. 4, p. 306.

[2] 'Glagolom zhgi serdtsa lyudei!' A. S. Pushkin, *Sobranie sochinenii* (Moscow, 1974–8), vol. 2, p. 83. I have slightly amended Maurice Baring's translation in his *Russian Lyrics* (London, 1943), p. 2.

At some point during the day, while the famous raconteur Andronikov was entertaining the company with an elaborate account of the Italian actor Salvini, Zinaida Nikolaevna drew me aside and begged me with tears in her eyes to dissuade Pasternak from getting *Doctor Zhivago* published abroad without official permission: she did not wish her children to suffer; surely I knew what 'they' were capable of. Moved by this plea, I spoke to the poet at the first opportunity. I said that I would have microfilms of his novel made, and cause them to be buried in the four quarters of the globe – in Oxford, in Valparaiso, in Tasmania, Haiti, Vancouver, Cape Town, Japan – so that a text would survive even if a nuclear war broke out; was he resolved to defy the Soviet authorities, had he considered the consequences?

For the second time during that week he showed a touch of real anger in talking to me. He told me that what I said was no doubt well intentioned, that he was touched by my concern for his own safety and that of his family (this was said a trifle ironically), but that he knew what he was doing: that I was worse than that Commonwealth diplomat eleven years ago who had tried to convert him to Communism; he had spoken to his sons; they were prepared to suffer; I was not to mention the matter again – I had read the book, I surely realised what it, above all its dissemination, meant to him. I was shamed into silence.

After an interval, perhaps to lighten the atmosphere, he said, 'You know, my present position here is less insecure than you seem to think. My translations of Shakespeare, for example, have been acted with success: let me tell you an amusing story.' He then reminded me that he had once introduced me to one of the most celebrated of Soviet actors, Livanov (whose real name, he added, was Polivanov). Livanov was very enthusiastic about Pasternak's translation of *Hamlet*, and, some years ago, wished to produce it and act in it himself. He obtained official permission for this and rehearsals began. During this period he was invited to one of the regular banquets in the Kremlin, over which Stalin presided. It was Stalin's habit, at a certain point in the evening, to walk from table to table, exchanging greetings and offering toasts. When he approached Livanov's table, the actor asked him: 'Iosif Vissarionovich, how should one play *Hamlet*?' He wanted Stalin to say something, anything; he could then carry this away under his arm and use it. As Pasternak put it, if Stalin had said 'You must play it in a mauve manner', Livanov could tell his actors that what they were doing was not mauve enough, that the Leader had distinctly ordered it to be mauve; he, Livanov, had alone grasped exactly what the Leader meant, and the director and everyone else would then be bound to obey. Stalin stopped and said 'You are an actor? At the Arts Theatre? Then you should put your question to the artistic director of the theatre; I am no expert on theatrical matters.' Then, after a silence, 'However, since you have put the question to me, I shall give you my answer: *Hamlet* is a decadent play and should not be performed at all.' The rehearsals were broken off on the next day. There was no performance of *Hamlet* until well after Stalin's death. 'You see,' said Pasternak, 'things have changed. They change all the time.' Another silence.

He then talked about French literature, as often before. Since our last meeting he had procured Sartre's *La Nausée* and found it unreadable, and its obscenity revolting. Surely after four centuries of creative genius this great nation could not have ceased to generate literature? Aragon was a time-server, Duhamel, Guéhenno were inconceivably tedious; was Malraux still writing? Before I could reply, one of his guests at lunch, a woman with an indescribably innocent and sweet expression of a kind perhaps more often found in Russia than in the West, a teacher who had recently returned after fifteen years in a labour camp, to which she had been condemned solely for teaching English, shyly asked whether Aldous Huxley had written anything since *Point Counter Point*; and was Virginia Woolf still writing? – she had never seen a book by her, but from an account in an old French newspaper which in some mysterious fashion had found its way into her camp, she thought that she might like her work.

It is difficult to convey the pleasure of being able to bring news of art and literature of the outer world to human beings so genuinely eager to receive it, so unlikely to obtain it from any other source. I told her and the assembled company all that I could of English, American, French writing: it was like speaking to the victims of shipwreck on a desert island, cut off for decades from civilisation – all they heard, they received as new, exciting and delightful. The Georgian poet Titsian Tabidze, Pasternak's great friend, had perished in the Great Purge; his widow Nina Tabidze, who was present, wanted to know whether Shakespeare, Ibsen and Shaw were still great names in the Western theatre. I told her that interest in Shaw had declined, but that Chekhov was greatly admired and often performed, and added that Akhmatova had said to me that she could not understand this worship of Chekhov: his universe was uniformly drab; the sun never shone, no swords flashed, everything was covered by a horrible grey mist – Chekhov's world was a sea of mud with wretched human creatures caught in it helplessly – it was a travesty of life. Pasternak said that Akhmatova was wholly mistaken: 'Tell her when you see her – we cannot go to Leningrad freely, as you probably can – tell her from all of us here that all Russian writers preach to the reader: even Turgenev tells him that time is a great healer and that kind of thing; Chekhov alone does not. He is a pure artist – everything is dissolved in art – he is our answer to Flaubert.' He went on to say that Akhmatova would surely talk to me about Dostoevsky and attack Tolstoy. But Tolstoy was right about Dostoevsky: 'His novels are a dreadful mess, a mixture of chauvinism and hysterical religion, whereas Chekhov – tell Anna Akhmatova that, and from me! I love her deeply, but I have never been able to persuade her of anything.' But when I saw Akhmatova again, in Oxford in 1965, I thought it best not to report his judgement: she might have wished to answer him; but Pasternak was in his grave. In fact, she did speak to me of Dostoevsky with passionate admiration.

But let me return to 1945 and describe my meetings with the poet (she detested the word 'poetess') in Leningrad. It happened in the following way. I had heard that books in Leningrad, in what in the Soviet Union were called 'antiquarian bookshops', cost a good deal less than in Moscow; the terrible mortality and the possibility of bartering books for food during the siege of that city had led to a flow of books, especially those of the old intelligentsia, into government bookshops. Some of the inhabitants of Leningrad, one was told, weakened by illness and undernourishment, became too feeble to carry entire books, and so had had torn out for them by friends chapters and pages of poems: books and fragments of books had found their way into the second-hand departments of the shops and were on sale. I should have done my best to go to Leningrad in any case, for I was eager to see again the city in which I had spent four years of my childhood; the lure of books added to my desire. After the usual delays I was granted permission to spend two nights in the old Astoria hotel, and in company with the British Council representative in the Soviet Union, Miss Brenda Tripp – a most intelligent and sympathetic organic chemist – I reached Leningrad on a grey day in late November.

III

I had not seen the city since 1920, when I was eleven years old and my family was allowed to return to our native city of Riga, the capital of a then independent republic. In Leningrad my recollections of childhood became fabulously vivid – I was inexpressibly moved by the look of the streets, the houses, the statues, the embankments, the market-places, the suddenly familiar broken railings of a little shop in which samovars were mended below the house in which we had lived – the inner yard of the house looked as sordid and abandoned as it had done during the first years of the Revolution. My memories of specific events, episodes, experiences, came between me and the physical reality: it was as if I had walked into a legendary city, myself at once part of the vivid, half-remembered legend, and yet, at the same time, viewing it from some outside vantage-point. The city had been greatly damaged, but still in 1945 remained indescribably beautiful (it seemed wholly restored by the time I saw it again eleven years later).

I made my way to the object of my journey, the Writers' Bookshop of which I had been told, in the Nevsky Prospekt. There were then – I expect there still are – two sections in certain Russian bookshops: the outer room for the general public, in which one asks for books across the counter, and an inner room, with free access to the shelves, for recognised writers, journalists and other privileged persons. Because we were foreigners, Miss Tripp and I were admitted to the inner sanctum. While looking at the books, I fell into casual conversation with someone who was turning over the leaves of a book of poems. He turned out to be a well-known critic and literary historian; we talked about recent events, and he described the terrible ordeal of the siege of Leningrad and the martyrdom and heroism of many of its inhabitants, and said that some had died of cold and hunger, others, mostly the younger ones, had survived: some had been evacuated. I asked him about the fate of writers in Leningrad. He said, 'You mean Zoshchenko and Akhmatova?' Akhmatova to me was a figure from a remote past; Maurice Bowra, who had translated some of her poems, spoke about her to me as someone not heard of since the First World War. 'Is Akhmatova still alive?' I asked. 'Akhmatova, Anna Andreevna?' he said: 'Why yes, of course, she lives not far from here on the Fontanka, in Fontanny Dom [Fountain House]; would you like to meet her?' It was as if I had suddenly been invited to meet Miss Christina Rossetti; I could hardly speak; I mumbled that I should indeed like to meet her. 'I shall telephone her,' my new acquaintance said; and returned to tell me that she would receive us at three that afternoon; I was to come back to the bookshop and we would go together. I returned to the Hotel Astoria with Miss Tripp, and asked her if she would like to meet the poet – she said that she could not, she was otherwise engaged that afternoon.

I returned at the appointed hour. The critic and I left the bookshop, turned left, crossed the Anichkov Bridge and turned left again, along the embankment of the Fontanka. Fountain House, the palace of the Sheremetevs, is a magnificent late baroque building with gates of exquisite ironwork for which Leningrad is famous, and built around a spacious court, not unlike the quadrangle of a large Oxford or Cambridge college. We climbed up one of the steep, dark staircases to an upper floor, and were admitted to Akhmatova's room. It was very barely furnished – virtually everything in it had, I gathered, been taken away – looted or sold – during the siege; there was a small table, three or four chairs, a wooden chest, a sofa and, above the unlit stove, a drawing by Modigliani. A stately, grey-haired lady, a white shawl draped about her shoulders, slowly rose to greet us.

Anna Andreevna Akhmatova was immensely dignified, with unhurried gestures, a noble head, beautiful, somewhat severe features, and an expression of immense sadness. I bowed – it seemed appropriate, for she looked and moved like a tragic queen – thanked her for receiving me, and said that people in the West would be glad to know that she was in good health, for nothing had been heard of her for many years. 'Oh, but an article on me has appeared in the *Dublin Review*,' she said, 'and a thesis is being written about my work, I am told, in Bologna.' She had a friend with her, an academic lady of some sort, and there was polite conversation for some minutes. Then Akhmatova asked me about the ordeal of London during the bombing: I answered as best I could, feeling acutely shy and constricted by her distant, somewhat regal manner. Suddenly I heard what sounded like my first name being shouted somewhere outside. I ignored this for a while – it was plainly an illusion – but the shouting became louder and the word 'Isaiah' could be clearly heard. I went to the window and looked out, and saw a man whom I recognised as Randolph Churchill. He was standing in the middle of the great court, looking like a tipsy undergraduate, and screaming my name. I stood rooted to the floor for some seconds. Then I collected myself, muttered an apology and ran down the stairs: my only thought was to prevent him from coming to the room. My companion, the critic, ran after me anxiously. When we emerged into the court, Churchill came towards me and welcomed me effusively: 'Mr X,' I said mechanically, 'I do not suppose that you have met Mr Randolph Churchill?' The critic froze, his expression changed from bewilderment to horror, and he left as rapidly as he could. I never saw him again, but as his works continue to be published in the Soviet Union, I infer that this chance meeting did him no harm. I have no notion whether I was followed by agents of the secret police, but there could be no doubt that Randolph Churchill was; it was this untoward event that caused absurd rumours to circulate in Leningrad that a foreign delegation had arrived to persuade Akhmatova to leave Russia; that Winston Churchill, a lifelong admirer of the poet, was sending a special aircraft to take Akhmatova to England, and the like.

I had not met Randolph since we were undergraduates at Oxford. After hastily leading him out of Fountain House, I asked him what all this meant. He explained that he was in Moscow as a journalist on behalf of the North American Newspaper Alliance. He had come to Leningrad as part of his assignment; on arriving at the Hotel Astoria, his first concern had been to get the pot of caviare which he had acquired into an icebox: but as he knew no Russian and his interpreter had disappeared, his cries for help had finally brought down Miss Brenda Tripp. She saw to his caviare and, in the course of general conversation, told him that I was in the city. He said that he knew me and that in his view I would make an excellent substitute interpreter, and was then unfortunately told by Miss Tripp about my visit to the Sheremetev Palace. The rest followed: since he did not know exactly where I was to be found, he adopted a method which had served him well during his days in Christ Church (his Oxford college), and, I dare say, on other occasions; and, he said with a winning smile, it worked. I detached myself from him as quickly as I could and, after obtaining her number from the bookseller, telephoned Akhmatova to offer an explanation of my precipitate departure and to apologise for it. I asked if I might be allowed to call on her again. 'I shall wait for you at nine this evening,' she answered.

When I returned, her companion turned out to be one of her

second husband's – the Assyriologist Shileiko's – pupils, a learned lady who asked me a great many questions about English universities and their organisation. Akhmatova was plainly uninterested and, for the most part, silent. Shortly before midnight the Assyriologist left, and then Akhmatova began to ask me about old friends who had emigrated – some of whom I might know (she was sure of that, she told me later; in personal relationships, she assured me, her intuition – almost second sight – never failed her). I did indeed know some of them: we talked about the composer Artur Lurié, whom I had met in America during the War; he had been an intimate friend of hers and had set some of her and of Mandel'-shtam's poetry to music; about the poet Georgy Adamovich; about Boris Anrep, the mosaicist (whom I had never met); I knew little about him, only that he had decorated the floor of the entrance hall of the National Gallery with the figures of celebrated persons – Bertrand Russell, Virginia Woolf, Greta Garbo, Clive Bell, Lydia Lopokova and others. Twenty years later I was able to tell her that in the meantime Anrep had added a mosaic of her too, and had called it 'Compassion'. She did not know this, and was profoundly moved; and showed me a ring with a black stone which Anrep had given to her in 1917.

She asked after Salome Halpern, *née* Andronikova, whom she knew well in St Petersburg before the First World War – a celebrated society beauty of that period, famous for her wit, intelligence and charm, a friend of Russian poets and painters of the time. Akhmatova told me – what, indeed, I knew already – that Mandel'shtam, who had been in love with her, dedicated one of his most beautiful poems to her; I knew Salomeya Nikolaevna (and her husband Aleksandr Yakovlevich Halpern) well, and told Akhmatova something of their lives and friendships and opinions. She asked after Vera Stravinsky, the composer's wife, whom I did not then know; I answered these questions only in 1965, in Oxford. She spoke of her visits to Paris before the First World War, of her friendship with Amedeo Modigliani, whose drawing of her hung over her fireplace – one of many (the rest had perished during the siege); of her childhood on the Black Sea coast, a pagan, unbaptised land, she called it, where one felt close to an ancient, half-Greek, half-barbarian, deeply un-Russian culture; of her first husband, the celebrated poet Gumilev, who had done a great deal to form her – he had thought it ridiculous that a poet should be married to another poet, and on occasion had harshly criticised her writing, though he never humiliated her before others. On one occasion, when he was returning from one of his journeys to Abyssinia (the subject of some of his most exotic and magnificent poems), she had come to meet him at the railway station in St Petersburg (years later she told the story again, in the same words, to Dimitri Obolensky and me in Oxford). He looked severe: the first question he put to her was 'Have you been writing?' 'Yes.' 'Read it.' She did so: 'Yes, good, good,' he said, his eyebrows unknitting, and they went home; from that moment he accepted her as a poet. She was convinced that he had not taken part in the monarchist conspiracy for which he had been executed; Gorky, who had been asked by many writers to intervene on his behalf, disliked him and, according to some accounts,[1] did not intercede for him. She had not seen him for some time before his condemnation – they had been divorced some years before; her eyes had tears in them when she described the harrowing circumstances of his death.

After a silence she asked me whether I would like to hear her poetry: but before doing this, she said that she wished to recite two cantos from Byron's *Don Juan* to me, for they were relevant to what would follow. Even if I had known the poem well, I could not have told which cantos she had chosen, for although she read English, her pronunciation of it made it impossible to understand more than a word or two. She closed her eyes and spoke the lines from memory, with intense emotion; I rose and looked out of the window to conceal my embarrassment. Perhaps, I thought afterwards, that is how we now read classical Greek and Latin; yet we, too, are moved by the words, which, as we pronounce them, might be wholly unintelligible to their authors and audiences. Then she spoke her own poems from *Anno Domini*, *The White Flock*, *From Six Books* – 'Poems like these, but far better than mine, were the cause of the death of the best poet of our time, whom I loved and who loved me . . .' – whether she meant Gumilev or Mandel'shtam I could not tell, for she broke down in tears and could not go on. She then recited the (at that time) still unfinished *Poem Without a Hero*. There are recordings of her readings, and I shall not attempt to describe them. Even then I realised that I was listening to a work of genius. I do not suppose that I understood that many-faceted

---

[1] For example, that of Nadezhda Mandel'shtam; see her *Hope Abandoned*, trans. Max Hayward (London, 1974), p. 88.

and most magical poem and its deeply personal allusions any better than when I read it now. She made no secret of the fact that it was intended as a kind of final memorial to her life as a poet, to the past of the city – St Petersburg – which was part of her being, and, in the form of a Twelfth Night carnival procession of masked figures *en travesti*, to her friends and their lives and destinies and her own – a kind of artistic *nunc dimittis* before the inescapable end which would not be long in coming. The lines about the Guest from the Future had not then been written, nor the third dedication. It is a mysterious and deeply evocative work. A tumulus of learned commentary is inexorably rising over it. Soon it may be buried under its weight.

Then she read the *Requiem*, from a manuscript. She broke off and spoke of the years 1937–8, when both her husband and her son had been arrested and sent to prison camps (this was to happen again), of the queues of women who waited day and night, week after week, month after month, for news of their husbands, brothers, fathers, sons, for permission to send food or letters to them – but no news ever came, no message ever reached them – when a pall of death in life hung over the cities of the Soviet Union while the torture and slaughter of millions of innocents were going on. She spoke in a dry, matter-of-fact voice, occasionally interrupting herself with 'No, I cannot, it is no good, you come from a society of human beings, whereas here we are divided into human beings and . . .'. Then a long silence. 'And even now . . .'. I asked about Mandel'shtam: she was silent, her eyes filled with tears, and she begged me not to speak of him: 'After he slapped Aleksey Tolstoy's face it was all over . . .'. It took some time for her to collect herself; then, in a totally changed voice, she said 'Aleksey Tolstoy liked me; he wore lilac shirts *à la russe* when we were in Tashkent, and spoke of the marvellous time he and I would have together when we came back. He was a very gifted and interesting writer, a scoundrel, full of charm, and a man of stormy temperament; he is dead now; he was capable of anything, anything; he was abominably anti-Semitic; he was a wild adventurer, a bad friend, he only liked youth, power, vitality, he didn't finish his *Peter the First* because he said that he could only deal with Peter as a young man; what was he to do with all those people when they were old? He was a kind of Dolokhov, he called me Annushka – that made me wince – but I liked him, even though he was the cause of the death of the best poet of our time, whom I loved and who loved me.'

(Her words were identical with those she had used earlier; it now seemed clear to me to whom, on both occasions, she was referring.)

It was, I think, by now about three in the morning. She showed no sign of wishing me to leave. I was far too moved and absorbed to stir. The door opened and her son Lev Gumilev entered; it was plain that his relation to his mother and hers to him were deeply affectionate; he explained that he had been a student of the famous Leningrad historian Evgeny Tarle, and his field of study now was the history of the ancient tribes of central Asia (he did not mention the fact that he was there originally in a prison camp); he had become interested in the early history of the Khazars, Kazakhs and earlier peoples; he had been allowed to join a prisoners' unit of anti-aircraft gunners and had just returned from Germany. He seemed cheerful and confident that he could once more live and work in Leningrad, and offered me a dish of boiled potatoes, which was all that they had. Akhmatova apologised for the poverty of her hospitality. I begged her to let me write down the *Poem Without a Hero* and *Requiem*. 'There is no need,' she said: 'a volume of my collected verse is to appear next February; it is all in proof; I shall send you a copy to Oxford.' The Party, as we know, ruled otherwise, and she was denounced by Zhdanov (in a phrase that he had not wholly invented) as 'half nun, half harlot',[1] as part of the condemnation of other 'formalists' and 'decadents' and of the two periodicals in which their work had been published.

After Lev Gumilev left us, she asked me what I read: before I could answer, she denounced Chekhov for his mud-coloured world, his dreary plays, the absence in his world of heroism and martyrdom, of depth and darkness and sublimity – this was the passionate diatribe, which I later reported to Pasternak, in which she said that in Chekhov 'no swords flashed'. I said something about Tolstoy's liking for him. 'Why did Anna Karenina have to be killed?' she asked. 'As soon as she leaves Karenin, everything changes: she suddenly becomes a fallen woman in Tolstoy's eyes, a *traviata*, a prostitute. Of course there are pages of genius, but the basic morality is disgusting. Who punishes Anna? God? No,

---

[1] A similar formula had been used, in a very different context, by the critic Boris Eikhenbaum, in *Anna Akhmatova: opyt analiza* (Petersburg, 1923), p. 114, to describe the mingling of erotic and religious motifs in Akhmatova's early poetry. It reappeared in 1930, in a caricatured form, in an unfriendly article on her in the Soviet Literary Encyclopaedia, whence it found its way into Zhdanov's anathema of 1946.

society; that same society the hypocrisy of which Tolstoy is never tired of denouncing. In the end he tells us that she repels even Vronsky. Tolstoy is lying: he knew better than that. The morality of *Anna Karenina* is the morality of Tolstoy's wife, of his Moscow aunts; he knew the truth, yet he forced himself, shamefully, to conform to philistine convention. Tolstoy's morality is a direct expression of his own private life, his personal vicissitudes. When he was happily married he wrote *War and Peace*, which celebrates family life. After he started hating Sofia Andreevna, but was not prepared to divorce her because divorce is condemned by society, and perhaps by the peasants too, he wrote *Anna Karenina* and punished her for leaving Karenin. When he was old, and no longer lusted so violently after peasant girls, he wrote *The Kreutzer Sonata*, and forbade sex altogether.'

Perhaps this summing up was not meant too seriously: but Akhmatova's dislike of Tolstoy's sermons was genuine. She regarded him as an egocentric of immense vanity, and an enemy of love and freedom. She worshipped Dostoevsky (and, like him, despised Turgenev); and after Dostoevsky, Kafka ('He wrote for me and about me,' she told me in 1965 in Oxford – 'Joyce and Eliot, wonderful poets, are inferior to this profoundest and most truthful of modern authors'). She said of Pushkin that of course he understood everything: 'How did he, how could he have known it all? This curly-haired youth in Tsarskoe, with a volume of Parny under his arm?' Then she read me her notes on Pushkin's *Egyptian Nights*, and talked about the pale stranger, the mysterious poet who offered, in that story, to improvise on themes drawn at random. The virtuoso, she had no doubt, was the Polish poet Adam Mickiewicz; Pushkin's relation to him became ambivalent – the Polish issue divided them, but he always recognised genius in his contemporaries. Blok was like that, with his mad eyes and magnificent genius – he too could have been an *improvisateur*. She said that Blok, who had, on occasion, praised her verse, had never liked her, but that every schoolmistress in Russia believed, and would go on believing, that they had had a love-affair – 'and historians of literature will believe this too – all this is probably based on my poem *A Visit to the Poet* which I dedicated to him in 1914; and perhaps on the poem on the death of *The Grey-Eyed King*, although that was written more than ten years before Blok died; there were other poems, too, but he did not like any of us' – she was speaking of the Acmeist poets, above all Mandel'shtam,

Gumilev and herself – and added that Blok did not like Pasternak either.

She then spoke about Pasternak, to whom she was devoted. She said that it was only when Pasternak was in a low state that he would express a wish to be with her; and then he would come, distraught and exhausted, usually after some passionate involvement, but his wife would swiftly follow and take him home. Both Pasternak and Akhmatova were apt to fall in love easily. Pasternak had occasionally proposed to her, but she had not taken this seriously; they had never been genuinely in love with one another; not in love, but they loved and adored each other and, after Mandel'shtam's and Tsvetaeva's deaths, felt themselves alone. The idea that the other was alive and at work was a source of infinite comfort to them both; they criticised each other, but permitted no one else to do so. She admired Tsvetaeva: 'Marina is a better poet than I am,' she said to me; but now that Mandel'shtam and Tsvetaeva were gone she and Pasternak were living in a desert, alone, even though they were surrounded by the love and passionate devotion of countless men and women in the Soviet Union who knew their verse by heart, and copied it and circulated it and recited it; this was a source of pride and delight to them, but they remained in exile. Their deep patriotism was not tinged by nationalism; the thought of emigration was hateful to both. Pasternak longed to visit the West, but not at the risk of being unable to return to his native land. Akhmatova said to me that she would not move: she was ready to die in her own country, no matter what horrors were in store; she would never abandon it. Both were among those who harboured extraordinary illusions about the rich artistic and intellectual culture of the West – a golden world, full of creative life – both wished to see it and communicate with it.

As the night wore on, Akhmatova grew more and more animated. She questioned me about my personal life. I answered fully and freely, as if she had an absolute right to know, and she rewarded me by giving a marvellous account of her childhood by the Black Sea, her marriages to Gumilev and Shileiko and Punin, her relationships with the companions of her youth, and of St Petersburg before the First World War. It is in the light of this alone that the succession of images and symbols, the play of disguises, the entire *bal masqué* of the *Poem Without a Hero*, with its echoes of *Don Giovanni* and the *commedia dell'arte*, can be understood. Once again she spoke of Salomeya Andronikova (Halpern), her beauty, charm, acute intelligence, her incapacity for being taken in by the second- and third-rate poets ('they are fourth-rate now'), of evenings at the Stray Dog cabaret, performances at the Distorting Mirror theatre; of her reaction against the sham mysteries of symbolism, despite Baudelaire and Verlaine and Rimbaud and Verhaeren, whom they all knew by heart. Vyacheslav Ivanov was infinitely distinguished and civilised, a man of unerring taste and judgement, of the finest imaginable critical faculty, but his poetry was to her chilly and unsympathetic; so was Andrey Bely; as for Bal'mont, he was unjustly despised – he was, of course, ridiculously pompous, and self-important, but gifted; Sologub was uneven, but interesting and original; far greater than these was the austere, fastidious Tsarskoe Selo headmaster, Innokenty Annensky, who had taught her more than anyone, even more than Gumilev, his disciple, and who died largely ignored by editors and critics, a great, forgotten master: without him, there would have been no Gumilev, no Mandel'shtam, no Lozinsky, no Pasternak, no Akhmatova. She spoke at length about music, about the sublimity and beauty of Beethoven's last three piano sonatas – Pasternak thought them greater than the posthumous quartets, and she agreed with him, she responded with her whole nature to the violent changes of feeling within their movements. The parallel which Pasternak drew between Bach and Chopin seemed to her to be strange and fascinating. She found it easier to talk to him about music than about poetry.

She spoke of her loneliness and isolation, both personal and cultural. Leningrad after the War was for her nothing but a vast cemetery, the graveyard of her friends: it was like the aftermath of a forest fire – the few charred trees made the desolation still more desolate. She had devoted friends – Lozinsky, Zhirmunsky, Khardzhiev, the Ardovs, Olga Bergholz, Lydia Chukovskaya, Emma Gerstein (she mentioned neither Garshin nor Nadezhda Mandel'shtam, of whose existence I then knew nothing) – but her sustenance came not from them but from literature and the images of the past: Pushkin's St Petersburg; Byron's, Pushkin's, Mozart's, Molière's Don Juan; and the great panorama of the Italian Renaissance. She lived by translating: she had begged to be allowed to translate the letters of Rubens, and not those of Romain Rolland – permission had finally been granted; had I seen them? I asked whether the Renaissance was a real historical past to her, inhabited by imperfect human beings, or an idealised image of an imaginary world. She replied that it was of course the latter; all poetry and art, to her, was – here she used an expression once used by Mandel'shtam – a form of nostalgia, a longing for a universal culture, as Goethe and Schlegel had conceived it, of what had been transmuted into art and thought – of nature, love, death, despair and martyrdom, of a reality which had no history, nothing outside itself. Again she spoke of pre-revolutionary St Petersburg as the town in which she was formed, of the long dark night which had covered her thenceforth. She spoke without the slightest trace of self-pity, like a princess in exile, proud, unhappy, unapproachable, in a calm, even voice, at times in words of moving eloquence.

The account of the unrelieved tragedy of her life went far beyond anything which anyone had ever described to me in spoken words; the recollection of them is still vivid and painful to me. I asked her if she intended to compose a record of her literary life. She replied that her poetry was that, in particular the *Poem Without a Hero*; and then she read it to me again. Once more I begged her to let me write it down. Once again she declined. Our conversation, which touched on intimate details of both her life and my own, wandered from literature and art, and lasted until late in the morning of the following day. I saw her again when I was leaving the Soviet Union to go home by way of Leningrad and Helsinki. I went to say goodbye to her on the afternoon of 5 January 1946, and she then gave me one of her collections of verse, with a new poem inscribed on the flyleaf – the poem that was later to form the second in the cycle entitled *Cinque*. I realised that this poem, in this, its first version, had been directly inspired by our earlier meeting. There are other references and allusions to our meetings, in *Cinque* and elsewhere.[1]

These allusions were plain to me when I first read them: but Academician Victor Zhirmunsky, Akhmatova's close friend, an eminent literary scholar and one of the editors of the posthumous Soviet editions of her poems, who visited Oxford a year or two after Akhmatova's death, went through the text with me and confirmed my impressions with precise references. He had read the texts with the author: she spoke to him both about the three dedications, their dates and their significance, and about the 'Guest from the Future'. With some embarrassment, Zhirmunsky

---

[1] For details see the appendix on pp. 253–4 below.

explained to me why the last dedication of the poem, that to myself – that this dedication existed was, so he informed me, widely known to readers of poetry in Russia – had nevertheless to be omitted in the official edition. I understood and understand the reason for this only too well. Zhirmunsky was an exceptionally scrupulous scholar, and a man of courage and integrity who had suffered for his principles; he explained his distress at being obliged to ignore Akhmatova's specific instructions in this regard, but political conditions made it essential. I tried to persuade him that this was of little consequence: it was true that Akhmatova's poetry was to a high degree autobiographical, and that therefore the circumstances of her life threw more light on the meaning of her words than was the case with many other poets; nevertheless, the facts were unlikely to be wholly forgotten – as in other countries under rigorous censorship, an oral tradition was likely to preserve such knowledge. The tradition might develop in various directions, and might not be free from legend and fable, but if he wished to be sure that the truth was known to a small circle of those likely to be interested, he could write an account of it all and leave it with me or someone else in the West to be published when it was safe to do so. I doubt if he followed my advice; but he remained inconsolable about his shortcomings as an editor under censorship, and apologised for it again and again, whenever we met during his visits to England.

The impact upon Akhmatova of my visit, such as it was, seems to me to have been largely due to the fortuitous fact that I happened to be only the second foreign visitor whom she had seen since the First World War.[1] I was, I think, the first person from the outside world who spoke her language and could bring her news of a world from which she had been isolated for many years. Her intellect, critical power and ironical humour seemed to exist side by side with a dramatic, at times visionary and prophetic, sense of reality; she seemed to see in me a fateful, perhaps doom-laden messenger of the end of the world – a tragic intimation of the future which made a profound impact upon her, and may have had a part in creating a new outpouring of her creative energy.

I did not see her on my next visit to the Soviet Union, in 1956. Pasternak told me that though Anna Andreevna wished to see me,

---

[1] Before me, she had met only one other non-Soviet citizen – Count Joseph Czapski, the eminent Polish critic, whom she saw during the War in Tashkent.

her son, who had been rearrested some time after I had met him, had been released from his prison camp only a short while before, and she therefore felt nervous of seeing foreigners, particularly as she attributed the furious onslaught upon her by the Party at least in part to my visit in 1945. Pasternak said that he doubted whether my visit had done her any harm, but since she evidently believed that it had, and had been advised to avoid compromising associations, she could not see me; but she wished me to telephone her – this was safe, since all her telephone calls were certainly monitored, as were his own. He had told her, when he was in Moscow, that he had met my wife and me, that he thought my wife delightful, and told Akhmatova that he was sorry that she could not meet her. Anna Andreevna would not be in Moscow long, and I was to telephone her at once.

'Where are you living?' he asked me. 'At the British Embassy.' 'You must on no account telephone her from there – you must use a public call box – not my telephone.'

Later that day I spoke to her over the telephone. 'Yes, Pasternak told me that you were in Moscow with your wife. I cannot see you, for reasons which you will understand only too well. We can speak like this because then they know. How long have you been married?' 'Not long,' I said. 'But exactly when were you married?' 'In February of this year.' 'Is she English, or perhaps American?' 'No, she is half French, half Russian.' 'I see.' There followed a long silence. 'I am sorry you cannot see me, Pasternak says your wife is charming.' Another long silence. 'Have you seen a collection of Korean poems translated by me? With an introduction by Surkov? You can imagine how much Korean I know – a selection of poems, it was not I who selected them. I shall send them to you.'

After this she told me something of her experience as a condemned writer: of the turning-away of some whom she had considered faithful friends, of the nobility and courage of others; she had reread Chekhov, whom she had once condemned so severely, and said that at least in *Ward No 6* he had described her situation accurately, hers and that of many others. 'Pasternak [she always called him so when speaking to me, as has long been the habit among Russians, never 'Boris Leonidovich'] will probably have explained to you why I cannot see you: he has had a difficult time, but not as agonising as mine. Who knows, we may yet meet in this life. Will you telephone me again?' I promised to do so, but when I did, I was told that she had left Moscow, and Pasternak strongly advised against attempting to ring her in Leningrad.

When we met in Oxford in 1965, Akhmatova described the details of the attack upon her by the authorities. She told me that Stalin was personally enraged by the fact that she, an apolitical, little-published writer, who owed her security largely to having contrived to live comparatively unnoticed during the early years of the Revolution, before the cultural battles which often ended in prison camps or execution, had committed the sin of seeing a foreigner without formal authorisation, and not just a foreigner, but an employee of a capitalist government. 'So our nun now receives visits from foreign spies,' he remarked (so it is alleged), and followed this with obscenities which she could not at first bring herself to repeat to me. The fact that I had never worked in any intelligence organisation was irrelevant: all members of foreign embassies or missions were spies to Stalin. 'Of course,' she went on, 'the old man was by then out of his mind. People who were there during this furious outbreak against me, one of whom told me of it, had no doubt that they were speaking to a man in the grip of pathological, unbridled persecution mania.' On the day after I left Leningrad, on 6 January 1946, uniformed men had been placed outside the entrance to her staircase, and a microphone was screwed into the ceiling of her room, plainly not for intelligence purposes but to frighten her. She knew that she was doomed – and although official disgrace followed only some months later, after the formal anathema pronounced over her and Zoshchenko by Zhdanov, she attributed her misfortunes to Stalin's personal paranoia. When she told me this in Oxford, she added that in her view we – that is, she and I – inadvertently, by the mere fact of our meeting, had started the Cold War and thereby changed the history of mankind. She meant this quite literally; and, as Amanda Haight testifies in her book,[1] was totally convinced of it, and saw herself and me as world-historical personages chosen by destiny to begin a cosmic conflict (this is indeed directly reflected in one of her poems). I could not protest that she had perhaps, even if the reality of Stalin's violent fit of anger and of its possible consequences were allowed for, somewhat overestimated the effect of our meeting on the destinies of the world, since she would have felt this as an insult

[1] Amanda Haight, *Anna Akhmatova: A Poetic Pilgrimage* (Oxford, 1976), p. 146.

to her tragic image of herself as Cassandra – indeed, to the historico-metaphysical vision which informed so much of her poetry. I remained silent.

Then she spoke of her journey to Italy in the previous year, when she was awarded the Taormina Literary Prize. On her return, she told me, she was visited by officials of the Soviet secret police, who asked her for her impressions of Rome: had she come across anti-Soviet attitudes on the part of writers, had she met Russian émigrés? She said in reply that Rome seemed to her to be a city where paganism was still at war with Christianity. 'What war?' she was asked: 'Was the USA mentioned?' What would she answer when similar questions were put to her, as they inevitably would be, about England? London? Oxford? Did the poet who was honoured with her in the Sheldonian Theatre – Siegfried Sassoon – have any political record? Or the other honorands? Would it be best to confine herself to speaking of her interest in the magnificent font which Tsar Alexander I had given to Merton College when he was similarly honoured by the University, at the end of the Napoleonic Wars? She was a Russian, and to Russia she would return no matter what awaited her there: the Soviet regime, whatever one might think of it, was the established order in her country; with it she had lived and with it she would die – that is what being a Russian meant.

We returned to Russian literature. She said that the unending ordeal of her country in her own lifetime had generated poetry of wonderful depth and beauty, which, since the 1930s, had for the most part remained unpublished. She said that she preferred not to speak of the contemporary Soviet poets whose work was published in the Soviet Union. One of the most famous of these, who happened to be in England at this time, had sent her a telegram to congratulate her on her Oxford doctorate. I was there when it arrived – she read it, and angrily threw it into the waste-paper basket: 'They are all little bandits, prostitutes of their gifts and exploiters of public taste. Mayakovsky's influence has been fatal to them all.' She said that Mayakovsky was, of course, a genius, not a great poet but a great literary innovator, a terrorist, whose bombs blew up ancient structures, a major figure whose temperament outran his talent – a destroyer, a blaster of everything; the destruction was, of course, deserved. Mayakovsky shouted at the top of his voice because it was natural to him to do so, he could not help it: his imitators – here she mentioned a few names of living poets – had adopted his manner as a genre and were vulgar declaimers with not a spark of true poetry in them, rhetoricians whose talents were theatrical, and Russian audiences had got used to being screamed at by these 'masters of the spoken word' as they were called nowadays.

The only living poet of the older generation about whom she spoke with approval was Maria Petrovykh; but there were many gifted young poets in Russia now: the best among them was Joseph Brodsky, whom she had, she said, brought up by hand, and whose poetry had in part been published – a noble poet in deep disfavour, with all that that implied. There were others, too, marvellously gifted – but their names would mean nothing to me – poets whose verses could not be published, and whose very existence was testimony to the unexhausted life of the imagination in Russia. 'They will eclipse us all,' she said, 'believe me, Pasternak and I and Mandel'shtam and Tsvetaeva, all of us are at the end of a long period of elaboration which began in the nineteenth century. My friends and I thought we spoke with the voice of the twentieth century. But these new poets constitute a new beginning – behind bars now, but they will escape and astonish the world.' She spoke at some length in this prophetic vein, and returned again to Mayakovsky, driven to despair, betrayed by his friends, but, for a while, the true voice, the trumpet, of his people, though a fatal example to others; she herself owed nothing to him, but much to Annensky, the purest and finest of poets, remote from the hurly-burly of literary politics, largely neglected by avant-garde journals, fortunate to have died when he did. He was not read widely in his lifetime, but then this was the fate of other great poets – the present generation was far more sensitive to poetry than her own had been: who cared, who truly cared about Blok or Bely or Vyacheslav Ivanov in 1910? Or, for that matter, about herself and the poets of her group? But today the young knew it all by heart – she was still getting letters from young people, many of them from silly, ecstatic girls, but the sheer number of them was surely evidence of something.

Pasternak received even more of these, and liked them better. Had I met his friend Olga Ivinskaya? I had not. She found both Pasternak's wife, Zinaida, and his mistress equally unbearable, but Boris Leonidovich himself was a magical poet, one of the great poets of the Russian land: every sentence he wrote, in verse and prose, spoke with his authentic voice, unlike any other she had ever heard. Blok and Pasternak were divine poets; no Frenchman, no Englishman, not Valéry, not Eliot, could compare with them – Baudelaire, Shelley, Leopardi, that was the company to which they belonged; like all great poets, they had little sense of the quality of others – Pasternak often praised inferior critics, discovered imaginary hidden gifts, encouraged all kinds of minor figures – decent writers but without talent – he had a mythological sense of history, in which quite worthless people sometimes played mysterious, significant roles – like Evgraf in *Doctor Zhivago* (she vehemently rejected the theory that this mysterious figure was in any respect based on Stalin; she evidently found this impossible to contemplate). He did not really read the contemporary authors he was prepared to praise – not Bagritsky or Aseev, or Maria Petrovykh, not even Mandel'shtam (for whom he had little feeling as a man or a poet, though of course he did what he could for him when he was in trouble), nor her own work – he wrote her wonderful letters about her poetry, but the letters were about himself, not her – she knew that they were sublime fantasies which had little to do with her poems: 'Perhaps all great poets are like this.'

Pasternak's compliments naturally made those who received them very happy, but this was a delusion; he was a generous giver, but not truly interested in the work of others: interested, of course, in Shakespeare, Goethe, the French symbolists, Rilke, perhaps Proust, but 'not in any of us'. She said that she missed Pasternak's existence every day of her life; they had never been in love, but they loved one another deeply, and this irritated his wife. She then spoke of the 'blank' years during which she was officially out of account in the Soviet Union – from the mid-1920s until the late '30s. She said that when she was not translating, she read Russian poets: Pushkin constantly, of course, but also Odoevsky, Lermontov, Baratynsky – she thought Baratynsky's *Autumn* was a work of pure genius; and she had recently reread Velemir Khlebnikov – mad but marvellous.

I asked her if she would ever annotate the *Poem Without a Hero*: the allusions might be unintelligible to those who did not know the life it was concerned with; did she wish them to remain in darkness? She answered that when those who knew the world about which she spoke were overtaken by senility or death, the poem would die too; it would be buried with her and her century; it was not written for eternity, nor even for posterity: the past alone had significance for poets – childhood most of all – those were the emotions that they wished to re-create and relive. Vaticination, odes to the future, even Pushkin's great epistle to Chaadaev, were a form of declamatory rhetoric, a striking of grandiose attitudes, the poet's eye peering into a dimly discernible future, a pose which she despised.

She knew, she said, that she had not long to live: the doctors had made it plain that her heart was weak, and therefore she was patiently waiting for the end; she detested the thought that she might be pitied; she had faced horrors and knew the most terrible depths of grief, and had exacted from her friends the promise that they would not allow the faintest gleam of pity to show itself, to suppress it instantly if it did; some had given way to this feeling, and with them she had been obliged to part; hatred, insults, contempt, misunderstanding, persecution, she could bear, but not sympathy if it was mingled with compassion – would I give her my word of honour? I did, and have kept it. Her pride and dignity were very great.

She then told me of a meeting with Korney Chukovsky during the War, when they were both being evacuated to cities in Uzbekistan. Her feelings towards him had for years been some-what ambivalent: she respected him as an exceptionally gifted and intelligent man of letters, and had always admired his integrity and independence, but did not like his cool, sceptical outlook, and was repelled by his taste for Russian populist novels and the committed literature of the nineteenth century, in particular for civic poetry; this, as well as the unfriendly ironies which he had uttered about her in the 1920s, had created a gulf between them; but now they were all united as fellow victims of Stalin's tyranny. She said that he had been particularly amiable to her on the journey to Tashkent, and that she was on the point of offering him a royal pardon for all his sins, when suddenly he said 'Ah, Anna Andreevna, that was the time – the '20s! What a wonderful period in Russian culture – Gorky, Mayakovsky, the young Alesha Tolstoy – that was the time to be alive!' The pardon she had so nearly extended was instantly withdrawn.

Unlike the survivors of the turbulent years of post-revolutionary experimentation, Akhmatova looked on these beginnings with deep distaste; to her it was a dishevelled, Bohemian chaos, the beginning of that vulgarisation of cultural life in Russia which sent true artists into bomb-proof shelters when they could find them: from which they emerged at times, only to be slaughtered.

Anna Andreevna spoke to me about her life with an apparent detachment, and even an impersonality, which only partially disguised passionate convictions and moral judgements against which there was plainly no appeal. Her accounts of the personalities and acts of others were compounded of sharp insight into the moral centre of both characters and situations – she did not spare her friends in this respect – together with a dogmatic obstinacy in attributing motives and intentions, particularly when they related to herself, which even to me – who often did not know the facts – seemed implausible, and indeed, at times, fanciful – but it may be that I did not sufficiently understand the irrational and sometimes wildly capricious character of Stalin's despotism, which makes normal criteria of what can and cannot be believed difficult to apply with confidence even now. It seemed to me that upon dogmatically held premisses Akhmatova constructed theories and hypotheses which she developed with extraordinary coherence and lucidity. Her unwavering conviction that our meeting had had serious historical consequences was an example of such *idées fixes*; she also believed that Stalin had given orders that she should be slowly poisoned, then countermanded them; that Mandel'shtam's belief, shortly before his end, that the food he was given in the labour camp was poisoned was well founded; that the poet Georgy Ivanov (whom she accused of having written lying memoirs after he emigrated) had at one time been a police spy in the pay of the tsarist government; that the poet Nekrasov in the nineteenth century must also have been a government agent; that Innokenty Annensky had been hounded to death by his enemies. These beliefs had no apparent foundation in fact – they were intuitive – but they were not senseless, not sheer fantasies; they were elements in a coherent conception of her own and her nation's life and fate, of the central issues which Pasternak had wanted to discuss with Stalin, the vision which sustained and shaped her imagination and her art. She was not a visionary; she had, for the most part, a strong sense of reality. She described the literary and social scene in St Petersburg and her part in it before the First World War with a sharp and sober realism which made it totally credible. I blame myself greatly for not having recorded in detail her views of persons and movements and predicaments.

Akhmatova lived in terrible times, during which, according to Nadezhda Mandel'shtam's account, she behaved with heroism. This is borne out by all available evidence. She did not in public, nor indeed to me in private, utter a single word against the Soviet regime: but her entire life was what Herzen once described virtually all Russian literature as being – one uninterrupted indictment of Russian reality. The widespread worship of her memory in the Soviet Union today, both as an artist and as an unsurrendering human being, has, so far as I know, no parallel. The legend of her life and unyielding passive resistance to what she regarded as unworthy of her country and herself, transformed her into a figure (as Belinsky once predicted about Herzen) not merely in Russian literature, but in Russian history in our century.

To return to the starting-point of this narrative: in a despatch for the Foreign Office written in 1945,[1] I wrote that, whatever the reason – whether it was innate purity of taste or the enforced absence of bad or trivial literature to corrupt it – it was a fact that there was, in our time, probably no country where poetry old and new was sold in such quantities and read so avidly as in the Soviet Union; and that this could not fail to act as a powerful stimulus to critics and poets alike. I went on to say that this had created a public whose responsiveness could only be the envy of Western novelists, poets and dramatists; so that if, by some miracle, political control at the top were relaxed, and greater freedom of artistic expression permitted, there was no reason why, in a society so avid for productive activity, in a nation still so eager for experience, still so young and so enchanted by everything that seemed to be unfamiliar or even true, above all a society endowed with a degree of vitality which could carry off blunders, absurdities, crimes and disasters fatal to a thinner culture, a magnificent creative art should not once again spring into life; and that the contrast between the appetite for anything that had signs of life in it, and the dead matter provided by most of the approved writers and composers, was perhaps the most striking phenomenon of Soviet culture of that day.

I wrote this in 1945, but it still seems to me to fit; false dawns have been many, but the sun has still not risen for the Russian intelligentsia. Even the most hateful despotism sometimes has the unintended effect of protecting the best against corruption, and of promoting a heroic defence of humane values. In Russia this has been, as often as not, combined, under all regimes, with an

[1] 'A Note on Literature and the Arts in the Russian Soviet Federated Socialist Republic in the Closing Months of 1945', in Public Record Office FO 371/56725.

extravagant and often subtle and delicate sense of the ridiculous, to be found in the entire field of Russian literature, at times at the heart of the most harrowing pages of Gogol or Dostoevsky; it has about it something direct, spontaneous, irrepressible, different from the wit and satire and carefully contrived entertainments of the West. I went on to say that it was this characteristic of Russian writers, even of loyal servants of the regime, when they were slightly off their guard, that made their bearing and their conversation so attractive to a foreign visitor. This seems to me to be no less true today.

My meetings and conversations with Boris Pasternak and Anna Akhmatova; my realisation of the conditions, scarcely describable, under which they lived and worked, and the treatment to which they were subjected, and the fact that I was allowed to enter into a personal relationship, indeed, friendship, with them both, affected me profoundly and permanently changed my outlook. When I see their names in print, or hear them mentioned, I remember vividly the expressions on their faces, their gestures and their words. When I read their writings I can, to this day, hear the sound of their voices.

APPENDIX

Some of the passages relevant to the 'Guest from the Future'[1] in the *Poem Without a Hero* occur in the poems listed below. References are to the collection in one volume of Akhmatova's poems edited by V. M. Zhirmunsky, *Stikhotvoreniya i poemy* (Leningrad, 1976) (hereafter Z). Included are page references to Anna Akhmatova, *Sochineniya*, ed. G. P. Struve and B. A. Filippov, 2 vols ([Munich], 1967 (2nd ed.), 1968) (hereafter SF I and SF II).[2]

Cinque, Z Nos 415–19: 1, 26 November 1945; 2 and 3, 20 December 1945; 4, 6 January 1946; 5, 11 January 1946 (Z pp. 235–7, notes pp. 412, 488; SF I pp. 283–5, notes p. 410).

A Sweetbriar in Blossom: From a Burnt Notebook (*Shipovnik tsvetet: iz sozhzhennoi tetradi*), Z Nos 420–33; 1, *Burnt Notebook* (*Sozhzhennaya tetrad'*), 1961; 2, *In Reality* (*Nayavu*), 13 June 1946; 3, *In a Dream* (*Vo sne*), 15 February 1946; 4, *First Song* (*Pervaya pesenka*), 1956; 5, *Another Song* (*Drugaya pesenka*), 1956; 6, *A Dream* (*Son*), 14 August 1956, near Kolomna; 7, untitled, undated; 8, untitled, 18 August 1956, Starki; 9, *In a Broken Mirror* (*V razbitom zerkale*), 1956; 10, untitled, 1956 (1957 in SF), Komarovo; 11, untitled, 1962, Komarovo (Z pp. 238–43, notes pp. 412–13, 488–9; SF I pp. 288–95, notes pp. 411–12).

Z No 555, untitled, 27 January 1946 (Z pp. 296–7, notes p. 499; SF I p. 295, printed (on the authority of Lydia Chukovskaya) as poem 13 of *A Sweetbriar in Blossom* (see above), notes p. 412).

[1] See p. 242 above.
[2] A third volume, edited by G. P. Struve, N. A. Struve and B. A. Filippov, was published in Paris in 1983. A complete English translation of Akhmatova's poems is also now available: *The Complete Poems of Anna Akhmatova*, trans. Judith Hemschemeyer, ed. Roberta Reeder (Somerville, Mass., 1989 [English text only: 2nd ed. 1992] and 1990 [with parallel Russian text]); this edition includes translations of many of Zhirmunsky's notes. Ed. 1997.

Midnight Verses: Seven Poems (*Polnochnye stikhi: sem' stikho-tvorenii*), Z Nos 442–50: *In Place of a Dedication* (*Vmesto posvyashcheniya*), summer 1963; 1, *Elegy Before the Coming of Spring* (*Predvesennaya elegiya*), 10 March 1963, Komarovo; 5, *The Call* (*Zov*) (originally published with the epigraph 'Arioso dolente', the title of the third movement of Beethoven's piano sonata, op. 110), 1 July 1963; 6, *The Visit at Night* (*Nochnoe poseshchenie*), 10–13 September 1963, Komarovo (Z pp. 247–50, notes pp. 414–15, 490; SF I pp. 303–6, notes pp. 414–15).

Z No 456, untitled, 15 October 1959 (October 1959 in SF), Yaroslavskoe Chaussée (Z p. 253, notes pp. 415, 491; SF I pp. 320–1, notes p. 418) (Professor Zhirmunsky has no doubt that it should be included under this heading; I feel less certain of its relevance).

From an Italian Diary (*Iz italyanskogo dnevnika*) (Mecelli), Z No 597, December 1964 (Z pp. 311–12, notes p. 502).

Z No 598, untitled, February 1965, Moscow (Z p. 312, notes p. 502).

A Song (*Pesenka*), Z No 601, undated (Z p. 313, notes pp. 422–3, 502).

Z No 619, untitled, undated (Z p. 318, notes p. 503).

Poem Without a Hero: A Triptych (*Poema bez geroya: triptykh*), Z No 648, 1940–62 (Leningrad–Tashkent–Moscow in SF): *Third and Last Dedication* ([*Posvyashchenie*] *Tret'e i poslednee*), 5 January 1956 (*Le jour des rois*); *1913: A Petersburg Tale* (*Devyat'sot trinadsatyi god: petersburgskaya povest'*), lines 133–45 ('The White Hall' ('Belyi zal'), 210 (Z pp. 354–5, 358, 360, notes pp. 427, 513–14; SF II pp. 102–3, 107 (lines 82–93), 109 (line 166), notes pp. 357–70, 603–5); *Epilogue* (*Epilog*), lines 40–50 (SF II pp. 130–1).

The reader should be warned that some of the figures who occur in the *Poem Without a Hero*, and in the other poems referred to above, may represent a fusion of two or more persons, real, imaginary or symbolic.

This is as much assistance to scholars as I am able to provide. There is nothing that I wish to add.

THE THREE STRANDS IN MY LIFE

WHEN THE NEWS of the award of the 1979 Jerusalem Prize became public, the Israel Broadcasting Service telephoned me in Oxford, and the interviewer asked me whether it was correct to say that I had been formed by three traditions – Russian, British and Jewish. I am not good at improvising answers to unexpected questions, and I was too greatly taken aback by this deeply personal enquiry to provide a coherent reply. I have never thought of myself as particularly important, or interesting as a topic for reflection, either to myself or others; and so I did not know what to answer. But the question itself lingered in my mind, and since it was asked, it deserves to be answered. I shall do my best to do this now.

I

To my Russian origins I think that I owe my lifelong interest in ideas. Russia is a country whose modern history is an object-lesson in the enormous power of abstract ideas, even when they are self-refuting – for example, the idea of the total historical unimportance of ideas in comparison with, let us say, social or economic factors. Russians have a singular genius for drastically simplifying the ideas of others, and then acting upon them: our world has been transformed, for good and ill, by the unique Russian application of Western social theory to practice. My fascination with ideas, my belief in their vast and sometimes sinister power, and my belief that, unless these ideas are understood, men can be their victims even more than of the uncontrolled forces of nature, or of their own institutions – these are reinforced daily by what goes on in the world. The French Revolution, the Russian Revolution, American democracy and American civilisation with its vast influence, the horrors of Hitler and of Stalin, the rise of the Third or decolonised World, of Islam, and the creation of the State of Israel – all these are transformations of world importance; and their effects in shaping men's lives are not intelligible without a degree of insight into the social, moral and spiritual visions embodied in them, whether noble and humane, or cruel and odious – or a mixture of the two – always formidable, often dangerous, forces for good and evil or for both. That is an element in my conception of history and society which I owe, I believe, to my Russian origins.

The oldest and most obsessive of these visions is, perhaps, that of the perfect society on earth, wholly just, wholly happy, entirely rational: a final solution of all human problems, within men's grasp but for some one major obstacle, such as irrational ideas in men's heads, or class war, or the destructive effects of materialism or of Western technology; or, again, the evil consequences of institutions – State or Church – or some other false doctrine or wicked practice; one great barrier but for which the ideal could be realised here, below. It follows that, since all that is needed is the removal of this single obstacle in the path of mankind, no sacrifice can be too great, if it is only by this means that the goal can be attained. No conviction has caused more violence, oppression, suffering. The cry that the real present must be sacrificed to an attainable ideal future – this demand has been used to justify massive cruelties. Herzen told us long ago that sacrifices of immediate goals to distant ends – the slaughter of hundreds of thousands today that hundreds of millions might be happy tomorrow – often means that hundreds of thousands are indeed slaughtered, but that the promised happiness of the hundreds of millions is no nearer, is still beyond the hills. Acts of faith – *autos-da-fé* – when they inflict misery and savage repression in the name of lofty ideals, have the effect of removing all sense of guilt from the perpetrators, but do not lead to the blessed state guaranteed to result from, and therefore the justification of, the appalling means. When all is said and done, we are never too sure – not even the wisest among us – of what is good for men; in the end we can only be reasonably sure of what it is that particular societies of individuals crave for: what makes them miserable and what, for them, makes life worth living.

Men's ultimate ends sometimes conflict: choices, at times agonising, and uneasy compromises cannot be avoided. But some needs seem universal. If we can feed the hungry, clothe the naked, extend the area of individual liberty, fight injustice, create the minimum conditions of a decent society, if we can generate a modicum of toleration, of legal and social equality, if we can provide methods of solving social problems without facing men with intolerable alternatives – that would be a very, very great deal. These goals are less glamorous, less exciting than the glittering visions, the absolute certainties, of the revolutionaries; they have less appeal to the idealistic young, who prefer a more dramatic confrontation of vice and virtue, a choice between truth and falsehood, black and white, the possibility of heroic sacrifice on the altar of the good and the just – but the results of working for these more moderate and humane aims lead to a more benevolent and civilised society. The sense of infallibility provided by fantasies is more exciting, but generates madness in societies as well as individuals.

II

An effective antidote to passionate intensity, so creative in the arts, so fatal in life, derives from the British empirical tradition. It was this civilised sense of human reality, a quality of life founded on compromise and toleration as these have been developed in the British world, that seemed so marvellous to the half-emancipated children of the oppressed and impoverished Jews of Central and Eastern Europe in the nineteenth century. I confess to a pro-British bias. I was educated in England and have lived there since 1921; all that I have been and done and thought is indelibly English. I cannot judge English values impartially, for they are part of me: I count this as the greatest of intellectual and political good fortune. These values are the basis of what I believe: that decent respect for others and the toleration of dissent are better than pride and a sense of national mission; that liberty may be incompatible with, and better than, too much efficiency; that pluralism and untidiness are, to those who value freedom, better than the rigorous imposition of all-embracing systems, no matter how rational and disinterested, or than the rule of majorities against which there is no appeal. All this is deeply and uniquely English, and I freely admit that I am steeped in it, and believe in it, and cannot breathe freely save in a society where these values are for the most part taken for granted. 'Out of the crooked timber of humanity', said Immanuel Kant, 'no straight thing was ever made.'[1] And let me quote also the words of the

---

[1] 'Idee zu einer allgemeinen Geschichte in weltbürgerlicher Absicht' ['Idea for a Universal History with a Cosmopolitan Purpose'] (1784): p. 23, line 22, in *Kant's gesammelte Schriften* (Berlin, 1900–), vol. 8.

eminent German-Jewish physicist, Max Born, who, in a lecture
delivered in 1964, said: 'I believe that ideas such as absolute
certainty, absolute exactness, final truth and so on are figments of
the imagination which should not be admitted in any field of
science ... the belief in a single truth, and in being the possessor
thereof, is the deepest root of all evil in the world.'[1] These are
profoundly British sentiments, even though they come from
Germany – salutary warnings against impatience and bullying and
oppression in the name of absolute certitude embodied in
unclouded Utopian visions. Wherever in the world today there is a
tolerable human society, not driven by hatreds and extremism, there
the beneficent influence of three centuries of British empirical
thought – not, unfortunately, of a good deal of British practice – is
to be found. Not to trample on other people, however difficult they
are, is not everything; but it is a very, very great deal.

III

As for my Jewish roots, they are so deep, so native to me, that it is
idle for me to try to identify them, let alone analyse them. But this
much I can say. I have never been tempted, despite my long
devotion to individual liberty, to march with those who, in its name,
reject adherence to a particular nation, community, culture, tradition, language – the myriad unanalysable strands that bind men into
identifiable groups. This seems to me noble but misguided. When
men complain of loneliness, what they mean is that nobody
understands what they are saying. To be understood is to share a
common past, common feelings and language, common assumptions, the possibility of intimate communication – in short, to share
common forms of life. This is an essential human need: to deny this
is a dangerous fallacy. To be cut off from one's familiar environment
is to be condemned to wither. Two thousand years of Jewish history
have been nothing but a single longing to return, to cease being
strangers everywhere; morning and evening, the exiles have prayed
for a renewal of the days of old, to be one people again, living
normal lives on their own soil – the only condition in which
individuals can live unbowed and realise their potential fully. No
people can do that if they are a permanent minority – worse still, a

---

[1] 'Symbol und Wirklichkeit' ['Symbol and Reality'], *Universitas*, German
edition, 19 (1964), 817–34, at p. 830.

minority everywhere, without a national base. The proofs of the crippling effect of this predicament, denied though it sometimes is by its very victims, can be seen everywhere in the world. I grew up in the clear realisation of this fact; it was awareness of it that made it easier for me to understand similar deprivation in the case of other people and other minorities and individuals. Such criticisms as I have made of the doctrines of the Enlightenment and of its lack of sympathy for emotional bonds between members of races and cultures, and its idealistic but hollow doctrinaire internationalism, spring, in my case, from this almost instinctive sense of one's own roots – Jewish roots, in my case – of the brotherhood of common suffering (utterly different from a quest for national glory), and a sense of fraternity, perhaps most real among the masses of the poor and socially oppressed, especially my ancestors, the poor but literate and socially cohesive Jews of Eastern Europe – something that has grown thin and abstract in the West, where I have lived my life.

These are the three strands about which the Israeli radio interviewer asked me: I have done my best to answer her question.

INDEX

Compiled by Douglas Matthews